Y0-AQV-830

An Educator's Guide to Understanding the Personal Side of Students' Lives

William L. Fibkins

A SCARECROWEDUCATION BOOK

The Scarecrow Press, Inc.
Lanham, Maryland, and Oxford
2003

A SCARECROWEDUCATION BOOK

Published in the United States of America
by Scarecrow Press, Inc.
A wholly owned subsidiary of the Rowman & Littlefield Publishing
Group, Inc.
4501 Forbes Boulevard, Suite 200, Lanham, Maryland 20706
www.scarecroweducation.com

PO Box 317, Oxford, OX2 9RU, UK

British Library Cataloguing in Publication Information Available

Library of Congress Cataloging-in-Publication Data

Fibkins, William L.
   An educator's guide to understanding the personal side of
students' lives / William L. Fibkins.
      p.   cm.
   "A ScarecrowEducation book."
   Includes bibliographical references and index.
   ISBN 1-57886-057-1 (pbk. : alk. paper)
   1. Teacher-student relationships.   2. High school students—
Psychology.   I. Title.
LB1033.F523   2003
371.102′3—dc21   2003008563

♾ ™ The paper used in this publication meets the minimum
requirements of American National Standard for Information
Sciences—Permanence of Paper for Printed Library Materials,
ANSI/NISO Z39.48-1992. Manufactured in the United States
of America.

Contents

1 The Need for Teachers to Understand the Personal Side of
Students' Lives   1

2 Why the Subject-Mastery Role Has Overshadowed the
Pedagogy Role of Teachers   21

3 Why Today's Students Need the Personal Involvement and
Understanding of Teachers in Their Lives: What Has
Changed?   72

4 The Reality of Teenage Life   151

5 Preparing Secondary-School Teachers to Be Effective
Advisors and Adult Role Models   245

Bibliography   269

Index   277

About the Author   280

The Need for Teachers to Understand the Personal Side of Students' Lives

The major goal of this book is to help teachers and other educators gain an understanding of several critical issues so they will be better prepared to help students improve academically and socially. Understanding these issues will help students take their places as contenders in an ever-changing and complex world and avoid a diminished future, as some marginal students now face. The following are the issues that must be addressed so educators can help students successfully navigate through the risks and challenges of adolescence and find and follow their star.

1. Why teachers have not utilized their bully pulpit and skills to lead the way in addressing the personal and well-being problems that interfere with student achievement and why they have turned over this role to, or as I suggest, let it be taken away by, other educators in the schools.

2. Why changes in our students' families and communities, and an increase in risky behavior, have created the need for teachers to reclaim their guidance and advisory roles and reassert themselves as the primary source of intervention for students who are underachieving and failing.

3. Why the emphasis on increasing student achievement has created the need for teachers to use their understanding of the personal side of their students' lives as an important tool in helping teachers assess, diagnose, and remediate their students' academic problems. For example, teachers understand how their students learn, how they develop, what their hopes and dreams are, and what personal and well-being issues may get in the way of learn-

ing. Put simply, teachers must learn how to help their students right themselves and become successful students.

4. Why school guidance counselors and social workers need to step back from their unattainable and specious roles as the primary source of intervention in students' nonacademic problems and begin to shift this role to teachers on the front lines, teachers who are better positioned to know students well, observe when academic and personal troubles first surface, intervene with simple, caring overtures, and advise students on how to proceed to find credible sources of help in the school and community to resolve their problems. In today's schools we need the school's student service personnel to act in support of, not in place of the teachers' personal and nonacademic involvement with students, a win-win situation, I believe, for both teachers and student service personnel.

5. How we can remove the barriers to closer teacher–student relationships such as lack of caring and attention to students by some teachers; personal and cultural differences that divide both teachers and students, labeling certain students at risk and ignoring those who develop problematic school relationships and need intervention; increased social distance between teachers and students; administrators who do not model or support closer teacher–student relationships; and the self-defeating attitude held by some teachers who say they can't be involved with students on a more personal level because of large class size.

6. Why we need to help teachers and administrators improve the quality of teacher–student relationships in their schools right now and not postpone intervention and remediation for students until secondary-school enrollments and class size are dramatically reduced. We cannot look to other special school models that have ample resources and patrons and are drawing national attention. These models are unattainable and unreachable for the vast majority of schools in America today, which lack the resources to reduce enrollment and class size and to develop new structures, such as formal teacher–student advisory systems. Some models promise closer teacher–student interaction but in fact may not deliver on this promise. As I argue in this book, going small does

not guarantee that teachers whose major focus is on teaching their subject will magically move to being more student centered just because class size is reduced and a formal advisory system is put in place. Removing the barriers to quality teacher–student interactions needs to be continually addressed.

It is very important for teachers to understand the personal side of their students' lives. Given the fact that so many middle, junior high, and high school students are at risk to personal and health problems, we need to prepare and expect teachers to be aware of what goes on in students' lives outside the walls of the classroom. As Joseph Sanacore, chairman of the Department of Special Education at Long Island University, suggests, each year educators work hard to meet the academic and personal needs of their students.[1] Compounding these challenges are social issues that affect children: high divorce rates, a rise in homes with two working parents, and an increase in single parents, who must work. This has resulted in home situations where children don't have a consistently available adult they can talk to about their daily stresses. I believe Sanacore is right on target with his assessment. Many teenage students in our schools are trying to navigate through life's challenges and risks without a consistently available adult to guide them. All too often, students without this necessary adult guidance slip into risky behavior that leads to underachieving, sometimes failing, school performance and related personal and health problems brought on by lack of self care.

Sanacore's assessment of the anonymity many teenage students are facing in our culture is also supported by the writer and education reformer Deborah Meier.[2] Meier reports that most children today are disconnected from any community of adults, including, absurdly, the adults they encounter in schools. Many young people literally finish four years of high school without knowing or being known by a single adult in the school building. Meier suggests that it is a striking fact that kids don't keep a lot of company these days with the kind of adults, in and out of school, who they might grow up to be (or who we might wish them to grow up to be). In fact, they don't keep genuine company with many adults beyond their immediate family. Our children don't work alongside adults in ways that, for good or bad, were once the norm for most young people. Meier warns that we've cut kids adrift without the support or nurturance of grownups, without the support of a community in which they might feel safe to try out various roles, listen in to the world of adults—a world they will someday join.

It doesn't have to be this way. These teens do have easily accessible adult resources to turn to. And these critical adult resources—the majority being teachers—can be found in the schools they attend each day. Meier's critique is a stinging, painful but honest indictment of what is now missing in many teacher-student relationships. It is absurd that we have failed to capitalize on the value of the teacher's role in modeling competent and caring adult behavior. It is ridiculous that we have ignored the powerful role of teachers to ensure that our students connect in an intimate way with an adult who is known to them and who can guide and advise them. In a very real sense we have squandered our most valuable adult capital—teachers—in a world that diminishes quality contact between adults and children. Our task, and a major argument in this book, is to find a way to harness these currently underused teacher resources and enlist them in a nationwide effort to back up the rhetoric of "not leaving one child behind" and "not letting one child fall between the cracks" with real, concrete, everyday support. We must pump a healthy dose of reality into these overused slogans.

How do we proceed? For me the implications in Sanacore and Meier's descriptions of the dramatic changes in our family, economic, and child-rearing lives are clear. Schools have become, like it or not, the one community institution that can provide consistently available adults that students can turn to for role models and advice. In most cases that consistently available adult is the classroom teacher—a professional on the front lines who is able to make daily contact with students and observe changes in behavior, health, and well-being that can negatively impact on the student's success. No, I am not suggesting that teachers become parent surrogates or personal counselors but rather professionals who are willing and able to intervene in their students' challenges of teen life. Professionals who, as Arthur Levine, president of Teachers College, suggests have a dual qualification in both subject matter and in pedagogy.[3] It is a role in which the teachers maintain their historical roles as masters of their subject area and gain an expanded role that encourages and expects them to understand the personal side of their students' lives and how each student learns and develops.

How do we sell teachers on the need for this new role? I suggest that the key is finding new ways to connect the personal lives and needs of today's students, their stories, and the personal experience and stories of teachers' own lives. After all, many of today's teachers have chosen their profession because they themselves were helped by teachers in their own life struggles. As Mark Edmundson, a professor of English, suggests, in becoming teachers we pledge to do for our students what our own best teachers did for us.[4] I believe Edmundson is right on target when he advises that "virtually all of us teachers got into the profession because we have been inspired by someone like my teacher at Medford High. We have become determined that, as Wordsworth put it, 'what we have loved, others will love' and we will teach them how."

Certainly life for today's students may be more complex than the teen experience of today's teachers. But many teachers have experienced what Sanacore is talking about: divorce, both parents working, single-parent homes, growing up in a home where there is no consistently available adult to talk to about their daily stresses. And as Edmundson suggests, many of today's educators did find a consistently available adult in their own teachers. They understand, many at a personal level, that available and caring teachers offer the best opportunity to help students stay connected to life in a positive way. That system works. In my experience, if teachers are given the opportunity to both understand and value the personal lives of their students, recall their own sometimes turbulent teen years, and remember how they were helped by a concerned teacher, they can begin to envision their powerful helping role. They can visualize a connection between their own personal lives and those of their students. They can understand that they and their students are more alike than different and that they do know something about being useful on a personal level to students in need. Indeed they've lived a life and their own personal experience— lessons in life—can be a powerful source of wisdom and guidance in helping their students resolve the many problems and crises that emerge in the lives of today's teenagers. The key, and a major argument in this book, is helping teachers become aware of their helping resources and be ready to use them.

I know some readers are already skeptical about my proposals. Many of you have toiled in our schools to bring about education reform and more child-centered schools. My guess is that you have experienced more failures than successes in this labor. You know first-hand the depths of resistance that teachers can and will display when asked or even expected to redefine their historical roles as subject-mastery teachers and take on a dual qualification as both subject teachers and personal advisors. And you understand that my proposals will be seen by some teachers as a cry to do more. Many teachers will say large classes, lack of time, and pressure to meet higher academic standards deter them from forming more caring and personal relationships with students. You've been there. You've heard these words before.

I agree. Encouraging and expecting teachers to reinvent themselves and move from subject-mastery roles to dual-qualification roles will not be a walk in the park. We need to keep in mind that teachers do have legitimate concerns and must be sold on the value of this new role. Some teachers will rightly ask, "What's in it for me? What's to be gained? Don't we have enough on our plates already, with the push to raise test scores and make sure students pass the competency tests that are put in place throughout the country?" Edmundson wisely reminds us that many teachers are being told that their primary task is to prepare students for fact-based tests, to stuff their charges with information. They are also being pressured to act as uncritical supporters, sometimes even cheerleaders, for our students. They are encouraged to inflate their grades, pushed to turn recommendations into exercises in Madison Avenue puffery, urged never to say or even imply a critical word about our students. More and more, the culture is asking teachers to be part of the service economy, providing our customers with what they think they want rather than what teachers believe they actually need.

Edmundson's vivid picture of the current consumer and test-obsessed state of American learning is supported by researchers Anne Marie Lenhardt and H. Jeanette Willert in the results of a collaborative project on school violence and safety in thirteen school districts in Niagara and Orleans (New York) counties.[5] Lenhardt and Willert report that adult focus groups in the study believed that increases in school standards have placed undue stress on the lives of their students, their families, and school personnel. This academic stress contributes to increased drug use, violence, and eventually to hopelessness. The groups complained of the increased stress brought on by national trends toward high-stake testing, more rigorous curricula, and increased requirements for graduation. The groups agreed that these demands create a disproportionate emphasis on cognitive versus developmental and emotional needs of the whole student.

So when teachers ask, "What's to be gained by having a better understanding of the personal side of our students' lives," they arrive at this question in chains—chained by a role that is increasingly dominated by a process of drilling information into their students' minds and testing who has mastered the information and who has not. A dual-qualification role that sets them free to understand and respond to the personal side of their students' lives is not considered available or important. We need to help teachers become aware of the negative barriers that are a part of the subject-mastery-only role, for both teachers and students, and understand that overcoming these barriers presents an opportunity for change. We must help them become more aware of the professional suffocation that comes with this kind of role. We must help them understand that a shift to a dual-qualification role as subject teacher and personal advisor has something in it for them and their students, a professionally enhancing opportunity for teachers and an opportunity for students to enhance their academic and social skills.

So what is the argument for a dual-qualification role that would make sense to teachers? I say to teachers, "You have a great deal to gain in the process of knowing more about each of your students." In knowing more about their students, teachers can begin to understand how they learn best, what gets in the way of learning, and how to maximize their students' chances to take advantage of the opportunities open to them in the school and community. Put simply, they can learn how to open doors to success and avoid poor choices and risks that can lead students down a dead end path. No school or teacher is perfect. But we know simple acts of concern by sensitive and aware teachers who know their students well can make a major difference in increasing motivation to learn, to belong, and to believe in one's own worth, wanting more for oneself. For example, a teacher's smile of support, a note of congratulations for a well-written paper, an inquiry about a sick parent, a birthday card and congratulations given with a McDonald's gift certificate, or a caring inquiry about a painful bruise on a student's face—each of these is a seemingly simple but important gesture in the everyday classroom exchange. They are gestures that send a message to students that their presence is valued and what happens in their lives matters, and they send students the message that they have a consistently available adult they can talk to about their daily stresses.

However, we also need to be straightforward with teachers and tell them up front that these seemingly simple gestures do not take place without skill and effort on the part of the teachers. Being concerned and caring is important but not enough to help students make a difference in their lives. Good intentions are just that—wishes to make things better. But wishes lack the hard effort and skill that is necessary to understand and help teens buffeted by life's problems, problems for the most part not caused by their own doing. Many problems have been laid at their innocent doorsteps by family and other adult relationships gone wrong. Students cry out for support and an acknowledgment that they are not the cause of these problems but rather victims of family lives gone wrong. All too often students affected by family crisis blame themselves. Somehow their poor grades, failures, or mischief making is the source of the family's problems. The victim becomes the source of the problem.

Who is the best resource to guide them out of the maze of personal distress? It makes sense to argue that trusted and concerned teachers, who are nearby and ready to help, are our best resource. It makes sense that we need to be about encouraging and expecting teachers to have closer personal interactions with their students and become aware that it is in their own self-interest and professional development to foster these kinds of relations. We should point out to teachers the value of assessing the data obtained by observing each student's readiness and willingness to learn and the personal issues he or she brings into the classroom each day. That data is not hard to come by. Observing and interacting with students for a few short minutes provides an opportunity for students to share with their teachers a slice of their lives, what's going on with them, their peers, family, and so on. In order to get at this important data, teachers need to be prepared to ask information-gathering questions. Simple questions work best, questions that don't put the student on the defensive but that are designed to encourage them to talk. Talking doesn't come easy for many students. For the most part, they need an opportunity to respond to queries that are gentle and safe. Ask simple questions like, "How is it going?" "Missed you in class the past few days . . . glad you're back. What kept you out of school?" "Met your mom in the principal's office yesterday. Everything OK?" In my experience with highly resistant students, however, sometimes hard-hitting, intrusive, and confrontational questions are necessary to gain a response. Remember, some students have never had the opportunity to learn how to respond to a caring inquiry. They've been told their responses don't matter by uncaring adults. As a result they have taken their distance from adults in general. Sometimes direct queries are required. Here's an example:

John, I've tried to make contact with you in every way I know. Nothing has worked. I'm tired of trying to get a response from you. But I'm not giving up. I want some kind of feedback from you, any kind. Tell me off, get mad, call me names. Take your pick. I can tell you have a lot of good stuff in you but you're going nowhere as long as you stay isolated from me and the class. What gives?

It is important in our discussion to keep in mind that this kind of inquiry by teachers takes a willingness, curiosity, energy, and problem-solving zeal. Teachers have to want to know, to understand, and to form pieces of what students say into an ever-changing mosaic of their lives. They have to be curious, unwilling to know students only from an academic standpoint. They need to recognize that this process requires effort and energy on their part. And they need to form and practice new habits for successfully connecting with their students on nonacademic and personal issues. Asking nonacademic questions of students is new and risky behavior for many teachers. It is not a process they learn in schools of education. In most schools it has not been an expected or valued part of teachers' work. It's unknown territory, a territory that takes practice to master. It takes a willingness to risk to step outside the role of academic teacher and dare to be available, ready to listen to students' views of their family life, health, and well-being issues; peer relationships; losses; setbacks and failures; involvement or lack of involvement in school and community activities; their views on the school and teachers; their hopes and dreams for the future; their views of themselves; their sense of where they fit in, where they are valued in the scheme of school, family, and community life.

And, yes, let's be honest with teachers. There are always failures and setbacks for teachers who set out to better understand the personal lives of their students. Rebuffs come in many forms. Silence, avoidance, and blunt "none of your business" responses from students come when teachers enter this new territory. Building trust with students requires many overtures. Why? As I have suggested, many students are not used to personal inquiries and attention from teachers. It's new territory for them as well. They, too, lack a road map on how to behave. Often their first response is uncertainty. What do these inquiries mean? Sometimes it is difficult for students to trust well-meaning and helpful overtures from teachers. Many have not experienced this kind of communication and connection with a meaningful adult in their past home, community, or school life. They are taken by surprise when an adult is interested in and wants to know more about their lives.

So when teachers set out to understand the personal lives of their students, it marks a new way of doing business in the classroom. It does take risks and, in the beginning, much stumbling around and fencing and getting to know this new role on the part of teachers and students. It takes time, practice, and some small successes to iron out the kinks in the process. But I believe this kind of more intimate and involved connection is a win-win situation for both students and teachers. For teachers it provides clues and insights into how best to motivate a student. For students it offers the opportunity to connect with a concerned and mature adult who has real life experiences, successes, losses, and failures that they can learn from. Both groups benefit.

Here is an example of this kind of mutual growth and learning experience for both students and teachers, modeled by Itzhak Pearlman, the violinist conductor and founder, along with his wife, Toby, of the Pearlman Music Program Summer Camp for teenagers on Shelter Island, New York. As writers Lois B. Morris and Robert Lipsyte report, while the students have been the focus of Pearlman's teaching efforts, they are not the only beneficiaries.[6]

By several accounts his early conducting of the campers in the beginning days of the summer camp program had nowhere near the virtuosity of his violin playing. But this summer on Shelter Island he teased out color, nuance, passion, subtlety, and personality from youngsters with a baton that seemed as familiar as his bow. Although the Pearlman Music ·Program is the dream of his wife, Toby, to provide a humane music education to shape future musicians aged eleven through eighteen, it has also reshaped Mr. Pearlman. "He has completely reinvented himself," Mrs. Pearlman said.

Although famously private, for his students he will sometimes peel down to the 13-year-old Itzhak who became an instant celebrity when he appeared on television on the *Ed Sullivan Show* in 1958. Maya Shankar, a 16-year-old recovering from a hand injury received while playing the violin at camp last year, remembers a session with Mr. Pearlman in which he revealed his own feelings of terror and competitiveness. "When we got to ask him questions about his childhood he said that for many years he was jealous. He'd worry, 'Oh, this person has learned many concertos so much faster than I have, and this person is playing concerts and I'm not performing. There's no way I am going to get anywhere in music.' From someone who turned out the way he did, that was so comforting for me to hear. Then he told us that we have our own inner clock and it ticks at a certain rate, and you're going to get to certain places at times different than anyone else is, but that doesn't make you any less a musician."

What he doesn't tell his students is how to play. "For me one of the great things about teaching is not so much what to say but to know what not to say. If someone is talented they contain a certain kind of magic, and that magic is very precious because it is on very precarious ground. It's like a very fine leaf that if you shake it too much it breaks. You have to let the branch grow until it becomes strong enough that if you shake it, it won't break."

At camp, when he is conducting, "That's a form of teaching, I suppose," he said. He is gentle and amusing, always trying to coax out of each individual in the group. "Don't play like a section," he exhorted the string players at a rehearsal for a benefit concert. "You are individuals playing together." He tells them not to hide in the music but to express their own vibrancy and intensity. He evokes the image of the Blue Angels, planes flying in formation yet each flying boldly.

Mr. Pearlman says he believes that listening to his students and orchestra players has changed his point of view about music and enhanced his ability to listen to himself. Sometimes he teaches a piece in the afternoon that he will play in performance that night. During the lesson he will urge the students to vary an interpretation. Later, onstage, he'll find himself thinking, "Why am I doing it this way? Just because I did it last week?"

There are many winners in this brief look into the relationship between teacher Pearlman and his students. He clearly is a model for Arthur Levine's dual-qualification teacher: master of his violin and baton but also personally involved, listening, coaxing his students. This teacher–student relationship encourages Pearlman to openly reveal his own feelings of terror, jealousy, and competitiveness he experienced as a teenager. And in revealing, sharing his personal story, Pearlman is able to connect with his students. His experience is a reminder that he and his students are more alike than different. Indeed, his teenage fears of not connecting, not succeeding, and not doing well strongly resonate with his students, many of whom are experiencing the same fears and vulnerable feelings. He is able to remind them that as learners they each have their own inner clocks that tick at different rates. They are going to get to certain places at different times from anyone else. Pearlman is able to grasp the vulnerability of his students and to remind himself that they, like a fine leaf, can break under certain conditions. He understands the work is to help them grow, become strong, so that like a fine leaf, they can survive when they are shaken by life circumstances, as with Maya Shankar's injury. Pearlman also grasps the notion of encouraging, coaxing, and allowing his students to be individuals first. He says, "You are individuals playing together, flying in formation, yes, but also each flying boldly."

In the process Pearlman becomes a better listener, teacher, and musician. His students find safety and belonging in the environment he has created, safety to learn and grow at their own pace. They also are able to learn by his sharing of wisdom that emerges from his lifelong creative experience as a performer and conductor. In a sense, Pearlman's experience provides some important clues on how teachers can proceed to better understand their students' personal needs and use this data to coax them into becoming better achievers. Let's review how he goes about connecting with his students:

1. He creates a safe and encouraging environment.
2. He reveals himself; he shares stories of his own angst as a teenager and how he survived.
3. He encourages his students to share their own stories and concerns.
4. He allows each student to grow and learn at his or her own individual pace.
5. He stresses that each student has his or her own inner clock and she or he will get to certain places at times different from anyone else.

This is a step-by-step prescription for the successful dual-qualified teacher/advisor. When teachers and students know each other in a personal way, the doors of learning are open. In the process, teachers become real people with rich lives of experience to share and call upon in advising their students. This can be a valuable addition to their teaching repertoire. They are now able to add a pedagogy dynamic to their subject-matter mastery. For students, knowing that their teacher, like Pearlman, has experienced terror, jealousy, and nagging competitiveness in growing up but has turned out OK is, as Maya Shankar suggests, comforting. It suggests that teacher and student do share a bond and common experiences as they try to successfully navigate through the risks and challenges that life offers.

Pearlman's experience has much to offer teachers stuck in a one-dimensional subject-mastery role. By becoming more personally involved with their students, teachers reinvent themselves and become better listeners and more involved. And in revealing more of themselves and asking the same of their students, teachers begin to enjoy their work in exciting new ways, finding ways for both themselves and their students to be lighter and have some fun, in their highly competitive worlds.

As I argue in this book, this process of understanding the personal lives of students is an important but often little-used tool in helping students to be more successful achievers. Clearly it should come as no surprise that identifying, understanding, and helping students resolve personal and health problems that are getting in the way of learning is a needed and important part of teachers' work. No other group in the schools—administrators, counselors, and so on—has more opportunity than teachers for ongoing, quality, intimate contact with students, contact that daily yields important data about students that provides insight into their learning and achievement process. Yet as I shall point out in the book, historically teachers have not been expected to embrace this aspect of their work, instead defining themselves solely as academic teachers. In a real sense, this dramatically limits the scope of their work and any opportunity to help students. Just as critical, even if they opted for more involvement in their students' lives, they lack the necessary habits and skills to be successful in this role. Teachers represent a resource that has been too long ignored and certainly underutilized in our efforts to increase achievement for all our students. Is this cost-effective? Hardly, when we have a process that suggests to teachers, "Don't look, don't ask, don't get involved in the personal issues of students. Teach your subject. And when the students' personal and well-being problems impact negatively on achievement, quickly refer them to some school or community resource. Get the troubled student problem off your back and out of your professional psyche, fast." The result? We've abandoned our most valuable intervention resource, our teachers, locking them into a role as neuters, onlookers, when their students run into personal problems. Teachers are left to feed on rumors and gossip about troubled students in the faculty room, perceiving they have no real role in their students' personal lives.

For me, allowing teachers to remain mired in this kind of process is costly for the school climate, the professional development of teachers, and for students in need of a positive adult relationship. In a real sense we have taken the risks out of the work of teachers. Once they master the academic side of teaching, there is no more challenge, no more growth opportunity. Yes, every year a few unnerving students and events intrude, but teachers know that helping these students is not part of their domain. These problems and problem students are usually easily dispensed with by a code blue cry to counselors and administrators.

Unfortunately this process leaves teachers without an expectation or the skills and commitment to better understand their students' personal lives. They remain onlookers to the process. It doesn't have to be this way. How do we proceed to change this limited view of teachers as academics? There are four reasons that I believe educators, parents, and community leaders need to throw their strong support to changing this isolated and isolating academic role.

Personal and well-being problems often get in the way of school achievement.   This should come as no surprise to any experienced educator, parent, or community leader. Personal and well-being health problems manifest themselves in poor school attendance; tardiness; school failure; addiction to alcohol, drugs, or tobacco; eating disorders; poor peer relationships; problems with authority; and isolation from the broader, productive school community. Concerned teachers on the front lines who have close and personal relationships with their students, who understand what's coming down in their lives, are ideally positioned to respond to minor problems before they break out in major crises. Teachers who have an understanding of the personal side of their students' lives are careful to observe, take notice, and listen carefully. They quickly zero in on changes of behavior, appearances, cuts and bruises that may be a sign of abuse, a sudden lack of interest in school and care of oneself, or a dramatic change in well-being such as weight loss. They understand that something isn't going right for the student and that something can become costly, even deadly, for the students and their chances of future school success. As we know, bad things do happen to teens who are trying to navigate through the various risks and pitfalls of adolescent life. That is true for students from every part of the school community—the best and brightest of our students, who are Ivy League bound, those who are economically well off and whose every physical and emotional need is catered to by overly involved parents; students labeled as troublemakers, who are constant visitors to the principal's office and detention room; the so-called average child who causes no waves; and those students who are usually no-shows, who are on the rolls and put in a few appearances but they are literally gone, forgotten. These last cause no trouble; they are just vacant seats waiting to be taken off the rolls and added to the dropout list.

Yet all of these student groups have something in common. As any educator who has worked intimately with teens understands, students from every group get hit by life's blows. No one is exempt. No one escapes. Pain and disruption, large and small, knows no boundaries. Parents get divorced; friends die in motor vehicle accidents. A once safe and secure family life gets turned upside down by alcohol or drug addiction. Peer relations, once so solid and connected in elementary school, become fragmented in junior high and high school. Temporary setbacks abound in our schools. One thing is certain in the complex world of today's students: personal, health, family, and peer problems will affect many of them every day. Some of these problems will strike blows that leave once well-adjusted kids reeling. Vulnerable teens can lose their way quickly without the guiding, informed, supportive hand of concerned teachers. Caring adults who are willing to become involved with teens' personal lives, hear and understand their stories, and offer credible advice are in great demand in our schools. It is important to keep in mind that every student, not just the ones labeled at risk, can experience temporary setbacks that impede academic achievement.

Teachers need to be trained and expected to make understanding of the personal side of their students' lives a top priority. Today's schools and students demand that teachers be more than just academic teachers. That is a limited role that leaves teachers poorly prepared to respond to the growing personal and health concerns of students, concerns that often lead to poor achievement and student failure. In a real sense, our present system has left teachers in a no-win situation, relying on a view of their job and skills that is out of date and out of sync with today's student population. While they clearly observe that things aren't right for their students, many do not know how to connect with them on a personal level—how to ask the right questions to encourage the students to share their stories, how to listen to so-called nonacademic and personal issues, and how to offer guidance, support, and advice for troubled students who desperately need the wisdom of a mature adult. They are caught between wanting to help and not knowing how to proceed, a double bind that limits the natural impulse of many teachers to understand the dilemmas the students experience and be helpful and of service.

I believe there is a culture in our schools, a way of doing business, that subtly suggests to teachers, "Don't get too involved in understanding the personal and outside of school lives of your students." If you do, and this often comes as a subtle warning from colleagues, you'll be expected to act, to do something about the situation, take some responsibility to help out and be of service. The warning is clear. If you get too involved, you'll be drawn into new and foreign territory, filled with pitfalls, a territory you know nothing about and don't have the skills to handle. You'll be over your head. And guess what? Your colleagues and administrators won't be around to help when you flounder. You're on your own. It's better to conform, stay with being an academic teacher, go along.

In these situations many teachers tend to look the other way. If they see signs of students who are troubled, many feel it is not their place to respond or intervene. Those who do respond usually do so with a referral to an already overworked counselor. It's a way of getting the problem off their hands, an act of contrition that seemingly absolves them of any responsibility, or even more subtly, absolves them of any wrongdoing. But teachers lose a lot in the process. They ignore, or worse give away, their natural desire and inclination, to personally connect with their students and be helpful. It's a little like observing someone hurt or in despair but not stopping to offer concern and support, continuing on about our business as if our intervention is not needed, assuming that someone more experienced and skilled than we are will soon come along. We, like many teachers, give up a chance to be human, be helpful, thinking it's not our role, our job. What we lose, and many teachers lose this each day, is our willingness to be of service, the skills to intervene and the belief that intervention matters. We settle for the role of observers and passers-by. We have for too long allowed teachers to continue to embrace the long-held myth that their involvement in understanding the personal sides of their students is of little importance in helping students to become successful learners.

Understanding the personal sides of their students' lives helps teachers to be more inclusive. The process of understanding the personal sides of their students' lives is a powerful force in helping teachers to focus on, and understand, all of the students in their classes. In the process of understanding their students, they begin to take down walls that they, and their students, have put up. Yes, many of us as teachers build walls to keep students out. We arrive at the classroom door with our own biases, judgments, and prejudices. We are human. We are threatened, made to feel uncomfortable, by students who are "different," in color, culture, appearance, ability, attitude, values, motivation, and so on. As teachers we tend to gravitate toward those students who are most like us, with similar backgrounds and values, and who we feel will be more responsive to our message. Conversely we tend to move away from those students who are different and some-times reject our message, either openly or in passive ways. An uneasy standoff takes place, sometimes lasting the entire school year. By understanding and learning more about students' family life, health and well-being, peer relationships, setbacks, losses, and failures, we begin to really know the students. Communication and trust begin to develop. We begin to develop a sense of the road this student has traveled, the problems and struggles he or she has witnessed, and where his or her hopes and dreams, no matter how beaten down and smothered, lie. We begin to develop a road map of the kinds of intervention and remedia-tion we need to be about in order to help a particular student be all he or she can be. In knowing and understanding, we begin to take down our walls and no longer feel unresponsive students are threats, a puzzle or someone who is "different" and thus difficult to deal with.

When teachers begin to understand the personal side of their stu-dents' lives and reduce the barriers, the social distance, with students who are "different," the students themselves learn a powerful lesson about inclusion. Students watch what teachers do and how they behave. They quickly pick up on the way teachers respond to different students. When they observe a teacher who has the ability to connect in a positive way with the various groups and personalities within the class, they learn an important lesson. They begin to understand that although everyone has a different story and comes from different neighborhoods and cultures, everyone counts and has a unique gift to bring to the table. Differences are valued and not allowed to become barriers and sources of isolation. What matters for students is showing up, taking part, sharing the special gifts of your culture, knowing you are a product of your past but also assimilated into this school commu-nity. You fit, you belong. This sense of belonging can be transferred to the broader school community when the majority of teachers get signed on to this process, a process that honors the "specialness" and "differentness" of each student, their customs, values, food, music, ways of communicating, learning, sharing, valuing, honoring, celebrating, and grieving. The process fosters the energy to know each other well.

Understanding the personal sides of students' lives has great benefits for improving student academic and social success, the professional development of teachers, and improving school climate. In the process of understanding and knowing students more fully, teachers, not unlike Itzhak Pearlman, are asked to recall and share their own life experiences, not all of them successful and pain free. And in this process teachers are asked to share with students their special gifts of caring and concern.

Researchers Lenhardt and Willert suggest that students want teachers to care. "The resounding message we heard from both middle and high school students was that they want to be listened to and taken seriously; most important they want to be respected. Connectedness, a sense of belonging, and feeling cared for were top priorities for students. They seemed to believe that there is a direct correlation between caring and learning. As one 10th grader noted, 'The teachers who care more than just giving an A grade look into your eyes and into your face and care.'"

Our work, and a major argument in this book, is to consider how we can make such a school climate a reality. We must consider what the barriers are and what we must do to overcome these barriers. What is the best way to begin helping teachers to understand their students' lives? And what kinds of ongoing support do teachers need to become effective in this work?

In chapter 2, I discuss some of the historical barriers that have led teachers far astray from the caring role suggested by Lenhardt and Willert and locked them into a limiting, one-dimensional subject-mastery role.

NOTES

1. Joseph Sanacore, "Home at School," *Newsday*, 2 August 2002, 20 (A).

2. Deborah Meier, *In Schools We Trust* (Boston: Beacon Press, 2002), 10, 12.

3. Arthur Levine, "Rookies in the Schools," *New York Times*, 29 June 2002, 15 (A).

4. Mark Edmundson, "Soul Training," *New York Times Magazine*, 18 August 2002, 8, 10 (6).

5. Anne Marie Lenhardt and H. Jeanette Willert, "Involving Stakeholders in Resolving School Violence," *NASSP Bulletin*, June 2002, http://www.nassp.org/news/bltn_invstake0602.html (accessed 5 May 2002).

6. Lois B. Morris and Robert Lipsyte, "What Itzhak Pearlman Learned at Camp," *New York Times*, 8 August 2002, 1, 5 (E).

CHAPTER 2

Why the Subject-Mastery Role Has Overshadowed the Pedagogy Role of Teachers

As I have suggested, there exists a tremendous need for children to connect with competent and healthy adult role models. Yet ironically, in today's culture the opposite is more often the case. The reality is that many children are disconnected from any community of adults, including the adults they encounter in schools. Why is this so? I suggest that this underutilization of teachers as one of our most significant, powerful, and precious adult resources is a byproduct of years of viewing teachers solely as subject-matter experts, not as professionals who are adult role models for their students and who understand their personal lives, how they learn and develop, and how to intervene to help them resolve personal and health problems that may impact on school success and achievement. Even in today's culture, where there is a pressing need for caring and competent adult models, some leaders in education, such as Education Secretary Rod Paige, conclude that state licensing of teachers should require more verbal and subject-matter competence.[1] Subject-matter knowledge has long been the benchmark for teacher training and teacher success. Understanding the personal sides of students' lives has not been given any real priority, either in training or in the schools.

How did this one-dimensional, academic, role of teachers emerge and what has sustained it to the present day? The following are some indicators as to why this view of the teacher's role emerged.

In earlier generations, teachers were not needed as adult advisors and role models. As Deborah Meier suggests, adult role models were more available to previous generations of children.[2] Meier points out that a century ago, or even less, children made the transition to adulthood early, steeped in the company of adults. Surely by fifteen or sixteen, when a majority of youngsters today are still years away from entering the adult world, most were already in the thick of adult lives—having children, earning a living. They spent their time in the midst of multiage settings from birth on, in small communities, farms, or workplaces where they knew grownups intimately and knew a lot about how they went about their work, negotiating their way through life. Most of the learning of how to be an adult took place in the company of grownups by working alongside them, picking up the language and customs of "grown-upness" through both instruction and immersion, much as they had learned to walk and talk.

But as education researcher James S. Coleman reports, over time the industrialization of American society eroded the close relationship between children and adult mentors.[3] Society no longer needed the labor of children, so it passed child labor laws removing them from the workforce. Because it could not have free-roaming children, it committed them to an institution where they could be kept out of the way and, hopefully, some of them would be trained for the new white-collar jobs—the public high school. Higher education shifted from a voluntary matter for the few going to college to an involuntary matter for all. In 1900, 11 percent of the high school–aged population was in school; in 1920, 32 percent; in 1930, 51 percent; in 1940, 73 percent; and today, 90 percent. As Coleman reports, this evolving system required teachers well schooled in the academic subjects of college; teachers whose primary concern was the content of what they were teaching and who were only secondarily concerned with the students being taught. If a child would not learn, he need not stay in school; his very presence implied a commitment on his or his parents' part toward learning. Thus, a teacher did not need to know how to teach; he needed only to know his subject.

Historically, there was no pressing need for teachers to be adult role models and to be knowledgeable and experienced, about the personal and well-being issues of students. The emphasis was on transferring knowledge of their subject matter to students and to prepare them for college and a career. What mattered were preparations for the future rather than living in the present, preparing students to play a key role in a growing American economy. Students who developed personal and academic problems were encouraged, sometimes strongly persuaded, to drop out of school and join the workforce or the armed services. In a sense the role created for teachers was a miniacademic. If the students wanted to achieve and learn, school was the place for them. If they acted up and failed to respond to the academic message of the teacher, they were shown the door. The tone set for the teachers suggested that knowledge of child development, how students learn, and how to address poor academic performance brought on by personal and well-being issues were not important, not a part of their job description. Author Robert Hampel captures the essence of the teacher subject-mastery role when he reports on the way teacher Leonard Covello describes his role:

> I am the teacher. I am older, presumably wiser than you, the pupils. I am in possession of knowledge which you don't have. It is my function to transfer this knowledge from my mind to yours. For the most efficient transfer of knowledge, certain ground rules must be set and adhered to. I talk. You listen. I give, you take.[4]

In the early development of our public schools, teachers had little pedagogical training and focused on their subject-mastery role, relying on lectures and recitation from textbooks.   As education historian Diane Ravitch suggests, in the closing years of the nineteenth century Americans prided themselves on their free public schools.[5] Unlike Europe, which was burdened with rigid class barriers, in America it was believed that the public schools could enable any youngster to rise above the most humble origins and make good on the nation's promise of equal opportunity for all. But in practice schools and teachers were ill-equipped to help students reach these lofty goals. For example, as Ravitch suggests, teachers seldom had much pedagogical training so they relied mainly on time-tested methods of recitation from textbooks. When the muckraker Dr. Joseph Mayer Rice visited public schools in thirty-six cities in 1892, he complained bitterly about the quality of education he saw. In St. Louis, teachers cut students off with remarks such as, "Speak when you are spoken to" and "Don't talk, listen." And, "Don't lean against the wall" and "Keep your toes in line." Education historians David Tyack and Elisabeth Hansot suggest the textbook teaching of the nineteenth-century common school undergirded the small scale of the time with an ideology that hard work, loyalty, and good character led to success, while poverty and failure were the result of personal defects.[6] Schools existed to give all children a fair chance to acquire knowledge and skills necessary for success in a specialized, credential-oriented society. Students with so-called personal defects or who didn't take advantage of their fair chance usually did not last long in the schools.

Yet as Ravitch suggests, there were efforts to break free from this model of seeing public schools as a conduit for children to be given a fair chance to acquire knowledge and skills necessary for success in a specialized credential-oriented society. John Dewey, leader of the Progressive Education movement, founded the Laboratory School at the University of Chicago in 1896.[7] The school was to be child-centered, a place where children could be involved in social activities in which they could explore, create, and find out about themselves. The teachers wanted children to have first-hand experiences but they did not neglect the accumulated knowledge and past experience of the race. The school was supposed to be like a home in which experienced adults lovingly guided children to develop social, physical, and intellectual capacities. The Dewey School sought to balance individual growth, social goals, and knowledge. As Dewey suggests, the emphasis of schools should be on the present, not on the future. And children did not need the kind of teaching that relied on recitation from textbooks. And they certainly didn't need teachers who cut them off constantly or harangued them with remarks like, "Speak only when you are spoken to."

In Dewey's school, there was no room for viewing students as failing to learn because of so-called personal defects. And there was not room for curriculum and teaching that prepared students to acquire knowledge needed to fit into a specialized, credential-oriented society. Rather, the work was helping students develop habits and an openness of mind that would in the present, and in the future, give them control over their environment. It encouraged habits involving thought, invention, and initiative in applying capacity to new aims. It was opposed to routine, which marks an arrest of growth. Because growth is the characteristic of life, education is all one with growing. The criterion of the value of school education was the extent to which it created a desire for continued growth and supplied the means for making the desire effective in fact.

But Dewey's schools, as Ravitch suggests, were like a Roman candle in American education, casting a vivid light of pedagogical dreams and possibilities, then disappearing to become legend. It was an exemplar of what might be done under ideal conditions. But it was never reproduced except in elite private schools and in a small number of public schools, and then only for relatively brief periods of time under the direction of charismatic leaders.

Surging school enrollment and the development of large secondary schools further solidified the subject-mastery role of teachers in spite of pressure from progressive educators for schools to concentrate on the students' personal, emotional, and social development rather than academic studies. Between 1880 and 1940, high school enrollment soared. In 1920 it stood at 2.2 million, doubled to 4.4 million by 1930, then reached 6.6 million by 1940. Ravitch points out that youngsters and their parents realized that the changing economy required more knowledge, skills, literacy, and numeracy. Here again this increased enrollment brought with it a cry from progressive educators that the "curriculum must be dynamic; that education had to embrace the total life experience of the child, that the goal of education was effective living for all; that the instruction had to shift from subject matter to the whole needs of the child's experience."[8] Ravitch suggests progressive reformers pressured the public high schools to serve as custodial institutions that met miscellaneous, socioeconomic needs, kept youth off the streets, provided a range of nonacademic curricula, and deemphasized the importance of academic curriculum for all but the college bound. The high schools that adopted these progressive reforms, as Ravitch suggests, became in the words of a major sociological study in 1944, "an enormous, complicated machine of sorting and ticketing and routing children through life," a conveyer belt that inspected young people and then directed them to different destinations, some to the outside world, some to college, others to different vocations.[9]

Getting teachers to help meet the nonacademic needs of students proved to be a tough sell. History was not on the side of the progressives' cry for a shift in teachers' job descriptions from subject-matter experts to include expertise in how to meet the needs of the whole child, or for schools, as the Progressive Education Association stated in the late 1930s, to encourage the nation's high schools to concentrate on their students' personal, emotional, and social problems rather than academic studies.

As Ravitch reminds us, schools are essentially conservative institutions, staffed mainly by teachers who are educated to teach specific subjects. Their curricula and practices responded slowly to progressive reformers. Demands for teachers to minimize their intellectual goals floundered. The strong allegiances of parents and teachers to the academic curricula slowed the implementation of radical changes even after superintendents announced them. Teachers knew they had to go along, join study groups, and give outward signs of compliance to their supervisors but they could always close their classroom doors and teach the subject they knew best.

The effort by progressive educators in the 1930s and 1940s to change the ways schools operate and teachers teach failed to sell teachers themselves on the need to help their students develop personally, emotionally, and socially and the notion that this kind of intervention could also increase their students' academic success; that they could be both subject-mastery teachers and personal advisors for students and acquire the dual-qualification role now heralded by Arthur Levine.[10]   In the end, in spite of great efforts from educators from schools of education and state education departments, teachers hung on firmly to their subject-mastery roles. This should come as no surprise. This is the work they knew and felt comfortable with. What was missing for many teachers in local schools was the fact that they were not included in this call for great change. They were onlookers, not real participants. The case for change was being made by progressive educators from stated education departments and colleges of education. Nor were teachers shown the "how's and why's" of adding the personal, emotional, and social development of students to their academic teaching repertoire and psyche. Again, it was no surprise that while they may have talked about getting on board and supporting the called-for reforms, in the end they closed their doors and taught their subject matter. Failure of these reform efforts, though, had more serious long-term ramifications that have carried over to the present day. Here are three ramifications to consider:

1. These failed reforms and attacks on the way teachers went about their work further solidified their one-dimensional role as sub-

ject-mastery teachers. The proposals for reform resulted in teachers and parents erecting even higher barriers to any change in their teaching methods. In fact, the progressive reform efforts served as a vehicle to strengthen the position of teachers that they weren't going to be pushed around by tinkerers from state education departments and colleges of education. Harold Alberty, a progressive professor of education at Ohio State University, put it well regarding teacher disaffection with the progressive reforms in the 1930s and 1940s.[11] Alberty complained that most high school teachers actually blocked reorganization. He said they were all too complacent, having been taught by subject-matter specialists in college and believing their job was to teach mastery of the cultural heritage to their students. Persuading teachers to go along with curriculum reform was never easy. After an administrator introduced a new program with directives, publicity, bulletins, and conferences, a few teachers would be interested. But many were apathetic and even hostile. Skeptical teachers would pretend to comply but were only going through the motions.

2. These failed reforms and the further isolating of teachers as subject-mastery specialists made it more difficult for students to get help in resolving their personal and social problems, problems that do impact on academic achievement and success. Teachers, in not buying the denigration of their academic courses and getting on board the progressive's life adjustment curriculum, stuck to the notion that helping students solve their personal and social problems was not their job. If students needed help, let the newly emerging field of guidance counselors take over.

3. In reality the few guidance counselors in the schools were already overly engaged in testing and sorting students into the various courses in the increasingly large secondary schools. While many counselors were trained in personal, one-on-one and group counseling, once they began work in the secondary schools they soon learned that their value and worth to the school organization, students, and parents was in testing and scoring, not in helping students develop personally, emotionally, or socially, even though the school's public relations material often described their role as such.

I believe that these negative ramifications from the progressive movement can offer some useful advice to the reader and to today's education reformers who buy into Meiers's argument that teachers need to be more involved with their students on a personal level. Clearly the progressives failed to help teachers see a connection, and a role for themselves, between the personal and well-being issues of students and academic achievement, or to believe that well-adjusted and healthy kids have a better shot for school success. What can we learn from the progressive experience? It doesn't work to tell teachers they need to change the way they teach unless they can see that the required changes have some academic payoff. For example, don't follow the progressive educators' approach and offer teachers some vague argument that they and the public schools are the fulcrum for social planning, designed to meet the needs of their communities. And don't tell them they and the schools must help students make friends, look attractive, prepare for family life and vocation, and achieve social success. And clearly, don't tell them the school is supposed to be like a home in which experienced adults lovingly guide children to develop social, physical, and intellectual capacities.

Those are no-win arguments with teachers and rightfully so. They have been trained as subject-matter experts. This is what they know. The kind of fuzzy and vague arguments described above turn teachers off because they lack any specific relationship to their work as subject-matter experts. These arguments come across to teachers as slogans and pep talks that have no staying power in the academic teacher's psyche and only serve to drive teachers into their classrooms and close the door.

Instead, I believe the argument that the progressives needed to make to teachers, and that we need to make today, is that becoming involved in understanding the personal lives of students, how they learn, how they develop, and as Dewey suggested, helping them develop successful personal well-being relationships and dream-building habits and skills, can help students become better achievers. In other words, we must help teachers to become aware that their personal intervention does have a subject matter and academic, payoff. Everyone—students, teachers, and parents—wins in this teacher dual-qualification role. This argument is a call for teacher activities that are tangible, doable, and possible within the four walls of the classroom, activities that can produce results such as increased student achievement that teachers can see is consistent with their mission as subject-matter experts. They must see it as something within their reach, not vague slogans that call on teachers to change and reshape our national, state, and community lives, chuck their curriculum and ways of working, and if they resist, result in being criticized by education professors such as Hollis Caswell, dean of Columbia University Teachers College, who suggested that the biggest obstacle to curriculum change is getting teachers to abandon their traditional ways of teaching.[12]

As authors Arthur G. Powell, Eleanor Farrar, and David Cohen suggest:

> Education reformers' scribbling rarely helped teachers to take the next step. It was easy for Dewey to write about the importance of experience in education. It was easy for Kilpatrick and others to stress activities, practicality and students' interest. But building serious classroom work around the interest and experience of students and teachers was difficult and demanding. Few of the reformers explained how to do it. John Dewey confessed, after a try at running a school, that he knew much less about it than he had thought. Teachers found it much easier to fall back on the familiar techniques, lectures, drill, question-and-answer, recitation, or to organize classes around activities that had little content.[13]

In my opinion teachers needed to be included in calls for change, shown the "how's" and "why's" of how to proceed, and helped to make the next step.

The emergence of Conant's large comprehensive high school model occurred.   In late October 1957 the Soviets launched Sputnik, the first space satellite. As Ravitch points out, Sputnik became an instant metaphor for the poor quality of America's schools. Overnight a clamor arose for higher academic standards and greater attention to mathematics, science, and foreign language in schools. In response to these criticisms, James B. Conant, former president of Harvard, wrote in his book *The American High School Today* that no basic changes were necessary.[14] Instead he recommended that small high schools should be eliminated and that no high school would have a graduating class of fewer than one hundred students. This meant reducing the number of high schools in the United States from 21,000 to 9,000. Conant strongly preferred large comprehensive high schools that offered multiple curricula—a strong academic program for the minority who were academically gifted and an array of vocational and general courses for the large majority who were not. Conant belittled small high schools that tried to provide an academic program for all students. Such high schools wasted time on students who were uninterested in academics instead of focusing on the top quarter of the class, who did not get the specialized attention they deserved.

Conant also suggested that every high school have a good counseling program to ensure that students were guided into the right program. He recommended that there should be one full-time counselor for every 250 to 300 pupils in the high school. They should be familiar with the use of tests and measurements to assess the aptitudes and achievement of pupils. In his vision, all students would take a basic required course of four years of English, three or four years of social studies, one year of science, and one year of math. Everything else would be an elective and it would be up to the guidance staff, using tests of aptitude and intelligence, to make sure the students chose the appropriate electives. Conant said that only 15 percent of high school students had the mental ability to take rigorous courses in mathematics, science, and foreign languages. Perhaps another 10 to 20 percent might stretch to take an academic program as well. But the 65 to 75 percent of students should take courses in marketable skills. He warned that ambitious parents might attempt to get their children enrolled in advanced mathematics, physics, and foreign languages but that school officials must resist their entreaties. Counselors would have to be prepared to persuade overly ambitious parents that their children were not academically talented. Conant, speaking primarily about suburban high schools, suggested that one of the main tasks of the guidance counselors (or officers, as he sometimes called them) was college placement. And in order to keep the lines of communication open with these institutions and to follow high school graduates to college, the services of one person working full time on college placement was required.

Conant's proposals put strong pressure on state and local officials to get rid of small high schools because they could not offer a full array of academic, vocational, and general courses. His report was welcomed by educators because its message was reassuring. Any changes needed were minor and would conform to the basic philosophical premise that had ruled American education for more than a generation.

Conant followed up his recommendations in 1967 with his book *The Comprehensive High School: A Second Report to Interested Citizens.*[15] But he found some disturbing data regarding his suggestion that there be one full-time counselor for every 250 to 300 students in high school. His research indicated that in only 3.4 percent of the 2,000 schools was the ratio 1 to 299 or less. In other words, as he suggested, in the vast majority of schools, his recommendations were far from reality. He indicated that he could not believe that staff in a school with only one counselor per four hundred students can function as well as a school of similar size with a hundred fewer students per counselor.

I suggest that the changes proposed by Conant were not minor. In fact, the creation of large schools had unintended consequences for both students and teachers. When students attended small high schools they were known by many adults in the school. They were not anonymous. When small high schools were abandoned in favor of large comprehensive high schools, the intimate environment of the small school was lost. In many cases students were now bused long distances to attend school. They interacted with large numbers of students from different communities, some with radically different cultures and values. It became far easier for students to become unconnected and be at the margins of the school. The same was true for teachers. In small schools they were able to interact on a personal and intimate basis with their students. They often lived in the community and acted as adult role models while serving as coaches and club leaders. When they moved to large comprehensive high schools often located in a distant community, they, like their students, left the school environment they knew and understood. They too had to interact with large numbers of colleagues and students from many different communities. Intimacy and connection for them, as with their students, became more difficult.

The result? Subject-matter teaching more and more defined their role. Intimate, supportive, and helpful interactions became the role of the counselors, at least on paper. But as Conant suggested, the primary role of the counselor was to guide students into the right program and to persuade overambitious parents that their children were not academically talented. Personal counseling for the majority of students was more often than not given a lower priority due to the demands of college placement, testing, and scheduling of students into the right classes. In assigning counselors tasks and allotting time, as Conant recommended, priority was given to college placement and only the most troubled students in crisis saw the inside of the counselor's office.

The plan for large comprehensive high schools did bring with it new facilities and multiple curricula offerings. But an unintended consequence was a further isolating of teachers and students from one another on a personal and intimate level, pushing teachers further into their one-dimensional subject-matter specialist role. This made it less important for them to observe and identify students who were experiencing personal and well-being problems that affected their academic performance. It became easier for students to be anonymous and have their problems not recognized for two main reasons. First, because counselors oversold what they could realistically accomplish in helping students resolve their personal and well-being issues. Yes, on paper the role of the counselor was to intervene and when necessary refer troubled students to credible sources of help. But in reality the few counselors working in the large high schools were performing the tasks that Conant recommended, guiding students into the right programs and holding so-called ambitious parents at bay. The result? Students with personal and well-being problems that were causing poor academic performance were often slotted into nonacademic programs to learn marketable skills or encouraged to drop out. Second, the helping and advising skills of teachers were underutilized. They were told, sometimes not so subtly, that helping and advising were the counselors' job, not theirs. They were subject-matter teachers only, period. Results? A no-win situation for overburdened counselors, teachers who might have been helpful in advising their students how to overcome problems, and students who found few open doors in the school where they could pass through and have meaningful contact with a caring adult.

As education historian Robert Hampel points out, guidance counselors became a powerful force in the schools despite Conant's disappointment that his recommendation concerning the ratio of counselors to students had fallen short. The counseling ranks increased faster than the student population in the 1950s and early 1960s. In 1951–1952, 17.2 percent of high schools had at least 1 person who devoted half of his or her time or more to counseling. By 1966, 65 percent of high schools had hired counselors. Interestingly, these major changes involved the replacement of teacher-counselors by full-time counselors. In the 1930s and 1940s, some teachers counseled for one or two periods as part of their teaching role and administrators often shared guidance work. By the mid-1960s these duties were seldom their responsibilities. The same was true for principals and assistant principals, deans of boys, and deans of girls, who were once much more involved with counseling. By 1960, guidance was carried out mainly by full-time specialists. The change spawned so many journals, associations, training programs, and certification laws that no one could look on counselors as superannuated teachers or popular coaches. Yes, as Hampel points out, the guidance departments, however large, were not clinics dispensing survival skills. Counselors never analyzed teenagers' emotions to the extent envisioned by many reformers. They were greeted as administrators who would help keep the peace, expanding school services rather than reshaping what was already there. By the time of Sputnik in 1957, helping students with course selection and advising on college placement were the priorities. Counselors thus became mediators between students and the school's bureaucracy with a physical and symbolic location closer to the administration. Their new position of power was described by Dr. James E. Allen, commissioner of education of the New York State Department of Education, this way:

> Guidance is looked upon by the laymen, as well as those in education, as an integral and vital part of the educational process. The education profession and the public have come to expect substantial contributions from guidance in assisting boys and girls toward optimum development for their own fulfillment and for their economic and social contributions.[16]

Yet the 1964 American School Counselor Association's (ASCA) Statement of Policy for Secondary School Counselors[17] describes counseling in a much different, less administrative way. The policy statement identifies the school counselor as working in a secondary-school setting, concerned with and accepting a responsibility for assisting all pupils, and having as his or her major concern the developmental needs and problems of youth. They see counseling as a dynamic relationship between counselor and counselee and cite directly the counselor's responsibility for becoming involved with pupils and their behaviors. The counselor's focus is on the growth and development of pupils and on helping pupils to enhance and enrich their personal development and self-fulfillment by means of making more intelligent decisions.

In reality counselors rarely analyzed teenagers' emotions to the extent envisioned by reformers or recommended by their professional associations. As Hampel suggests, the counselor's role in the new comprehensive high school was as a quasi-administrator charged with scheduling, college placement, testing, and the like.

The emergence of shopping mall high schools increased teacher–student social distance and further locked counselors into a quasi-administrative role. As Powell, Farrar, and Cohen suggest, these newly created large high schools evolved into what they call "Shopping Mall High Schools." They suggest that secondary education is another consumption experience in an abundant society and compared these new comprehensive high schools to shopping malls that attract a broad range of customers with different tastes and purposes. Some students, like shoppers, know just what they want and efficiently make their purchases. Others come simply to browse. Still others do neither; they just hang out. The mall and the school are places to meet friends, pass the time, get out of the rain, or watch the promenade. Powell, Farrar, and Cohen report that teachers in these contemporary high schools, many of which even look like shopping malls, often regard themselves as sales people. Their business is to attract customers and persuade them to buy. Teachers compete with one another for the business of students.

In the process of selling themselves and their subjects and maintaining their enrollment, many teachers found their potential role as an adult model and advisor smothered by an increasing array of social services manned by counselors, school nurses, and increasing numbers of school security officers who addressed student health, adjustment, and safety issues. I believe these issues are augmented by the campus-like design of schools, large enrollments, and subsequent anonymity and disconnectedness among students coming from different communities.

Powell, Farrar, and Cohen provide a good example of how the teacher's potential role as an adult model and primary resource on the front lines of the school further dissolved. They point out that advising students is usually regarded as a specialized professional function of counselors. Counselors usually believe that teachers are inadequate for the advising task because they lack training in counseling and knowledge about the full variety of opportunities within the school. Counselors carry the brunt of advising and they prefer things that way. Unfortunately, the philosophy of well-intentioned counselors negated the value of teachers' involvement in the personal and well-being issues of their students, leaving teachers to feel, "OK, that's the way it is. One less thing to do. My involvement isn't wanted. Besides, these counselors think I don't have the knowledge and skills to advise my students."

This well-intended but unfortunate rejection of teachers' potentially valuable advising role had many unintended consequences for students, teachers, and counselors themselves, as Powell, Farrar, and Cohen vividly point out in a vignette describing a conversation between two high school students, Derek and George. Both students agreed that whenever they consulted any of the adults who were supposed to help them—counselors, nurses, social workers—the adult's assumption was that something must be very wrong. All they wanted was to talk to a caring adult, but the price of a conversation was that they would be considered a problem case. "It just scared me," said Derek. "She asked me so many questions it just made me scared. I don't ever want to go back there again." George reported, "Your counselors say they are there if you need help. But I don't agree with that. They should be there for you whether you need help or not."

As this conversation reveals, when students like Derek and George sought out a counselor as a way to "simply talk to a caring adult," they were viewed as problem students, not just kids trying to navigate through school academic and personal issues. In a sense, we created a system in which everyone loses. Caring teachers, often ideally situated to hear a student's concern and possibly bring clarity and hope, are out of the loop. Counselors are stuck in a role in which they are constantly buffeted by the school organization's demands to assess the aptitude and intelligence of students; advise them on course selection, gradua-tion requirements, and post high school career and college choices; and with the little time left serve as crisis counselors for the most troubled students. They are often placed in a situation in which they are overex-tended and trying to do too much. Being required to take leadership in the sorting, placing, and "credentializing" of students is politically demanding for counselors, with grave implications if they don't deliver. This process also produced a lose-lose situation for students. If they wanted to talk to a caring adult, they more often than not found teachers who were reluctant to step outside their subject-mastery role and counselors who were either too busy or too quick to assume that students who showed up at their door must be troubled.

As Powell, Farrar, and Cohen suggest, these perceptions are widely shared. The advising received by most students is dominated by the logistics of scheduling and meeting graduation requirements. "It's like you don't even know your counselor," one teenager complained. "You see him at the beginning of the year and that's it. You might as well not be here as far as he's concerned." "You see a counselor once," another reported. "You doing OK?" "And I'll say OK." A girl regarded her counselor as a kind of traffic cop who told her when to go and when to stop, which roads were open and which were blocked. "If I had a prob-lem he'd be the last one I would go to." The reason she gave was, "He doesn't know me. He wouldn't be able to help."

Part of the problem is, as Powell, Farrar, and Cohen point out, sheer numbers. At one school, the student-to-counselor ratio was 420 to 1. The objective of many counseling departments is to see each student once a year in a conference that typically, as one counselor suggests, takes ten minutes. In addition to sheer numbers, counselors complain with equal vehemence about the paperwork loaded upon them. One estimated that fully 75 percent of her time was spent keeping records, and others pointed to the significant scheduling and monitoring activi-ties required by special needs legislation. Yet, despite these odds, some of the nearly eight thousand counselors trained at university counselor education institutes sponsored by the National Defense Education Act in the 1960s did try to change their quasi-administrator role.[18] As coun-selor educator David R. Cook states, they were called change agents who could serve as creative critics, feedback agents, ombudsmen/student advocates and managers of conflict in addition to their regular guidance duties.[19] Their work was to help the school organization understand and respond to increasing racial conflicts and student unrest. They tried to implement new counseling approaches—such as group counseling and sensitivity training for teachers, group counseling for students, and training students as peer helpers—into their guidance programs. But in my experience with training school counselors in the 1960s, these bold and risky efforts by a small cadre of counselors to add a more personal connection between teachers and students was doomed to failure because of the pressing organizational demands identified by Powell, Farrar, and Cohen. Yes, counselor educators such as Cook could suggest that the guidance counselor who presumes that he can fulfill his role in the school by remaining in his office and seeing students one at a time is already an anachronism. When some counselors did move out of their offices and begin to offer group counseling to teachers and students, they encountered great resistance from colleagues who were more comfortable with their sorting and selecting role. They often found themselves without cover and political support from directors of guidance and school administrators who wanted these counselors back in their offices, dealing with the nuts and bolts of the guidance operation, not offering counseling to teachers and students that might bring calls for changes in the existing and increasingly vulnerable school climate. I believe it is safe to say that these pioneer counselors were out of step with the selecting and sorting counseling model that took hold in the 1960s and still exists today.

Counselor educator Harold L. Munson[20] describes the lost opportunity to utilize the helping and advising role of teachers with the emergence of counselors as *the* primary source of help for students. He suggests that teachers do have very specific classroom opportunities to become engaged with individual students in ways that not only facilitate the learning process of an individual student but also in ways that can be personally relevant and enhancing to him or her. He also suggests that teachers who care about a student or students who care about a teacher (or feel that a teacher cares about them) are more apt to communicate about very meaningful and sometimes confidential topics. They may develop very significant relationships. Such communication should be encouraged. Teachers are human. They can be accepting, understanding, and trusting. Some teachers, if we can accept the reports of youth, are better at providing these conditions than some school counselors. If a teacher can relate to a student in this manner, he or she should be free to do so. To restrict such relationships is to infringe on the freedom of the teacher and destroy the humanness of the teaching-learning process. Perhaps his or her communication skills and techniques are not professionally developed, yet he or she has the potentiality for a human relationship with every student. Communication about the student's progress, ability, and interest in the subject may spill over to personal matters outside the usual realm of teacher concern and responsibility. This should be anticipated and when the teacher feels capable and confident to deal with these issues, he or she should be encouraged to do so. This is counseling, even though it may be limited to the topics relevant to the individual's learning experience.

Munson cautions, however, that this role is rapidly being taken away from teachers. He suggests that while many students are seeking to communicate with teachers, with increasing frequency teachers are urged to refer students with learning irregularities, with unsatisfactory achievement, and with a host of other concerns to the school counselor. As Munson wisely suggests, the danger here lies in absolving the teacher of his or her rightful and expected guidance responsibilities. The message, while not always overt or openly expressed, has become rather clear. Even when this is calculated only for students with problems that extend beyond the proficiency of the teacher, the expectation that students are "treated" in the guidance office leaves the developmental needs of youth too often unattended in the classroom. And it raises considerable doubt, fear, and guilt in the mind of teachers who respond or feel they must respond to students. Teachers have been warned repeatedly that they are not counselors and thus, with the advent of guidance, they have become increasingly wary and cautious. Counseling has increasingly been a territorial claim of the school counselor, accordingly reducing the involvement of many teachers in any communication with their students that could be interpreted as counseling. As the guidance movement has developed, and particularly as the counseling function has become a more important and significant element in the total guidance activity, arguments against teacher involvement in student counseling have been cited. It is almost as if teachers have been warned against any kind of human involvement wherein they can communicate with their students about goals, interests, abilities, values, feelings, and behaviors. It is no wonder that some teachers have become disenchanted with the guidance movement. It is no wonder that they have become less sure of their own human relationships with their students. It is no wonder they have become cautious and concerned.

Munson's cogent observations about the negating of teachers' helping and advising role is on target. Munson's comments, made in 1971, could accurately describe the flawed helping relationships that exist in today's secondary schools. Yet I believe that counselors didn't intentionally set out to develop the flawed helping and advising system that remains alive and well in today's secondary schools. As the American School Counselors Association's policy statement suggests, the original goal of counseling in the secondary schools was to assist all students with their developmental needs and problems.[21] But other powerful forces were at play that forced counselors into a quasi-administrative role. The needs of the nation in the post–World War II and Sputnik era demanded that the schools guide students into the right courses, colleges, and vocations. Students were seen as resources to keep our nation strong militarily and economically. Counselors became the point persons in carrying out the school's new mandate. As Cook suggests, counselors emerged as one of the main functionaries in implementing the sorting and allocation of functions in the school. They were caught up in a system that left little time for personal counseling. Counselor educator Harold C. McCully says guidance became a nuts and bolts operation.[22] The nuts and bolts were the individual inventory, educational, and occupational information; counseling for a realistic future; matching of individual traits with occupational opportunities; and placement and follow up. As Cook suggests, general education counseling emerged as the main counseling concern in the schools. As he wisely observed, many counselors who might be adequate to the task of therapeutic counseling found that the demands of the school's situation made it difficult, if not impossible, to carry out this kind of counseling. Cook backs up his assertions with data from the New England Assessment Project:

1. When students were asked, "Has your school counselor helped you find better ways to solve problems about school and other things

you've had to face?" 68 per cent of students said no and 32 per cent said yes.

2. "Did you get help in understanding yourself from your school counselor?" Sixty-one per cent said no; 31 per cent said yes.

3. "Do you know yourself better as a student as a result of visiting your school counselor?" Sixty-four per cent said no; 36 per cent said yes.

4. "Can you talk about your real feelings about things with your school counselor?" Forty-three per cent said yes; 57 per cent said no.[23]

Cook suggests that for the past several years, counselors have been wrapped in an identity crisis, struggling with the question, "What is our role?" He suggests that professionalization of school counseling has become something of a box in which the school counselor is trapped.[24] The counselor has been seduced into functioning on behalf of the bureaucratic structure of the school. Despite a mountain of rhetoric about meeting the needs of "pupils," the reality is that it was the increasing bureaucratization of our school systems that created the demands for guidance services.

I believe Cook, writing in 1971, accurately described conditions for many fine counselors in 2003. The same conditions exist thirty-plus years later. As he suggested then, many counselors who might be adequate to the task of therapeutic counseling find the demands of the school situation make it difficult, if not impossible, to carry out this kind of counseling. And as it exists today, despite a mountain of rhetoric about meeting the needs of "pupils," the reality is that it was the increasing bureaucratization of our school system that has created the demands for guidance services.

And, I would add, it's no wonder, as Meier suggests, that most children today are disconnected from any community of adults including, absurdly, the adults they encounter in school. Many young people literally finish four years of high school without knowing or being known by a single adult in the school. I believe students, their teachers, and counselors themselves are victims of a helping and advising system that is itself disconnected from the personal, emotional, social, and well-being needs of students. They are existing in a school climate that is focused on the future, what students should and might become, rather than emphasizing, as John Dewey suggests, learning how to live in the present, learning how to develop habits and an openness of mind that would in the present, and in the future, give them control over their environment.

I believe the observations of Powell, Farrar, and Cohen, Munson, and Cook provide educators with a road map to begin correcting this out-of-date and flawed counselor-based helping and advising system. In particular let's remind ourselves of Munson's sound advice concerning why we need teachers in the helping and advising role:

> Teachers do have very specific classroom opportunities to become engaged with individual students in ways that not only facilitate the learning process of an individual student but in ways that can be personally relevant and enhancing to him. Teachers who care about a student or students who care about a teacher are apt to communicate about very meaningful and sometimes confidential topics.
>
> Such communication should be encouraged. Teachers are human. They can be accepting, understanding and trusting. Some teachers, if we can accept the reports of youth, are better at providing these conditions than some school counselors. If a teacher can relate with a student in this manner, he should be encouraged to do so. To restrict such relationships is to infringe on the freedom of the teacher and to destroy the humanness of the teaching-learning relationship.[25]

I believe that the kind of teacher model that Munson describes can emerge in our schools. In fact there are teachers who operate this way because they have a natural desire and commitment to engage their students on a personal as well as academic level. They know both areas are vital to students' achievement and healthy social and emotional development. Maybe their communication skills and techniques are not professionally developed but by being accepting, understanding, and trusting, they connect with their students. What we need to be about is focusing on these positive teacher models, how they go about their work, and consider how we can expect and empower other less skilled teachers to follow their model. As Powell, Farrar, and Cohen report, most students and most teachers do prefer relations they see as open, friendly, and caring. No student definition of a good teacher was more common than someone who could "relate" to them. "When you have a good relationship with someone it is much easier to come to school," said one student. In a different school a particular teacher seemed, "the best, not an asshole like every other teacher." But another teacher, who admittedly knew her subject extremely well, was considered "a drip, a wet blanket" because she was so introverted. "She only gives a certain amount to the class." Students would have liked her better "if you knew something about her." Relating well requires self-revelation as well as friendliness. Teachers like her had "a steel wall around them. They know the kids can't relate to them but they don't care, and they don't try to relate to kids." Teachers tended to agree. One said, "You've got to be personal; you've got to be friendly. It helps the kids get interested. You can't be nasty." Another summed up the general mood. "Kids want to be dealt with openly, and they want people to be straight with them. I find that dealing with things directly, getting angry, taking the kids seriously, giving and taking and being vulnerable, is what teachers need in order to get along with kids in school today. The kids want to know they're cared for."

I believe we need to increase the kind of positive teacher role model described above. The goal is to encourage and empower the kind of teacher who, as vividly reported about, knew her subject extremely well but who was a "drip, a wet blanket." "Students would like her better if you knew something about her." I would agree with the student's assessment that teachers like this know the kids can't relate to teachers who lack understanding of their students' lives and how to connect with them, can't be both straight and caring, and know they lack these powerful components in their teacher repertoires. Most teachers know when they are not connecting, even though they have mastery of their subject matter. And for most teachers facing this kind of painful classroom experience is personally and professionally debilitating, a situation that encourages anonymity on the part of both students and teacher, each withdrawing to his or her own isolated camps, a situation where the subject matter itself becomes the guiding force and personal relationships don't exist.

I believe our students' assessment that teachers who know the kids can't relate to them "don't care" is not accurate. Most teachers do understand that being able to relate to students is a powerful way to increase student interest and desire to show up in class and learn.

Teachers with poor relating skills do observe other teachers who have effective relating skills and, I believe, secretly desire to be like them. I say "secretly" because teachers like the expert subject-mastery teacher described above don't know how to go about understanding the personal side of their students' lives, how they learn, how they develop, and what works to get them involved. They lack data on what goes on with students outside the classroom, what their hopes and dreams are, what failures and setbacks they have experienced. As a result, they lack the necessary information that could be used in creating helpful conversations with each student and, lacking a means of knowing more about their students, how to question them and how to reveal their own professional and personal self, being forced to settle for being one-dimensional subject-mastery teachers who tend to build steel walls around themselves and surround themselves with like-minded subject-mastery colleagues who spend their careers bemoaning the lack of student achievement. What is needed are effective ways for subject-mastery teachers to gather personal and well-being data about their students, understand how to reveal themselves as persons and be more like the teacher Mrs. Austin. As Powell, Farrar, and Cohen report, Mrs. Austin says, "It feels good to walk down the hall and be able to say hello to people and know who they really are; they're not just faces."

Powell, Farrar, and Cohen conclude that personalization has a human and a professional dimension. The human side involves knowing students from the point of view of a concerned adult friend, while the professional side adds the element of specialized knowledge about particular strengths and weaknesses in learning. In the end, what students need are adults who know them as unique learners, complex and distinctive.

The kind of teacher personalization called for by Powell, Farrar, and Cohen was hard to come by in the 1960s and 1970s, just as it is today. As author and researcher Larry Cuban suggests in reporting on research carried out by John I. Goodlad in the late 1960s, in sixty-seven schools in thirteen states, the classrooms the research team observed were marked by teachers "telling students."[26] Goodlad and his research team, in looking behind the classroom door, found a dreary sameness, a "flatness." Reforms were "blunted at the school and classroom door." The report concluded that in subject matter, materials, and teaching practice the 150 classrooms were "geared to group norms rather than individual differences." Cuban also cites a survey of research studies commissioned by the National Science Foundation in curricular and instructional changes that had taken place in science, math, and social studies between 1955 and 1975. The survey found:

- In math the teacher talks about two-thirds of the time. Telling and questioning, usually in total class groups is the prevailing practice.
- In science at the secondary level there is less lecture and more student centered activity than there used to be but lecture and discussion is the predominant method used by teachers.

Cuban also reports on research he conducted in classrooms in North Dakota, New York City, Washington, D.C., and scattered sites around the country. He concluded that there is very little evidence to show that classroom practice in regular high schools between 1967 and 1975 varied substantially from that of a generation earlier. The picture of high school teaching that emerges from these accounts is unmistakably teacher centered and remarkably akin to what showed up three or four decades earlier. Cuban also concluded that teachers continued to monopolize classroom verbal exchanges. In high school pedagogy since 1900, the five academic subjects altered very little except for formal recitation. Raising hands, yelling out answers, and informal discussion techniques replaced standing at one's desk or in front of the room to answer the teacher's questions. Whole group discussion, teacher-controlled classroom, little student movement, and little variety in tasks captured the high school classrooms in the 1970s.

Cuban argues that this behavior should not come as a surprise. He suggests that the occupational ethos of teaching breeds conservatism and resistance to change in instructional practice. This conservatism (i.e., preference for stability and caution toward change) is rooted in the people recruited into the profession, how they are informally socialized and the school culture that itself is a primary ingredient. Cuban points out that teachers believe students learn best in well-managed, noiseless classrooms where limits are made clear, academic rigor is prized, rules are equitably enforced, and the teacher's authority,

rooted in institutional legitimacy and knowledge, must be paid respectful attention. These and similar beliefs are held by most teachers, especially in high schools. They account for the perseverance of such
teaching practices as reliance upon textbooks, little student movement,
and a concern for tranquil classrooms marked by the "hum of knowledge." Beliefs, then, shape what teachers choose to do in their classrooms and explain the core of instructional practices that have endured
over time. But Cuban suggests the argument of a teacher culture
explains nicely the durability of a core of teaching practices. It
accounts for high school classrooms especially retaining the look and
smell and activities of previous generations.

The social, cultural, and political eruptions in the beginning of the
1960s acted to further isolate students from personal and intimate
connections with teachers.   As Ravitch suggests, the 1960s began
with no hint of troubles ahead for schools and society.[27] Educators
enjoyed a keen sense of success. They had come closer to providing
universal access to high school education than in any generation before
them. In 1900, it was a rare youngster, only six out of every one hundred, who earned a high school diploma. By 1960, an astounding 70
percent of high school students received a diploma. For years the system had worked as planned, sending appropriate proportions of students to colleges, farms, factories, shops, domestic service, and
homemaking. But that keen feeling of success and pride fell apart in
many high schools in the 1960s. The upheaval of the 1960s changed
the public schools in important ways. Confronted with violence, disci-
plinary problems, and litigation, school officials backed away from acting "in locus parentis." In an effort to reduce conflict, academic
demands were minimized; students were increasingly left to fend for
themselves, without adult guidance.

Author Gerald Grant describes the chaos and lack of control at Hamilton High, the placid and coherent school community of the 1950s that
was destroyed by the turbulence of the 1960s.[28] In 1960, Hamilton
High was regarded as the leading school in the area. The school was
orderly; hallways glistened and lateness to class was a rarity. Students
showed deference to teachers and seldom needed more than a stern
glance to correct behavior. But, after taking steps to increase racial
integration, the school was convulsed with riots and violence from

1968 to 1971. Discipline dissolved, respect for teachers evaporated, racial separation increased, many white middle-class students left the school, and administrators had to devote most of their time to disciplining unruly students. In a school that once prided itself on its keen sense of community, adult authority collapsed. As Grant suggests, fearful of litigation, the adults at Hamilton High retreated to their classrooms and closed their doors. The school added new specialists to the staff for counseling and various social activities. As a result the school became more bureaucratic and teachers distanced themselves from their authority as adults. The school's organization operated under the flawed interpretation I cited earlier in the chapter, a belief that counselors would handle problems and teachers would teach. Students were increasingly left to fend for themselves, without adult guidance.

A survey by the National Association of Secondary School Principals in January 1969 revealed that 59 percent of a national sample of high school principals had experienced some form of student activism in their schools.[29] Many who had not experienced any activism expected they would shortly. Large suburban schools seemed to be the most affected, with 81 percent reporting activism. But large urban schools were also subject to activist incidents in 74 percent of those reporting. Estimates in late spring of 1969 placed the incidence of protest activities as high as two thousand high schools. This is how a superintendent of schools describes the school system of that era:

> Our schools are organized on a semi-prison approach. We have a lack of trust, sign-in and sign-out slips. Detention systems, wardens and jailers, fear of escape, regimentation, limited opportunities for choice, barricaded or locked toilet rooms, cell-like classrooms. Why are we surprised that some youngsters rebel? Is it not surprising that more of them do not?[30]

This withdrawal of adult guidance in the 1960s was also documented in research by James Coleman.[31] He reported that adults were retreating from their responsibility for monitoring the character and civic behavior of young people, leaving them without adequate supervision and without moral benchmarks. One result, as Ravitch points out, was that in the 1960s and 1970s the rates of drug and alcohol use among teenagers soared, as did homicides, suicides, and out of wedlock births. During this period the schools experienced increasing difficulties in maintaining discipline and student disrespect for teachers became commonplace.[32]

Author Rosemary C. Salomone[33] joins Coleman in this view of adults in the schools and community leaving children without adequate supervision and moral benchmarks when she reports that during the 1960s and 1970s, in classrooms across the country, teachers no longer taught right and wrong as moral absolutes bur rather led students to define and clarify their own values, which did not necessarily reflect those of their parents.

By the 1980s, Coleman's prediction of an American society in which many children are increasingly left on their own without needed adult guidance and role modeling was becoming the norm. He had predicted, as Ravitch suggests, the emergence of a social structure in which no one would be responsible for children and in which busy parents would view their daughters and sons as burdens and treat them with indifference. The exodus from city to the suburbs, he forecast, meant busy parents would work far from home. As the home ceased to be the center of social life and became "psychologically barren," he said women would join their husbands in the workforce. Children would remain behind, cared for by hired help or state agencies or given the latchkey to an empty home, abandoned to their own devices and lacking responsible adult supervision. Children would learn how to behave from other children and from television and movies. Under such circumstances they would absorb myriad random cues about how to conduct themselves rather than being systematically imbued with consistent norms. Yet consistency of norms was critical in the socialization of children, Coleman explained, because norms "establish within the child a sense of what is 'right' and what is 'wrong.'"[34] If that content is inconsistent, the norms conflict with one another and the child has a less fully developed sense of what is right and wrong.

The publication of **A Nation at Risk** *(1983), calling for higher standards and an increased academic emphasis for students, served to reinforce the subject-master role for teachers.* In the 1980s, there developed a growing consensus that something had to be done to improve education standards. *A Nation at Risk* warned that the schools had not kept pace with the changes in society and the economy and that the nation would suffer if education were not dramatically improved for all children. As education historians David L. Angus and Jeffrey E. Mirel suggest, the *A Nation at Risk* report, prepared by the National Commission on Excellence in Education, focused on a host of indicators, all of which revealed a profound crisis in public education, with problems of the high schools receiving the lion's share of attention.[35] These problems included an exceptionally low ranking by American students in international comparisons of student achievement. The commission urged states and local districts to mandate that, at a minimum, all students seeking a diploma take, as part of a four-year high school education, "(a) four years of English; (b) three years of mathematics; (c) three years of science; (d) three years of social studies; and (e) one-half year of computer science. For the college bound, two years of foreign language in high school are strongly recommended in addition to those taken earlier." The commission decried the "cafeteria-style" curriculum in which students could get a large portion of their credits for graduation through such courses as physical and health education, work experience outside of school, remedial courses, and personal service and development courses such as training for adulthood, bachelor living, and marriage.

However, as Angus and Mirel argue, children come to school with diverse abilities, backgrounds, talents, and problems. They learn different things at different rates and at different times in their development. It was a given that schools emphasizing high academic standards will succeed only if educational professionals create developmentally appropriate, challenging course material and methods for all students at every grade level. Much of the failure of modern American education lies in our avoiding the formidable task of discovering how to teach difficult subjects in ways that are both accessible to young people and yet true to the complexity and richness of the material.

What was missing in the *A Nation at Risk* report was the need for teachers to understand students with diverse backgrounds, talents, and problems and how to use this data to assess "how" to make difficult subjects accessible to the young. The message to teachers was to increase their subject-matter competence. Instead, what I believe teachers needed to hear was the practical advice offered by Powell, Farrar, and Cohen, that personalization of the teacher–student relationship is the key to successful achievement. As they said, personalization has a human side that involves knowing students from the point of view of a concerned adult friend and a professional side that adds the element of specialized knowledge about particular strengths and weaknesses in learning. In the end what students need are adults who know them as unique learners, complex and distinctive. However, as Meier points out, what occurred when the recommendations of *A Nation at Risk* were implemented was an increase in students' tuning out and dropping out for those at the bottom of the school's achievement and economic ladder. And, I would add, the report's call to minimize graduation credits awarded for courses that served to improve the well-being of students, such as health and physical education, ignored rising student health problems, such as being overweight, developing anorexia, and being at risk for alcohol, drug, and tobacco addiction. The report's call for cutting back the opportunities for students to receive credit for work experience outside the school also served to reduce the availability of positive adult mentors found in the workplace.

The relentless pursuit of credentials by students for personal advancement has served as yet another vehicle to lock teachers into their subject-mastery role and reduce the opportunity for meaningful personal contact and advising between teachers and students. As researcher David Lararee reports, the growing disengagement of students from the learning process, one of the primary problems confronting educators today, can be traced to the increasing dominance of the view that education is primarily a mechanism for producing credentials, not knowledge.[36] More than ever before, the publicness of public education is being called into question, so it is increasingly acceptable, even canonical, to think of education as a community whose purpose is to meet the needs of individual consumers. In the process the pursuit of educational advantage has inadvertently threatened to transform the public education system into a mechanism for personal advancement. The generous public goals that have been so important in defining the larger societal interest in education, to produce potentially capable and socially productive citizens, have lost significant ground to the narrow pursuit of private advantage at public expense. The result is that the common school has become increasingly uncommon, with a growing emphasis on producing selective symbolic distinction rather than shared substantive accomplishments, and the community interest in education has lost ground to the individual interests in education as private property. The relentless pursuit of education credentials in the name of social mobility is gradually consuming our system of education.

Lararee supports his argument of increasing student disengagement from the learning process by utilizing research by author Laurence Steinberg that identifies student disengagement as the central problem facing education in the United States. Drawing on a study of twenty thousand high school students, Steinberg concludes that an extremely high proportion of American high school students do not take school, or their studies, seriously. The root of the problem, he says, is in the kind of rewards that schools have available to them to motivate academic efforts. Steinberg says most of the time what keeps students going to school is not intrinsic motivation, motivation derived from the process of learning itself, but extrinsic motivation, motivation that comes from real or perceived consequences associated with success or failure, whether these consequences are immediate (in the form of grades, the reactions of parents, or the response of friends) or delayed (in the form of anticipated impact in other educational settings or in the adult world of work). Over the course of their educational careers, students are increasingly exposed to extrinsic motivation. As a result, teachers find themselves in the position of gatekeepers and dispensers of grades, credits, and degrees, dealing with students who have a belief system that all that counts is graduation. As Steinberg suggests, the urge to get ahead has transformed the basic function of U.S. education from public service to private service and this transformation has brought significant consequences for the people who attend, work in, pay for, and, in various ways, depend on American schools.

I contend that this process has helped to further cement the teacher's role as subject-matter specialist. A role in which they are perceived by some students as a tool to be used, and abused, in their hurry to get ahead in our credentialized world. Teachers are, in a sense, hemmed in by self-serving students and students who pressure them to provide high grades, produce high test results, and provide the necessary credentials for star students to enter elite colleges. It is a role in which it becomes all too easy to ignore low-achieving students who know they have little chance to participate in a school or society where credentials rule.

These eleven indicators offer evidence as to why it should come as no surprise that many of today's teachers do not see their role as adult role models and key players in advising students how to resolve personal and health issues that impact negatively on their school performance. While the indicators I have listed can help us better understand why teachers have been stuck, sometimes forced, into their one-dimensional subject-mastery roles, I believe we need to put a real face on the way teachers perceive the barriers to carrying on more personal contact with each of their students. Education reformer and writer Theodore E. Sizer provides us with a vivid picture of both the problem and the opportunity as represented by Horace Smith, a fifty-nine-year-old veteran English teacher from Franklin High School.[37] Among parents and graduates, he is widely considered a star faculty member of this inner-suburban high school of 1,350 pupils. His student load is 132. As Sizer suggests, Horace recognizes that he does not know many of his kids well enough to really understand how their minds work, how and why they make mistakes, and what motivates them, what stars they seek to reach or whether each hankers after a star at all. He perceives most of his students as "acquaintances" as they hail him in the hallway. But does he know them well enough to teach them powerfully, know the ways of their minds and moods? No, not even close. Horace compromises. He gets to know a few students very well, usually those who interest him especially or who press themselves to him. The kids in the middle remain a genial blur. Indeed, Horace wryly admits that most of them cherish their anonymity. "If Mr. Smith really knew me, he might find out that . . ."

During the school day, the students come to Horace by "classes"— ninth grade, tenth grade, and the rest. A student is in a particular class on the basis of her or his birthday. To be out of step, sixteen in the ninth grade or fourteen in the eleventh grade, is cause for comment, usually contemptuous—Dummy, Nerd. One of those kids. The assumption behind the system is that kids of the same age are essentially alike, more or less teachable in the same way and properly held to similar standards. Horace knows better. Young people grow intellectually, physically, and socially at different rates, often with mysterious spurts and stops along the way. As Sizer suggests about Horace, one copes largely by not being careful, by deliberately not attending to the record and specialness and stage of growth and disposition of each youngster. They are all ninth-graders so treat them the same—the same curriculum, same textbook, same pedagogy, same tests, same standards, same everything. It defies common sense.

I believe Sizer's observations about Horace give educators insight into why teachers, even star teachers like Horace, keep their social distance from the majority of their students and remain one-dimensional subject-matter specialists. While I agree with Sizer's assessment that one factor in Horace's choice not to have close contact with the majority of his students is large student loads and school size, I believe student numbers are not the primary reason for his choice, his compromise. I argue that Horace's belief that the way to make Franklin High more student-centered is to redesign the school structure is off the mark. As researchers Robert L. Sinclair and Ward J. Ghory suggest, many school reform efforts have been doomed to failure because of their focus on creating new structures rather than assessing "how" to improve the ways in which teachers relate to students.[38] In fact, Sinclair and Ghory observe that well-intentioned changes in school structure carried out by school reformers did not result in "how" educators thought about or acted toward students who were struggling to learn. The basis for Horace's dilemma is that he is locked into a stagnant role that is out of date in today's complex schools. And there is no one in the school—colleagues or administrators—who is available to show him how to connect with all of his students, some who are "different" and hard to reach, and expect him to add these new strategies to his teaching role. He is a star teacher and no one seems to observe that a major factor in his compromise is the fact that his skills may be out of date and ineffective in responding to the needs of today's students. No one, including Horace, expects him to change the way he teaches. They think the problems at Franklin High are dictated by the system, not the current teacher–student interactions. Here are some examples of how some of Horace's response to his students is holding him back from making quality student contact. His is a role that may have worked in the past for Horace but now limits his opportunities to be a successful teacher for all his students.

1. While he recognizes that he does not know many of his kids well enough to understand how their minds work, how and why they make mistakes, and what motivates them, he seems to accept and believe that the primary reason for this is the large number of students he has to deal with. Yes, he seems to care and recognize the problem. He wants a reduced student load for both himself and his colleagues so they can deal more effectively with individual students. He doesn't want to retire. As Sizer suggests, Horace believes, perversely, he often thinks, that Franklin High is not nearly what it could be. He wants to stay on and make it better. However, in my view of Horace, he, like many teachers, is stuck in a career pattern where someone says he or she wants to do more to connect with students but sees it as impossible until class sizes are dramatically reduced. "There are just too many students to serve." The bottom line is that Horace lets the numbers dictate his response. As a result, he decides, chooses, that he can become personally involved with only a small percentage of his students. He compromises. As Sizer suggests, he gives a little, gets along, compromises. In my opinion, he is handcuffed, neutered, by his response. He will do what he can but the odds are against him, he thinks.

2. His role with the majority of his students is an "acquaintance" role, a relationship defined by Webster as one in which a person knows another but not intimately. While he is hailed in the hallway, he has created a distance, a void, with the majority of his students.

3. Horace decides on the few students—the chosen few—whom he gets to know very well. They are usually the ones who interest him or who press themselves to his attention. This choosing of whom he interacts with is, in my opinion, human but in his own self-interest. His needs for human contact are being met in this compromise, not the needs of the majority of his students. He creates a close social distance with students who have special gifts and who have interests, perhaps even backgrounds and values,

that are more like his own. He is in sync, comfortable, even safe with these students. He is forced into human contact with students who press themselves on him, assertive or aggressive students who refuse to be part of the "genial blur" or put off, who demand from Horace the grades and recommendations that will give them one leg up in the competitive race to get into elite colleges and universities.

4. The rest of his students are a "genial blur" and generally remain anonymous. While Horace suggests that these students cherish their anonymity, I argue that it is Horace himself who promotes it. I suggest that in his students' perception, Horace himself is seen as a "genial blur" and as a person who cherishes his own anonymity. Horace is the director casting this scene. Perhaps in choosing anonymity, he hopes these isolated students won't notice that he is safer and more comfortable communicating with students who interest or who pressure him. Maybe they won't get the message that in this school climate they are in fact valued less by Horace and maybe by other teachers as well. Let them be and then let them move on.

5. Although he knows better, Horace copes by deliberately not attending to the record and specialness and stage of growth of each youngster. They are all ninth graders so treat them the same. It's a "better not to know" philosophy and way of interacting with students, by keeping himself and his students anonymous. Then maybe he won't have to notice, understand, and feel when students begin failing, having personal and well-being problems, acting up, missing school, becoming troubled, and heading toward the margins of school life and even dropping out.

But give Horace credit. He knows that some of the school's practices defy common sense and he recognizes that he goes along. His compromise is part of the problem. But he doesn't just sit it out. He becomes chair of a committee to review the purposes and practices of Franklin High School. He believes, as Sizer suggests, that the school itself must be rethought and redesigned and that his compromises must be addressed and remedied. Horace advocates that lowering class loads to a reasonable and workable number is a priority in rethinking and redesigning schools. One can sense Horace's strong belief that high student load is the primary reason for his inability to know each of his students well when, during a committee meeting, his principal suggests that "the trick is in getting to know each one well enough to provide each one attention. Her voice swelled as she stressed 'each one.'" Horace's response is strong and candid. "How in the hell do you expect me to do that with 130 kids? Until we have a realistic chance of knowing each kid well, we'll be stuck with our nasty stereotypes and the kids will fall in right behind us, little self-fulfilling prophesies."

My question for Horace, and for teachers in general, is, "Will reducing student loads to eighty students motivate you to have closer personal relationships with your students?" Will reducing class size motivate Horace to know all his students better, including the students in the middle whom he now treats as a "genial blur"? Will reducing class size help Horace to gain an awareness that maybe it is he, not the students in the middle, who is creating this social distance between him and these anonymous students? Will Horace be motivated to grapple with the hard work necessary to make these changes or will he expect this close contact with students to somehow magically take place once class size is reduced? Put simply, will he demand of himself that he take responsibility for knowing his students well, what star they seek, and begin to offer encouragement to those students who have long ago given up on finding their star? I have my doubts. I argue that reducing class size holds no sure guarantee that quality teacher–student personal contact will follow. It is only one part of the equation. My own experience as an educator suggests that other more subtle factors are at play. For example, while many teachers like Horace protest that only a reduction in class size will enable them to have a personal connection with their students, many, because of the indicators I have identified earlier in this chapter, have in fact hesitated to buy into the notion that this kind of personal interaction is an important part of their job and ultimately has a potential payoff for their subject-mastery role. As a result, they have had little practice in how to proceed to form the kinds of personal connections with students that I am advocating. This has little to do with the size of the student load. In order to change the way many teachers view their work, we are going to have to help teachers change current belief systems and practices by:

1. raising their awareness as to why they have traditionally resisted interacting with students on nonacademic issues,
2. selling them on the notion that understanding the personal side of their students' lives will serve as a vehicle to help students improve their academic success as well as their well-being,
3. assisting them in learning and practicing concrete ways to interact on a personal level with their students.

I also believe that we need to bring to light and examine other, more subtle, long-held reasons as to why teachers, even star teachers like Horace, have distanced themselves from close relationships with students and settled for an "acquaintance" role. These reasons go beyond the historical indicators I have addressed earlier in this chapter that have worked to limit teachers to their one-dimensional subject-mastery role. They go beyond the notion that quality teacher–student interaction for every student will only occur with redesigning our present educational delivery system and reducing school and class size. Most important, I believe teachers are not always conscious of these reasons; they are not on their radar screen. Here are examples of some of the more subtle, hard to observe reasons that we need to bring to light in order to help teachers better understand why they have limited their contact with all of their students:

Using reasons such as high student load as the primary motive and defense as to why teachers distance themselves from personal involvement with their students allows educators to settle for an easy answer to a more complex problem. By suggesting that high student loads are the primary reason that teachers don't become personally involved with their students, we have prevented educators from examining other compelling reasons for this distancing. It is an equation that needs reworking. I believe that for far too long we've allowed this specious argument to go unchallenged. And for far too long we have allowed teachers to hide behind this argument as to why they cannot get more personally involved with students. Large student loads do not automatically have to lead to teacher and student anonymity. There are other reasons, the dark side of teaching I call them, for this phenomenon.

When teachers like Horace are left on their own to make choices about what students they interact with, they block out the opportunity to learn how to deal with students whom they avoid.   One of the key phrases describing Horace's compromise is "he cannot be expected to know every one of his students well." Let's zero in on the work "expected" and ask just "who" is expecting Horace to add this important work to his teaching menu. Clearly there is no administrator bearing down on this star teacher to get on with the work of knowing his students well. And clearly this kind of behavior is not called for at Franklin High School, although the school's public relations talk about "taking each child individually" and claiming that caring teacher–student relationships are a hallmark of the schools success. No, it is Horace himself who chooses to remain a distant "acquaintance" and forego a closer relationship in which he just might learn how his students' minds work, how and why they make mistakes, and what motivates them. Yes, on the surface Horace is a star teacher and is hailed in the hallways. But in choosing to distance himself from the majority of his students, he has boxed himself into a situation with little opportunity for growth. For example, he gets to experience only those students who interest him or bang on his door. He doesn't get to know or understand the other students who seemingly hold no interest for him or who easily withdraw, not wanting to be involved. It's a lose-lose situation for both Horace and his students.

Horace loses because he doesn't have to learn how to make quality contact with many of his students and successfully motivate them to become involved and perhaps more successful students. Maybe he thinks he has arrived at the top of his career. He's a star teacher. He believes by lowering class size and redesigning the school, all will be well. It is the system that is at fault. He doesn't have to change or learn new strategies. The system is making him compromise. Horace's marginal students lose because they know they can remain uninvolved and not be expected to reveal more of themselves or make a commitment to the learning process. And let's not forget the students who interest or press themselves on Horace. They, too, lose because they may begin to believe that the special attention they receive from Horace may continue in all future high school and college classes.

In my view, Horace's choices and compromises result in creating a teaching role that is safe, comfortable, and relatively risk free. But the role has a huge downside as it is lacking in challenge and the opportunity for new learning on how to improve on his personal relationships with students. He doesn't have to relate to each student and he knows it. He doesn't even have to try. All he has to say is that the numbers are too high. For me, Horace's response to the growing need for teenagers to have caring and concerned adults in their corner is as harmful to his professional growth as it is to his students' personal and academic growth. He gets away with being less of a teacher than he can be. As Sizer suggests, Horace copes largely by not being careful, by deliberately not attending to the records and specialness and stage of growth and disposition of each youngster. They are all ninth graders; treat them the same—same curriculum, same textbooks, same pedagogy, same tests, same standards, same everything. It defies common sense. But he goes along. He knows in the daily practices of the school's organization, there is virtually no attempt to get thorough information to a student's new teacher about the youngster's history. Students do have files someplace but Horace knows that teachers don't read them and they are not encouraged to do so. Better to treat them all the same or accept someone else's judgment about how swift a kid is and go with it. Expect more or expect less, compromise with your common sense. The kids are different but we can't admit this, even to ourselves.

Making classroom decisions based only on compromise, common sense, and the judgments of other educators is not in the best interest of students or teachers like Horace.   Common sense is not enough. We need up-to-date data about each student—how he or she learns, his or her strengths and abilities, areas that need attention, his or her home and family life, relations with peers, past successes and failures, and hopes and dreams. Teachers need to make these assessments on a regular basis and not settle for someone else's judgment about how swift a kid is. To his credit, Horace does recognize the need to know more about his students but he blames his inability to do so on large classes. His compromise is with less. And as Sizer suggests, he resents his compromises and derides himself for making them. As a result he can't be counted on when a parent asks, as Sizer observes, "Does anybody know my children well and care for them? Will there be a future for my children and is the school helping them to achieve?"

Another part of this equation, a dark and usually not discussed area, is Theodore R. Sizer and Nancy Sizer's observation that educa-

tors can be selfish.[39]   If an institution claims to be responsive to a variety of constituencies but essentially serves only one, then it becomes hypocritical. Many teachers think of what "their" students need but others have come to be content with thinking of what *they* need. It is true that teachers need to feel comfortable in order to serve children well, but how comfortable? For example, remember Horace's claim that Franklin High School uses plenty of public relations talk about "taking each child individually, but the school's practices belie the boast." It's simply not fair to students, parents, and well-intended teachers to claim to be a child-centered school, not let one student fall between the cracks, and in reality allow a portion of students to remain anonymous. It is bad practice to allow some teachers to come and go, their eyes glued to the floor as they hurry through the hallways, only satisfying their own need for safety, no confrontations, no involvement, and clearly no commitment other than showing up and teaching their subject matter, fostering and serving as a model for a school climate in which their own needs come first, and being allowed to choose to avoid students who make them uncomfortable, who are different, and who in the teacher's mind have a dark side that may lead to mischief and confrontation. This conscious decision, which allows teachers to choose which students they wish to connect with, is the highest level of hypocrisy and an insult to those parents who honestly ask of teachers, "Does anyone know my children well and care for them?" And it is an insult to hard-working teachers who, in spite of large class sizes, do see as their job to connect individually with students and through conversations learn what stars they seek to reach and, when that star is missing, encourage students to begin believing that finding their star is possible and to get on with the work. Hypocritical, self-centered, and selfish teachers who seek only to satisfy their own needs are bad medicine for a positive school climate. They can avoid quality contact with their students by hiding behind the argument that their class sizes are too large. Their behavior is not a compromise but a cover-up for not doing what is needed for students in a changing world. Allowing the behavior of teachers who are selfish to go unchallenged gives off a powerful negative message to concerned teachers who see this travesty taking place in some of their peers, new teachers who may adopt this role model, administrators who look the other way and allow these behaviors to go on, and most of all, vulnerable students who may see these kinds of personal avoidances by teachers as personal rejections, particularly "different" students who because of color, culture, ability, and so on often have had more than their share of rejection in their homes, communities, and schools.

No, I don't believe Horace is self-centered or selfish. Rather, I believe the more subtle and less understood reasons for his compromises and choices are being driven by teaching practices that were successful in his earlier teaching life but no longer work for today's students and by the lack of professional development opportunities to learn new teaching strategies that would help him regain his professional footing. If he is going to exit his career being a successful teacher, he is going to need to develop new skills to meet these changing times. Sizer suggests that a teacher cannot stimulate a child's mind any more than a physician can guide ill patients to health without knowing the patient's physical condition. Tendencies, patterns, likelihoods exist, but the course of action necessary for an individual requires an understanding of the particulars.

As I have said, structural changes to the school's organization won't in themselves help Horace obtain these necessary skills. Remember the advice of Sinclair and Ghory that changes in school structure do not necessarily result in changes in "how" educators thought about and acted toward students who were struggling to learn. While Sizer argues for the need for structural changes that would reduce student loads, create opportunities for teachers to share information about students, and set aside time for teachers to confer with students and parents, he wisely reminds us that even if schools were to adopt these measures, most barriers to change, to doing business in a different way, are more personal and poignant. Teachers would have to teach differently, and even if they could imagine the prospect, they fear doing so. They are ill-trained to shift the way they work, having been studiously prepared in the universities for an unchangeable school world. To get the load of students down to an acceptable level, most would have to collaborate with colleagues, an unsettling business. Working alone in the castle of one's classroom is preferable to exposing to peers what one thinks of individual students and how one would teach them. Some "specialist" would have to carry out more broadly defined jobs, ones that would challenge them and challenge the mystery of their specialty.

Therefore, in reviewing the impact of some of the historical indicators and subtle reasons as to why many teachers have distanced themselves from personal contact with their students, it should come as no surprise that today's teachers are ill-trained to shift the way they work. As Sizer suggests, most barriers to change, doing business in a different way, are personal and poignant. Teachers would have to teach differently and even if they imagined the prospect, they fear doing so. And they would have to begin viewing teaching as a constantly changing process, acquiring new skills in order to respond to today's students and abandoning comfortable skills that no longer work. They would have to learn how to communicate with all their students and colleagues rather than only those who offer comfort and safety. Specialists, such as guidance counselors, would have to take some of the professional mystery out of their work and, as counselor educator Harold Munson suggests, encourage, not negate, teachers' personal contact with students.

I believe Sizer's use of the word "mystery" is very helpful to my argument. It is clear in reviewing the historical indicators and subtle reasons that have kept teachers locked in their subject-matter role that the process of how teachers should proceed to make personal contact with students has been shrouded in mystery. There has been little expectation or concrete training for teachers to add pedagogy to their subject-mastery role. As a result the helping and advising skills now needed in today's teacher–student relationships have remained unexplained and unknown to teachers and kept secret by specialists such as counselors. It's no wonder that faulty assumptions about helping and advising have been allowed to exist for decades. Let me list and hopefully demystify some of these faulty assumptions that have been long held by teachers and bring some reality and encouragement to the teacher–student advising process.

1. In the process of better knowing and understanding their students, teachers will somehow become personally responsible when trouble occurs. In fact, the opposite is true. By becoming

more personally involved with students, teachers can help their students resolve small problems before they become crises.

2. In the process of knowing and understanding their students, teachers have to become minicounselors and learn a whole new set of intervention and helping skills. Again, this is far from reality. Creating opportunities to talk with students, hearing and respecting their stories, and being willing to offer advice and direct them to other sources of help is not rocket science. One does not need an advanced degree in counseling or professional techniques to perform these tasks. Nor does one have to take on a parent surrogate, friend, or messiah role to save troubled children. Rather, teachers have to offer to students simple overtures that send a message of caring and concern and not expect immediate positive responses.

3. Counselors are the only professionals who are expected to become personally involved with students. In fact, given the large counselor-student ratio in today's high schools, counselors spend far less time with individual students than do teachers. Most committed and interested teachers do have an understanding of the particulars of each child, how their minds work, where they come from, what pressures them. This can't be said for overworked counselors, who constantly are being buffeted by pressure from scheduling, college placement, and so on. Many teachers do know how to listen, be nonjudgmental, and provide useful feedback and modeling for students. What is needed, indeed required, in today's schools is the recognition that we need to turn on the green light and say to teachers that this personal involvement is a needed part of their job. Yes, they will make mistakes and experience failures. But the risks are worth it if we are serious about removing the barriers of anonymity that exist between teachers and students and in the process, remove the barriers of anonymity that exist between students of different groups, cultures, and ethnicity. In the process we would also relieve counselors of the burden of being hypocritical and pretending that they alone are the only professionals trained and qualified to help students, a promise they could never deliver on given the realities of today's com-

plex school culture. This process challenges the "mystery" of their specialty and makes the helping process more visible and available, no longer hidden behind the closed doors of the counselor's office.

4. Most students want to remain anonymous; that's the way they like it. In fact, most students want to be known. For many students that's the main reason they come to school, not just to be merely an acquaintance with the teacher but to have ongoing quality contact in which both teacher and student reveal their lives, the ups and downs, the good and bad, in simple, informal and usually brief ongoing conversations. The conversations are not counseling sessions but simple acts of acknowledgment and respect. They are acknowledgments to students that their presence counts and if they are absent they will be missed. Helping students to avoid perceiving themselves as uncared for, not valued, is best accomplished with concrete acts. As Sizer suggests, it takes special loyalty to a student when you make a telephone call to his or her home on your quarter in a public pay phone in the hallway. It takes doggedness to insist that your student come for a one-on-one chat when you have neither a private place nor dependable hours. Remember, as Sizer and Sizer remind us, "They watch us all the time."[40] The students, that is. They listen to us, sometimes. They learn from all the watching and listening. They attend to us more than we usually realize. And I would suggest that they are looking for signs of loyalty, respect, acceptance, and inclusion.

5. Most teachers want to remain anonymous. That way they can come and go without taking on the so-called personal baggage that students bring to class. In the students' eyes they wear a "don't ask, don't share, leave me out of it, see a counselor if you need help" sign. In fact, most teachers long for a personal connection with their students and want to learn how to accomplish this goal, not just with the students who interest them or pressure them. Yes, teachers are human. Teachers arrive at the classroom door with mental and emotional baggage from their backgrounds, training, and ways of looking at the world. We all have a dark side, a side that if not recognized, accepted, and

dealt with can allow us to create self-imposed barriers to connecting to people who are different—different color, values, cultures, gender, behaviors, physical appearance, ability, motivation, and the like. The work of every teacher is to recognize these conditions and move toward knowing and understanding those students who are different and who do not buy into their offerings, not leave them anonymous and outside the school community.

6. It is not possible to know and respect every student. As Sizer suggests, so much about what makes up a good school is simple, obvious, and supported by common sense and often by research. The pity is that many schools, and the system as a whole, often seems to operate with different rules. For example, he points out the following:

   a. People tend to copy those whom they respect. People of all ages are likely to work harder when they feel they are valued and respected. The essence of respect is being known.

   b. If people have the right tools and the appropriate time to use them, they do their jobs better.

   c. People who are distracted work poorly. People who feel that their workplace is hostile or unsafe cannot be effective. Most people like to care about the communities in which they work.

   d. The joys and pressures of each part of one's life affect the other parts. The worker who is frightened by a situation at home works poorly.

   e. Respecting people means attending to their special needs.

   f. Respect means assuming that the file of a student, test scores, and personal data is a bare beginning in an understanding of that student.

   g. Respect is modeled.[41]

7. If teachers become dually qualified in both their subject matter and understanding their students' personal lives, they will lose their academic edge. In fact, by knowing more students on an individual basis, teachers no longer, as in the case with Horace, focus only on the students they find interesting and those who pressure them for attention. They are able to reduce the self-

imposed barriers that keep them at a distance from those students who upon first observation seemed difficult to know and deal with. In knowing, we increase the opportunity for contact, conversation, and mutual interest. Students are no longer a blank page or a genial blur. In the process of knowing and understanding, teachers too become learners. In my experience, teachers learn a great deal from students who are different, resist their intervention, and make them sweat, work hard, try out new strategies, to get them involved. Clearly they learn more from these resisting students than from students who are more like themselves, sharing similar interests, safe students who don't unsettle the teacher.

8. Teachers who become personally involved with their students will somehow lose control over their classes; in knowing students well, the professional boundaries between teacher and student become blurred. As Sizer suggests, respect comes with knowing. When students know and respect their teachers they tend to get on board with what is expected in class and teachers' less than efficient practices and discretions are accepted.

9. Administrators, department chairs, and teacher leaders should leave teachers alone and encourage them to use their own judgment when responding to students, letting them work alone in the castles of their own classrooms. Unfortunately this approach is very similar to Horace's allowing his middle students to be anonymous. Teachers who are left on their own have their own voice that is based on their background, training, and experience to counsel and advise them. As a result teachers, even star and experienced teachers like Horace, lack awareness and understanding concerning the barriers they erect with some students and colleagues. Even the best of our teachers need quality supervision and insight to help them stay at the top of their professional game; they don't need to be left using strategies and skills that no longer work.

10. Teachers will change their behaviors if they are given lower student loads, time to share with colleagues, and time to meet with students and parents. Yes, these major changes should provide ample opportunity for teachers to know each of their students

and serve as helpful role models. But all too often these changes don't result in changed teacher behavior. In reality they are only cosmetic changes that hide the fact the teachers are going about their business and teaching in the same old way.

How do we alter these faulty assumptions and myths, these mysteries, and encourage, expect, teachers to become more personally involved with their students? First of all, I believe we need to follow Larry Cuban's advice, that in encouraging teachers to take on a dual-qualification subject-mastery and pedagogy role that change will be better for children, not undercut the teacher's authority, and can be adapted to the current setting. Where modest changes have occurred, they have occurred because teachers have absorbed rival beliefs that compete with existing ones. They embraced different ways of viewing the classroom. They can begin to practice new approaches and form habits that can help them deal successfully with their ever-changing student population.

Changing beliefs can lead to teachers' forming new habits. With an increased understanding of why it is important to become personally involved with students, teachers will be able to focus on new habits and ways of interacting with all their students. Dewey stressed the need for students to develop useful and wise habits as a way to gain control over their ever-changing environment. He suggested that active habits involve thought, invention, and initiative in applying capacity to new aims.[42] Clearly the same can be said for teachers. Clearly new habits are needed by teachers to address the needs of our changing student population and the world they live in. But forming new habits is no easy task, even for the highly motivated and committed among us. We all tend to stay with what we know, what is comfortable, even when we know it's not working and change is necessary. We can easily settle into becoming that anonymous, distant teacher who, as one student put it, "doesn't even know my name, anything about me. I might as well be dead." Some teachers are, as Alfie Kohn suggests, more interested in what they're teaching than in what students are learning, more focused on the subject matter than on the kids.[43] But as Cuban suggests, when teachers are persuaded that change will be for the better and they are able to absorb rival beliefs that compete with existing ones, new

ways of acting and interacting can take place.[44] They can begin to practice new approaches and form habits that can help them deal successfully with their ever-changing student population and ever-changing
culture. For example, as Powell, Farrar, and Cohen suggest, personalization has a human and a professional dimension.[45] The human side
involves knowing students from a standpoint of concerned friend,
while the professional side adds the element of specialized knowledge
about particular strengths and weaknesses in learning. Teachers need
time and practice to grow into this role and form new habits. They also
need the institutional expectation that they can learn to behave in new
ways.

I would suggest that one way to convince teachers that this kind of
change is better for children, will not undercut their authority, and can
be adapted to the current setting is by putting a real face on what it's
like for children to search for and find their star, to be told by parents
and siblings to give up on that dream and then have a caring, concerned
and tough teacher help rekindle that dream and advise them on how to
find their place in that world. The film *Billy Elliot* captures the realities
involved in taking a road that is filled with barriers and responses dominated by "no, you can't do that."[46] As the CinemaSense.com movie
review suggests, films sometimes open our vision to what is possible
for our lives. In *Billy Elliot*, the story weaves the allure of magic
through the innocent determination of a teenage boy whose passionate
dancing challenges him and those around him to move beyond the con-
fines and false security of class and gender stereotypes. In Billy's
world, the most he should hope for is to grow up strong enough to earn
his place next to his father and his older brother in the coal mining pits.
Not only are Billy, his dad, and his brother scrambling to pull their
lives together after the loss of Billy's mother, but they are also in dire
financial straits because of a prolonged miners' strike. However, far
worse than the loss of a loved one or even the fear of starvation is Billy's decision to trade in his boxing gloves for ballet slippers. Even if
there were any future in ballet, real men don't do it.

Here is the story. Billy is a teenager growing up in the tough, blue-
collar projects in a small coal-mining town in England. His beloved
mother is dead. His dad and older brother are hard-nosed union people
enduring a lengthy coal miners' strike. Billy's dad wants him to
become a boxer. While at boxing class Billy notices a girls' ballet class

going on in the same gym. After he is knocked out in the match he wanders over to the ballet class and becomes fascinated with the dances. He returns the next day and hangs around, hoping to somehow get involved. The dance teacher, Mrs. Wilkinson, notices his interest and after some negotiations encourages him to become part of the class. Billy thrives in this environment and from the dedication of his teacher, who both affirms him and also drives him to improve. It is his secret and he dares not tell his father and brother. But the secret comes out. His father and brother, both proud, macho types, think that Billy's new interest in ballet is for "poofs." Billy is ordered to stop the ballet classes and get back to manly kinds of things. But again Mrs. Wilkinson comes through, convincing the father and brother over time that Billy is following his star. He has talent. He could go places. Billy eventually tries out for the Royal Academy of Dance in London and is accepted. He tearfully leaves his now-accepting and -affirming father and brother, his much-admired teacher Mrs. Wilkinson, and his friends to begin a new life in which he eventually becomes a star.

These kinds of real-life stories do happen. And they happen in our schools every day when vulnerable students like Billy come in contact with experienced teachers like Mrs. Wilkinson, who are real advocates for children. There are teachers who affirm their students and at the same time drive them to improve, teachers who know how to deal directly with anxious parents who are trying to extinguish their children's dreams because they see them wanting to enter a world different from their own. There are teachers who know how to proceed to search out opportunities for children to get the best training available. Most importantly, there are teachers who know when it's time to say their good-byes and encourage the Billy's of the world to move on and find their place in the world.

As Ravitch advises, it is a fundamental truth that children need well-educated teachers who are eclectic in their methods and willing to use different strategies depending on what works best for which children.[47] It is another fundamental truth that adults must take responsibility for children and help them develop as good persons with worthy ideas. As Kohn remarks, children are likely to grow into caring people if they know they themselves are cared for.[48] A warm, nurturing environment is the sine qua non of positive development. If children feel safe, they can take risks, ask questions, make mistakes, learn to trust, share their feelings, and grow. If they are taken seriously, they can respect others. If their emotional needs are met they have the luxury of being able to meet other peoples' needs. In the story of Billy Elliot, Billy feels safe with Mrs. Wilkinson. He is free to take risks and enter an all-girls ballet class, turn aside his father and brother's disapproval, and be taken seriously thanks to her intervention.

I believe we need more Mrs. Wilkinson's in our schools. There are many teachers who could be advisors, thoughtful companions, mentors, adult friends, and guardians for our teenagers if they were encouraged, expected, and trained to do so. As Diane Ravitch and Joseph Viteritti suggest, children need to be in schools where there are many adults who know their names and care about them, know when they are absent, know if they have a problem, think about their futures and expect to talk frequently with parents or guardians.[49]

In chapter 3, I present an argument as to why the personal involvement of teachers is so needed in today's complex school world.

NOTES

1. Arthur Levine, "Rookies in the Schools," *New York Times*, 29 June 2002, 15 (A).

2. Deborah Meier, *In Schools We Trust* (Boston: Beacon Press, 2002), 10, 12.

3. James S. Coleman, *Adolescents and the Schools* (New York: Basic Books, 1965), 6–7.

4. Robert Hampel, *The Last Citadel* (Boston: Houghton Mifflin, 1986), 7–8, 51–53.

5. Diane Ravitch, *Left Back: A Century of Failed School Reform* (New York: Simon and Schuster, 2000), 19, 21, 171–73, 239, 241, 273, 282–83, 336, 338, 361, 367, 406, 456–57.

6. David Tyack and Elisabeth Hansot, *Managers of Virtue* (New York: Basic Books, 1982), 110.

7. John Dewey, *Democracy and Education* (New York: Macmillan, 1916), 62.

8. Ravitch, *Left Back*.

9. Ravitch, *Left Back*.

10. Levine, "Rookies in the Schools."

11. Ravitch, *Left Back.*

12. Ravitch, *Left Back.*

13. Arthur G. Powell, Eleanor Farrar, and David Cohen, *The Shopping Mall High School* (Boston: Houghton Mifflin, 1985), 8–9, 34–37, 46–49, 86, 91, 268–69, 318.

14. James B. Conant, *The American High School Today* (New York: McGraw-Hill, 1959), 44, 78, 81, 93–94, 96.

15. James B. Conant, *The Comprehensive High School: A Second Report to Interested Citizens* (New York: McGraw-Hill, 1967), 26.

16. Harold L. Munson, "Guidance in Secondary Education: Reconnaissance and Renewal," in *Guidance for Education in Revolution*, ed. David R. Cook (Boston: Allyn & Bacon, 1971), 179.

17. Munson, "Guidance in Secondary Education."

18. Edward Joseph Shoben Jr., "Guidance: Remedial Function or Social Reconstruction?" *Harvard Educational Review* 32, no. 4 (Fall 1962): 430.

19. David R. Cook, "Guidance and Institutional Change," in *Guidance for Education in Revolution*, ed. David R. Cook (Boston: Allyn & Bacon, 1971), 478–81, 489.

20. Harold L. Munson, "Guidance and Instruction: A Rapprochement," in *Guidance for Education in Revolution*, ed. David R. Cook (Boston: Allyn & Bacon, 1971), 337, 341–43.

21. Munson, "Guidance in Secondary Education."

22. David R. Cook, "The Future of Guidance as a Profession," in *Guidance for Education in Revolution*, ed. David R. Cook (Boston: Allyn & Bacon, 1971), 517, 523–24, 529–31, 548.

23. Cook, "The Future of Guidance as a Profession," 530.

24. David R. Cook, "Guidance and Student Unrest," in *Guidance for Education in Revolution*, ed. David R. Cook (Boston: Allyn & Bacon, 1971), 493.

25. Harold L. Munson, "Guidance and Instruction."

26. Larry Cuban, *How Teachers Taught: Constancy and Change in American Classrooms 1890–1980* (New York: Longman, 1984), 196–201, 243–45.

27. Ravitch, *Left Back.*

28. Gerald Grant, *The World We Created at Hamilton High* (Cambridge: Harvard University Press, 1988), 196.

29. Cook, "Guidance and Student Unrest."

30. Helen B. Shaeffer, "Discipline in Public Schools," *Editorial Research Reports* 2, no. 8 (1969): 637–38.

31. Ravitch, *Left Back.*

32. Ravitch, *Left Back.*

33. Rosemary C. Salomone, *Visions of Schooling: Conscience, Community, and Common Education* (New Haven: Yale University Press, 2000), 3.

34. Ravitch, *Left Back*, 456.

35. David L. Angus and Jeffrey E. Mirel, *The Failed Promise of the American High School 1890–1995* (New York: Teachers College Press, 1999), 166–67, 201.

36. David F. Lararee, *How to Succeed in School without Really Learning* (New Haven: Yale University Press, 1997), 12–13, 251–52, 258.

37. Theodore E. Sizer, *Horace's School: Redesigning the American High School* (Boston, Houghton Mifflin, 1992), 1, 4–6, 8–9, 12–14, 30, 40–43, 122–24.

38. Robert L. Sinclair and Ward J. Ghory, "Last Things First: Realizing Equality by Improving Conditions for Marginal Students," in *Access to Knowledge: An Agenda for Our Nation's Schools*, ed. John I. Goodlad and Pamela Keating (New York: College Entrance Examination Board, 1990), 137.

39. Theodore R. Sizer and Nancy Faust Sizer, *The Students Are Watching* (Boston: Beacon Press, 1999), xvii.

40. Sizer and Sizer, *The Students Are Watching*.

41. Sizer, *Horace's School*.

42. Dewey, *Democracy and Education*, 62.

43. Alfie Kohn, *The Schools Our Children Deserve* (New York: Houghton Mifflin, 1990), 25.

44. Cuban, *How Teachers Taught*.

45. Powell, Farrar, and Cohen, *The Shopping Mall High School*.

46. Craig Sones Cornell and Anna-Maria Petricelli, CinemaSense.com Review of film *Billy Elliot*, 2000 http://www.cinemasense.com/Reviews/billy_elliot.htm (accessed 28 September 2002).

47. Ravitch, *Left Back*.

48. Kohn, *The Schools Our Children Deserve*.

49. Diane Ravitch and Joseph P. Viteritti, eds. *New Schools for a New Century* (New Haven: Yale University Press, 1997), 255.

CHAPTER 3

Why Today's Students Need the Personal Involvement and Understanding of Teachers in Their Lives: What Has Changed?

The main focus of this chapter is to make the case of why teachers' understanding and involvement in their students' lives is so needed in today's school and society. As I suggested in chapter 2, teachers whose primary focus is on their subject-mastery role and who design their classroom interactions with students around this role are, in my view, unprepared for teaching in today's schools. Yes, teachers need to have subject-mastery skills, but they also need understanding of child development, how children learn, and how their personal lives impact on their achievement. In other words, as Arthur Levine, president of Columbia University Teachers' College, advocates, there must be a kind of dual qualification that cannot be reserved only for affluent suburban children in places like Scarsdale, New York; Lake Forest, Illinois; and Palisades, California.[1] In these school systems, the job of teaching is seen as something akin to the job of a doctor. They are professionals, as Theodore R. Sizer suggests, who know their students, know them well enough to understand how their minds work, know where they come from, what pressures buffet them, what they are and are not disposed to do.[2] They are professionals, as Gene I. Maeroff says, who are capable of knowing and diagnosing a youngster's learning condition in much the same way a physician does with physical condition.[3] This role moves a teacher from the limited, handcuffed role of subject-matter specialist into a role, as Sizer suggests, that requires an understanding of the "particulars" about each student. These teachers have developed finely tuned habits that enable them to daily observe and gather informal data about what is going on with their students. For example, is he succeeding in his school work; what are her strengths; what areas need intervention and work; how are his peer relationships going; what about her health and well-being; what are her fears and failure issues; does he know how to unwind and have fun; can he be a kid instead of a miniadult? This kind of informal data gathering is an important part of teachers' daily work, developing an ever-changing composite of each student so that when academic and personal setbacks occur the changes are clearly visible to the concerned teacher. As educator Lilian Katz suggests, we cannot teach anything important to someone we do not know.[4]

In today's world there are important reasons for teachers to become dually qualified as subject-matter specialist and in understanding the personal side of their students' lives. Following are some reasons that teachers need to embrace this new role and be supported by administrators, counselors, teacher leaders, and colleagues:

1. By understanding the personal sides of students' lives, teachers can spot academic and personal trouble early on and help the students get the help they need right away. Early assessment and diagnosis are the keys in both medicine and teaching.

2. By understanding the personal side of students' lives, knowing them more fully, teachers become more effective academic teachers because they have up-to-date data on how best to approach, motivate, and support their students' academic progress.

3. By understanding the personal side of students' lives, teachers are able to reduce their self-erected barriers brought on by their own biases, background, conditioning, and valuing. They are better able to relate to students who are "different"—in color, culture, gender, abilities, appearance, motivation, achievement, values, and learning styles. Teachers are better able to deal with the entire class, not just those students who interest them and are more like them, well-behaved and the best and brightest, zeroing in on a Harvard destination.

4. The process of being able to relate more fully to every student in the class can help teachers serve as models of inclusion for their students, models that proclaim that each person, each group in the classroom has merit and value and should be respected. By knowing each other more fully, we can learn that we are more

alike than different. And our "differentness," our uniqueness, adds excitement and interest to our daily contact, making each of us special and worth knowing.

5. The process of understanding the personal side of their students' lives allows and encourages teachers to share their own life experience with students, to use their own life stories. How they navigated through their teen years and found and followed their stars are useful tools in guiding their students. For example, what problems and barriers did they face and how were they overcome? What kind of guidance, words of wisdom if you will, helped them to successfully navigate through their ever-changing world? In this revealing process, they can demonstrate and model the important lesson that teachers and students are more alike than different. Yes, they are different in age but they are connected through a common bond of how best to respond successfully to life's ongoing challenges.

6. By understanding the personal side of students' lives, teachers are able to reduce the anonymity that often comes with large comprehensive high schools. Students who have been left out of the school's mainstream can be known and welcomed aboard, valued for their presence, contributions (no matter how small), and uniqueness, given a seat at the table and told that they too can become contenders, be in the game, not looking in from the outside.

I am advocating that these teacher qualities are very much in demand in today's world. It is not a secret that today's students need the intervention of a concerned adult more than earlier generations. As author and researcher Jane M. Healy says, there is a need for teachers and other adults to be "thoughtful companions."[5] Others call for teachers to be "advisors," "mentors," and "adult friends." Webster defines "companion" as "a person who is associated with or accompanies another."[6] A mentor is a wise, loyal friend, advisor, and coach. A friend is a person who knows one well and is fond of this intimate relationship, a person who is on the same side of the struggle, a supporter, and a sympathizer. An advisor is one who recommends a course of action and implies that the giver of advice has knowledge of the experience. I believe all these definitions work well when describing the kind of adult much in demand by students. However, based on my experiences in the schools and my work with teachers, I believe the best label for the close relationship I am calling for is "advisor"—an easily accessible and inviting teacher who can recommend a course of action and has experience and knowledge about the situation. This is the label I will be ascribing to teachers in the remaining chapters. Why? I believe this is a label teachers can easily buy into, as recommending a course of action is very much a part of the student–teacher learning process. This is a process teachers know and understand. It is not a vague, fuzzy, counselor-ish, or therapeutic label. I believe this label allows teachers to envision how to form a bridge between their academic role and pedagogy role that calls for their personal understanding of students. I also believe the other labels such as thoughtful companion, adult friend, and mentor may be difficult for teachers to buy into, as these labels suggest a role that may be too intimate and move the student–teacher relationship into uncharted territory that has professional risks, such as becoming a surrogate parent, friend, or savior.

Therefore, it is extremely important in the teacher–student advisor role I am advocating that the emphasis be on understanding the personal side of students' lives as a way to help them to improve their academic performance and clearly discouraging teachers from trying to behave as surrogate parent, intimate friend, savior, or quasi-therapist. We need to keep in mind John I. Goodlad's prudent advice "that teachers want to teach and that the role they have in mind is a far cry from nurturing students in the personal and social non-academic aspects of their lives in school."[7] What I am asking teachers is to take notice of their students when trouble begins to surface, hear the student's view of the perceived problem, communicate their concern to the student, offer the student some kind of diagnosis—blueprint, if you will—to solve the problem, and help them connect with credible sources of help in the school and community to resolve the problem. And most importantly, the teacher must accompany the student on this journey, serving as a steady source of ongoing support. The key is to convince teachers that this kind of concerned intervention is necessary because personal and health troubles often impact negatively on academic achievement. As Goodlad suggests, "If awareness, diagnosis, and remediation of individual student's difficulties go hand in hand with progress in learning then this kind of personal attention appears to be part and parcel of the instructional function."[8] Our task and a major argument in this book is to convince teachers that understanding the personal and social, nonacademic aspect of students is a useful and important part of the teacher's awareness, diagnosis, and remediation of individual student difficulties. It is part and parcel, as Goodlad says, of the instructional function, an educative, not therapeutic, role that can pay off with increased student academic success.

But what is causing the need for envisioning this new way of looking at the teacher's role? What is the imperative? What has changed? What new issues are bringing about the cry on the part of students and parents for a more concerned, caring, and available teacher? Presented below are the issues that are powering the need for increased teacher understanding and personal connection with students, a connection that administrators, teacher leaders, parents, and most of all, students, must expect teachers to address if schools and students are to reach their goals of inclusion, academic success, and personal well-being.

More than half of Americans surveyed (52 percent) think that helping youngsters get a good start in life ought to be society's most important goal, even considering such competing priorities as protecting citizens from crime (18 percent) and creating more jobs (16 percent).   This survey was conducted by Public Agenda and is part of their report *Kids These Days: What Americans Really Think about the Next Generation.* In this study the authors, Steve Farkas and Jean Johnson suggest that in finding after finding across all demographic groups, Americans are intensely concerned about young people but their concerns center directly on youngster's moral well-being.[9] Americans worry about deficits in character and values. Here is what the adults in the study say about teenagers:

1. For many adults teen behavior is more than disappointing; it can be intimidating. When asked what first comes to their minds when they think about today's teenagers, two-thirds of Americans (67 percent) immediately reach for negative adjectives such as "rude," "irresponsible," and "wild."

2. In the study, there were rare complimentary comments about teenagers. Only a handful (12 percent) describe teens positively, using terms such as "smart" or "helpful."

3. Adults in the study also reported that it is very common for teenagers to get into trouble because they have too much free time. Four in ten Americans (41 percent) say it's very common to find teenagers who have poor work habits and lack self-discipline.

4. As the survey results show, even the people who have regular contact with teens are as critical as everyone else, if not more. Two-thirds (65 percent) of those with a lot of contact describe teenagers disapprovingly.

5. Only about one in five Americans (22 percent) say it's common to find parents who are good role models. Many Americans believe that too many parents put their own personal needs and challenges above the needs of their children.

6. Yet four out of five Americans say it's much harder for parents to do their job these days. They are profoundly conscious of dramatic changes that have made the job of parenting tougher than ever before. For example, three in four people believe it is very common for mothers to give up time with their kids to work to make ends meet. By an almost two to one margin (63 percent to 32 percent), Americans believe that "most parents face times when they really need help raising their kids."

7. Only 12 percent of parents in the survey say teens are friendly and helpful, and only 9 percent say teens treat people with respect. Parents probably, or hopefully as the survey suggests, have more sympathetic and complimentary views of their own teenagers, but they have little praise for other teens they come across.

8. Americans think these are uniquely difficult times for kids; more than eight in ten (83 percent) say it's harder to be a kid growing up in America these days. For example, Americans are extremely concerned about threats endangering all kids: drugs and crime, sex and violence in the media, and public schools that often fail to deliver education in a safe and orderly way.

The study suggests there seems to be a breech between teenagers and adults with adults looking at teens, preferably in their minds, from a safe distance, with anxiety and disappointment, not at all certain that this generation bodes well for their communities or for the country. And this public dissatisfaction and disapproval extend beyond the nation's teenagers. Even young children are viewed in a negative light. Many Americans think that children are spoiled and out of control, not friendly, helpful, or engaging. And people apply criticisms to children across a broad economic spectrum, children from disadvantaged backgrounds as well as children from the middle and affluent classes.

The significant and surprising message of this study is that teenagers and younger children do not inspire instinctively positive feelings from adults. Across history and across various cultures, people have often considered the next generation as the best hope for the future. But for Americans in the 1990s, this bedrock belief seems to have been shaken to the core. This growing disappointment with youth has also carried over into the schools, promoting a belief that schools no longer offer the safe haven of structure and discipline that young people need in order to thrive. However, as a key element in the study suggests, notwithstanding their extensive criticism of young people, Americans refuse to give up on kids. They care deeply about their well-being and believe that tackling the issue is of paramount importance to our society. Most encouraging, they are stubbornly optimistic about the chances of reclaiming the lives of even the most troubled teens. Americans demonstrate surprisingly high levels of caring and sympathy toward young people. In fact, Americans display an extraordinary, almost stubborn, refusal to write young people off as unsalvageable. Almost three quarters (72 percent) say that "given enough love and kindness, just about any kid can be reached."[10] Even the toughest youngsters, teenagers already in deep trouble, can be redeemed given the right effort. And 74 percent say that given enough help and attention, just about all youngsters can learn and succeed in school.

What are the implications of this data for teachers? I believe there is good news and opportunity for teachers in knowing that more than half of Americans think that helping youngsters get a good start in life ought to be society's most important goal. And despite their negative feelings about teenagers, younger children, and parents, most Americans are aware, and accept, that fundamental changes in our society have made it harder to be a kid growing up in America these days and more difficult to be an effective parent. Though they may be displeased with today's youth, many Americans care deeply about kids and their well-being and are committed to reclaiming the lives of even our most troubled teenagers.

I believe the key words for teachers to hear in this study are that American citizens have a strong desire to help kids get a good start in life, to provide kids with enough love, kindness, help, and attention so that just about any one of them can succeed, to redirect kids in trouble academically and personally and teach them alternatives. My reading of the study suggests that Americans want teachers to pay attention to students in new ways that are very personal, to be kind, helpful, attentive, and even loving toward students. It is interesting that citizens want teachers to be loving. Maybe they sense that's a good quality for teachers to have, a quality that maybe they missed along the way as teenagers and in retrospect wish they had received. It's a quality that may have made a difference in their teenage lives. Yes, many teachers would say, "Yes, I can be kind, helpful and attentive, but loving is going too far." However, in my school and classroom observations I do see many teachers who daily provide their students with Webster's definition of loving—showering their students with deep and tender feelings of affection and attachment. In fact, when Americans want teachers to be loving, many do reciprocate. It happens each day in many classrooms. I believe that it's not a process to be hidden or looked upon by teachers as being unprofessional. Our work, and a major argument in this book, is to convince teachers that it's OK to allow deep emotions about their students into their teaching psyche. Let the barriers down. Be human.

No, this does not mean being a surrogate parent. It is a truism about teachers that many feel they want to take a troubled child home to provide the care needed. As we get closer to our students we all can get pulled in that direction. It goes with the territory and can't be avoided. Teachers see a lot of pain and despair in their daily work with children. That pain can be seen in schools that serve affluent, middle-class, or poor children. Trouble knows no geographic or economic boundary. When we teachers connect intimately with students, the adrenaline flows and a part of our professional psyche desperately wants to make things right for each of our students. It is a process that can't be accomplished with half measures or facades. It is a total commitment to the child, giving them our best. However, there are professional boundaries we all must keep too. We are educators, not saviors. But that doesn't mean we can't care for, even love, our students in the few precious hours we have with them. Better, I say, to be loving than to be distant, uninvolved, or just pretending to care, mouthing the words but delivering no substance. I believe this is the way to go in order to help our students learn to solve their problems, take care of themselves, and not be at the margins of school life. The goal is to help each of our students to become better achievers and better people and then let them move on from our care, set them free if you will, thereby allowing us to shift our care and guidance to other students in need of our wisdom and guidance.

And I believe Americans want teachers to help students in ways that they no longer believe they can offer. As the Public Agenda study suggests, many people seem to have lost confidence that the human-to-human interaction involved in helping will be comfortable, natural, and trouble free. Respondents in a focus group repeatedly expressed fears that their good intentions might be misread, rejected, and even turned against them. Perhaps this is a reason that so many Americans, torn by being both concerned and disapproving in the same breath, choose to remain distant and have little contact with teenagers. They seemingly have lost their way in how to communicate with today's youth. As we all know from personal and professional experience, failure to communicate leads to stereotyping and isolation, the establishing of walls and barriers rather than a sense of community. They look to the school, teachers, and other community leaders to provide a connection with youth that they seem unable or unwilling to forge themselves. To me this honest assessment of the breakdown of linkages between America's adults and youth is sad. But looking at the glass as half full rather than half empty, I sense an opportunity here. I feel that America's adults are hopeful that teachers can provide connections that we are unable to provide right now.

My guess is that many Americans sense that the fundamental changes in our society for youth and parents require a more intimate relationship between teachers, the one constant adult figure in our communities, and students in search of caring adults who are not, like the broader community, disapproving, judgmental, and uncomplimentary, skeptical of their value to the present and future needs of the community and nation. We need a relationship in which teachers, again unlike many community adults who have lost confidence in the human-to-human interaction involved in helping, are willing, able, and expected to become personally involved in guiding students even at the risk of being misread, rejected, and even turned against. As many experienced teachers who are striving to understand their students' personal lives know, not every student–teacher interaction is comfortable, natural, and trouble free. Many initially resist, throw up roadblocks, seek haven in anonymity, make negative judgments, or act up. Yes, students need love, kindness, help, and attention but sometimes they need tough love, confrontation, and feedback that, although uncomfortable, is on target.

The picture is clear. Most Americans are saying that we don't particularly like today's youth, nor do we want to be around them, nor are we comfortable trying to know and help them. Yes, we are frightened for these children and frightened of these children, but we do care deeply about them and want the schools to engage these kids and help them succeed. As the Public Agenda study suggests, Americans stubbornly resist giving up on individual youngsters or abandoning an entire generation. They believe that teachers and schools, in concert with parent and community groups, can straighten them out and guide them into responsible adulthood.

Are teachers up to the task of seeking out new ways of communicating with students? Will they see this data as an opportunity to expand their one-dimensional subject-mastery role? Let's put on our reality glasses, tone down our sales pitch, and take a hard look at what needs to be done to help teachers embrace this broader, more inclusive and, I say, more personally and professionally fulfilling role. First, let's admit that not every teacher is a natural helper. Like the American adults in the Public Agenda study, many are looking for easy, smooth connections with students, warm and fuzzy interactions that are safe, comfortable, natural appearing, trouble free, and most important, nonconfrontational. They want no rough waters or uncharted territory. They don't want uneven, unsettled, problem-centered, or confrontational interactions. Smooth is the key word. And they don't want to be misread, rejected, or have their good intentions turned against them. Let me suggest that this is all very natural. We all seek the easy road, a pass when it comes to some of the complex relations between students and teachers. We are professionals and many of us carry the naïve illusion that as professionals we don't have to grapple and joust with our students. We are in charge; what we say goes; and our conversations with students should be civil, polite, and our advice and wisdom always received by students with a thank you, even praise. This is often the case for teachers new to the field who haven't tasted, or been tested by, battle, or veteran teachers who think that because of longevity they deserve only respect and civility from students. Both groups tend to find comfort—their own, I might add—by creating social distance from the fray, the real world of students. They are uncomfortable with the awkwardness, unevenness, fencing, even messiness that are a large part of many student–teacher interactions. They wrongly expect these conversations to be linear—present the problem, offer a solution, end of conversation. When that doesn't happen they feel misread, rejected, their good intentions and advice wasted.

The work, and a major argument in this book, is to help these teachers to lower their comfort zone and to become aware that quality student–teacher interactions don't always have to be nice and agreeable and have a happy ending. Not unlike many teachers, not every student wants to be involved and have a human connection with a teacher. The process often requires many overtures, often failing ones, by persistent teachers who consider it their business to understand the personal side of their students' lives. Concerned teachers need to keep their doors open and be accepting. But they also have to be assertive in their desire to involve students who have a school record of distancing themselves. Students need to be sought out and asked to be involved, often repeatedly. Teachers need to send the message that they are not going to go away, withdraw, and they are ready and able to deal with students' resistance to forming a human relationship. In other words, they intend to hang tough, change strategies that aren't working, look for openings that can bring about a beginning dialogue. Remember, this is not the time to reach into your teacher education case studies and textbooks for help. You are flying in fog; things aren't clear; you're looking for cracks in the visibility to make contact. And yes, let me emphasize again, realistically, not every teacher overture to connect on a personal level with his or her students will work. However, that is no excuse not to try. In a sense overtures to resisting students can have an incremental effect. At some point down the road one teacher overture, one invitation to talk, get to know the many sides of the students' lives, may succeed. Trying and not succeeding doesn't spell failure for the teacher. As many master teachers would say, it goes with the territory.

This is what teaching and student learning is all about—finding a way to understand the particulars of what works to make a connection with each student, finding a way to help students become responsible and successful students and people. As I have suggested, in finding "the way" teachers sometimes need to be assertive and confrontational, to be persistent with the students in telling them, "I think you're a person of worth. I value your presence, as do other members of the class. I am here to hear your story, help you strengthen your academic talents and shore up your weaknesses. But that requires something from you—a response!" Even an angry response is a beginning. What we need to be about is demystifying the student–teacher interaction; we need to shine some light on the realities involved and help teachers to become aware that smooth, light, superficial conversations usually yield no data about our students' lives and are mere fluff. What counts are interactions that have some meat, that yield some real stories and that, yes, may unsettle us, make us uncomfortable, and make us more human to both ourselves and our students.

I believe most teachers are capable of such interactions. What is needed is an expectation that they behave in this way. It requires work, practice, and the forming of new habits that are needed in today's complex school world. And yes, as I have stated, this process requires some humility, knowing that sometimes when they attempt to provide quality help it may not be appreciated. They need to know that when they provide quality advice, the student may do a complete turnaround, abandon the advice and pursue a risky path. Understanding that good intentions to be personally involved with their students are not enough. It simply isn't effective to continually support teachers armed only with good intentions who are constantly fearful of being rejected, misread, or tuned out, teachers who dabble in helping a few students but who for the most part keep the majority of their students at a distance so they can come and go unencumbered by the throbbing emotions of students that fill our schools. Our work is to reduce the number of such teachers, one by one.

How do we proceed in this important work? I believe we need to approach this issue by tapping into the developmental history of teachers themselves. My own work with schools has convinced me that many teachers have a difficult time dealing with intimate contact with their students because they forget what it was like when they were teenagers. They need to be reminded of how they were helped as a teenager by a concerned teacher or coach and empowered to reciprocate, give back, if you will, this kind of quality relationship with their current students. This process will help them remember their teenage voices and who was available to hear them. That life, for them, was often as complex as it is for today's students. Yes, it was a different time but many of the same issues had to be faced. For example, critical decisions about school, peers, family, and future plans are required. Many teachers will remember advisors who were present and available and offered credible advice at just the right moment. And they will remember also advisors who promised help but who weren't able to deliver on the promise, advisors who failed them.

What I am advocating is a simple process. It doesn't take a training program, a glossy manual with a step-by-step, surefire way to connect with students, or the creation of a formal teacher advisory. What we need to do is to help teachers temporarily remove themselves from their daily battles, go back in time to their own adolescent years and remember all those false starts, failures, fears, misadventures, even lost loves, that many experienced—all experiences that helped them become resilient, follow their own stars—and most of all remember those adults, often educators, who said yes, you can, or the ones who said no, that's not possible. The lives of teenagers can turn on a dime, for good or for bad, when they heed adult advice, advice that sometimes is not credible.

I will provide the reader with a road map on how to proceed in Chapter 5, where I discuss how to help every teacher in every secondary school become an adviser, not just the teachers in the few schools who have the resources to establish a formal student–teacher advisory system in which teachers meet daily with small groups of students. I believe the process of helping students connect with caring adults can be accomplished in simple and direct ways. Yes, resources can help. They can be the driving force in creating formal advisories. But we all need to remember that resources can't magically turn teachers into caring adults. Resources can't buy the hearts, souls, and courage we need our teachers to have. What we need to be about is shoring up our teachers' commitment to help young people maximize their academic and personal lives, find their niches. We must drive home the point to teachers that their daily human contact with students matters and matters a lot. Their daily presence is a powerful force for creating climates of hope, not despair. Their efforts to connect with students of all economic classes and abilities, the best and brightest and those on the margins and headed toward dropping out, can save lives being buffeted by issues not of their making and save souls that are being slowly drained of hope.

Am I saying that every teacher will become a competent advisor? Of course not. However, that should be our goal, the benchmark we are struggling to achieve—to drive home the point that the advisor role can work in the vast number of so-called ordinary, unheralded secondary schools, right now.

The increase in family mobility and immigration has led to increased student anonymity. E. D. Hirsch Jr. suggests that the most important single task of an individual school is to ensure that all children within the school gain prior knowledge they will need for the next grade level.[11] It is more difficult with children who must change schools in the middle of the year. Hirsch says that about one-fifth of all Americans relocate every year. In a typical community the average rate at which students transfer in and out of schools during the school year is nearly one-third. Hirsch also says that one-sixth of all third graders attend at least three schools between first and third grade. Mobility is high in our society. In our high mobility environment, it is easy for students to lose out on a sense of safety, continuity, and belonging and in moving into new schools, especially large comprehensive high schools, to become unknown and anonymous.

As researcher James A. Banks suggests, American classrooms are experiencing the largest influx of immigrant students since the beginning of the twentieth century.[12] About a million immigrants are making the United States their home each year. More than six million legal immigrants settled in the United States between 1991 and 1996. Language diversity is increasing among the nation's student population. In 1990, 14 percent of school-age youth lived in homes in which English was not the first language. The result? Many newcomers are coming into our schools with little or no experience on how to fit in and belong. Like the children of families who are on the move to find employment in our tough economic times, these immigrant students are literally thrown into a new school culture where it's sink or swim. As author Geneva Gay reports, many immigrant families and their children are caught in a paradox.[13] They come to the United States to escape poverty and persecution and to improve the general quality of their lives. In doing so they often suffer deep affective losses of supportive networks and familial connections. The formal schooling of many of these children prior to immigration was sporadic and fragmented. After arriving in the United States, some immigrant families experience frequent changes in residence, which interferes with the children's educational continuity. They have to adjust to a new culture, language, style of living, and educational system. This geographic, cultural, and psychoemotional uprootedness can cause stress, anxiety, feelings of vulnerability, loneliness, isolation, and insecurity. All these conditions can have a negative effect on school achievement.

Gay also points out the hostility that newcomers often face when she cites research by P. N. Kiang and J. Kaplan, who record the experiences of Vietnamese students at a Boston High School. The students told about encountering racial conflicts daily that included being rendered irrelevant and invisible; being ridiculed for speaking Vietnamese; being called derogatory names and subjected to racial slurs; witnessing and experiencing harassment on a regular basis; feeling threatened and angry; and being teased and insulted.[14]

What are the implications of this data for teachers? As any master teacher knows, teachers can easily provide a sense of safety, welcoming, and support for students new to their schools. This is an important teacher activity but one that doesn't receive a high priority in our busy schools. Simple kinds of connections work best—creating time and a ceremony to welcome students; introducing them to savvy peers who can show them the way; assessing their strengths and areas to be worked on, past school and family history, extracurricular interests, passions, fears, and hopes—and these can all be accomplished in simple, short, ongoing conversations. The key for teachers is in wanting to welcome and know new students, to see this work as important. They must want to serve as a helpful bridge for newcomers as they settle in and begin to find their place in this new and different environment. Newcomers need a road map to follow that is best provided by a concerned and informed teacher who knows the landscape, a concerned teacher who can enlist other students to be of service to newcomers and show them the ropes, not turn their backs and use newcomers as a source of hostility and targets and remain tied to their insulated groups. That is not the way to create a healthy school climate for both students and newcomers. Newcomers offer all of us—teachers, students, administrators, and parents—the ongoing opportunity to open up our doors and hearts to those in need of safety, protection, new hope, and new opportunity, to help every member of the school community to move beyond their own self-centeredness and serve as models of welcoming and inclusion. That, I suggest, is what being an American is all about.

Changing family and community connections and structures has also led to increased student anonymity. As Robert D. Putnam suggests, there has been an erosion of America's social connectedness and community involvement over the last several decades.[15] First, the American family structure has changed in several important and relevant ways. The downturn in civic engagement coincided with the breakdown of the traditional family unit—Mom, Dad, and the kids. Because the family itself is, by some accounts, a key form of social capital, perhaps its eclipse is part of the explanation for the reduction in joining and trusting the wider community. Putnam suggests the evidence of a loosening of family bonds is unequivocal. The century-long increase in divorce rates and the more recent increases in one-parent families has resulted in the doubling of one-parent households since 1950. Putnam says that the fraction of adults who are married and have children at home, the archetypal Ozzie and Harriet, was sliced by more than one-third, from 40 percent in 1970 to 26 percent in 1997. The traditional family unit is down, a lot. Putnam suggests that there are other factors also that have contributed to the decline in civic engagement and social capital. Here are some of those factors:

1. There has been an erosion of social capital over the last several decades. That is a decline in the norms and networks of trust and reciprocity that foster collective action. It's the friendship, professional circles, clubs, neighborhoods, churches, and alumni organizations where you help the group or fellow members because you care about and trust the group and know your actions will ultimately benefit all.

2. Pressure of time and money, including the special pressures on two-career families, contributed measurably to the diminution of our social and community involvement. The fraction of married Americans who definitely say "our whole family usually eats together" has declined a third from about 50 percent to 34 percent in just the last two decades.

3. The increase in movement to the suburbs and creation of unattractive sprawling landscapes also played a supporting role in this process.

4. The effect of electronic entertainment, above all television, on our leisure time has been substantial. Students are part of the TV Generation.

5. Decline in PTA membership over the past several decades reflects many parents' disengagement from their children's schooling. PTAs nationwide plummeted from a membership high in the early 1960s of almost fifty members per one hundred families with school-age children to less than twenty members per hundred in 1997.

6. Generalized trust also has evaporated. While 55 percent of American adults in 1960 believed others could be trusted most or all of the time, only 30 percent did in 1998, and the future looks bleaker because the decline was the sharpest among our nation's youth.

Putnam's research doesn't offer a pretty or hopeful picture of the barriers facing the healthy development of today's youth. He observes that a considerable amount of research dating back at least fifty years has demonstrated that trust, networking, and norms of reciprocity within a child's family, school, peer groups, and larger community have wide-ranging effects on the child's opportunities and choices and hence, on his behavior and development. As seen above, the emergence of two-career and one-parent families, pressures on time and money, longer commutes to work, and the increase in passive TV watching have led to a decline in parental involvement with children's schooling and an increase in the amount of time children are on their own and vulnerable to others' behaviors. As Putnam suggests, when parents are involved in their children's education, children do better in school and the schools themselves are better. But when parents are absent, who is to fill in?

The result, as Thomas H. Sanders and Robert D. Putnam suggest, is mounting isolation.[16] We are bowling alone. Sanders and Putnam observe that while a record number of Americans bowl today, bowling in organized leagues has plunged 40 percent from 1980 to 1993. They point out that the civic watering holes, such as bowling leagues, fraternal organizations, choral societies, and thousands of other places where Americans regularly met fellow citizens, talked periodically about issues of civic importance, and learned to trust others and work together are drying up. They say much of the decline in civic connectedness is generational. Today's children (and their parents) are much less engaged in community life than their grandparents' cohort. Sanders and Putnam suggest that establishing mentoring programs is one way to close this decline.

What are the implications for teachers? As Sanders and Putnam suggest, every child needs an adult to play Batman to his or her Robin, someone who can coach, provide a "toolbox," and ultimately protect. They need adults who, as C. Gregg Petersmeyer, father of the 1000 Points of Light, suggests, can share their passions with kids.[17] In a world where students are increasingly feeling the pressures and risks that come with the lack of connections to community and family, teachers represent the one constant adult presence they have access to in schools every day. In a sense, this situation provides teachers with an unprecedented opportunity to coach, provide a "toolbox," and protect, to become a beacon and port in the storm as other family and community sources of support are disappearing. Is this too much for teachers to handle? I say no. The trick is in helping teachers become aware of the powerful role and the gifts they can offer their students in their disconnected world. I say this is a role of honor that can help establish teachers as leaders in our changing communities who know, understand, and act as guides for our youth. They can be the right person at the right time.

Large schools are a fact of life in the United States.   Given our current environment as described by the Public Agenda study, Hirsch, Gay, and Sanders and Putnam, I believe educators need to get on with the work of finding better ways to address the needs of their students, rather than saying they can't change until the school size and class load numbers are significantly reduced. Let's face facts. Large comprehensive secondary schools are not going to disappear in the near future, in spite of the movement toward smaller schools and lower student loads for teachers. I believe there is an urgent need to challenge and redirect the limiting, long-held belief of educators that they cannot get to know their students on a personal basis because the schools are too large and their student load is too high. I argue that there are alternatives to this limiting way of perceiving the teacher's role. We need to quiet and change the institutional voice that says our hands are tied and nothing can be done to improve the situation until structural changes, such as the size of the school and student load, are made. We need to discourage the practice that encourages and allows teachers to be selective about what students they let into their world, a practice that allows teachers like Horace to choose to work closely only with the students that interest and pressure him while allowing most students to remain anonymous. We can't allow them the weak, specious excuse that they are compromising due to the size of their student load. That's not good for the Horaces of this world's professional development or for those anonymous students, their parents, and colleagues who may buy into the Horace model.

Yes, I agree with Horace that smaller schools and reduced student loads would help reduce anonymity and make it easier for teachers to connect with all their students. But that's talking about what "might" be, not the realities of today. As I suggested in chapter 2, even with the advent of smaller schools and reduced student loads, there is no guarantee that teacher behavior would automatically change and teachers would miraculously embrace the concept of knowing all their students well. That's an unknown. At best, a maybe. I believe we need to stay in the present and look for ways to better understand and address the personal needs of our students right now. Putting all our energy and commitment into arguing for structural change is an approach doomed to failure. Instead, let's redirect this energy and commitment to address the needs of our students right now, not postpone our intervention to some future day that may never come, living a professional life of postponement rather than a life of action.

As writer Rick Allen documents, large schools are a fact of life in the United States.[18] Although the issue of school size and its link to academic achievement and social and emotional well-being has been debated continually in the wave of school reform, Allen wisely says the arguments are taking place in an educational landscape of big schools that is unlikely to change soon. As I have suggested, arguing that we can't get to know our students better because of too high a student load is a prescription for no action. It's like saying to students and parents, "Sorry, my student load is too high, don't expect me to get to know and understand your personal life and how it impacts on your academic performance. End of story." This argument allows, gives permission, for teachers to remain unengaged with their students and look the other way when students seek, sometimes demand, their attention. Allen reminds us that more than 70 percent of U.S. high school students attend schools of more than 1,000 students.[19] Large middle schools are also on the increase. Between 1968 and 1996, middle schools of more than 800 students increased from 16 percent to 30 percent. Making a large school feel personal is a challenge for schools with thousands of students. But size need not be a major deterrent. As Donald Hoecherl, principal of G. Holmes Braddock Senior High School in Miami, Florida, tells Allen, "I do not find school size a deterrent. I find it a great strength. Being big doesn't mean we expect less."[20] Joy Hellard, who teaches English to gifted students, describes Braddock, which has a student population of 4,730, this way: "It's a huge school. The bell rings and nearly 5,000 kids move to the next class in five minutes. It's a mall. A large two-story mall. But the kids are friendly and the teachers are friendly. There's a feeling of safety, despite the size."[21]

Down country from Braddock, Alberto Rodriguez, principal of American Senior High School, which has an enrollment of 2,900 students, tells Rick Allen that he believes that even in a school of thousands, "You can treat each child with nurturing and caring." However, as principal Norman Wechsler of De Witt Clinton High School in New

York City's Bronx borough wisely insists, "Small will only succeed if other changes take place as well."[22]

I believe Wechsler is right on target. As Kirk A. Johnson, a senior policy analyst for Heritage Foundation, suggests, from the attention and financial support given to class size reduction by politicians and the public, one might assume that research has shown small class size to be essential to positive academic outcomes.[23] Proponents of class size reduction claim that small classes result in fewer discipline problems and allow teachers more time for instruction, individual attention, and more flexibility in instructional strategies. But, as Johnson reports, evidence of the efficacy of class size reduction is mixed at best.

What are the implications for teachers? Developing smaller schools and reduced class size may be a long time in coming. Again, this is not to say these changes are not needed. But it is important for teachers not to delay their personal investment with students because of what might be, someday, down the road. What happens in our schools today, now, is what matters. And we need to encourage, expect, teachers to begin to see that as principal Hoecherl suggests, "I do not find school size a deterrent. I find it a great strength." There is no reason that teachers in large schools, as teacher Hellard suggests, can't be friendly and open and create a feeling of safety, despite the school's size. And as principal Norman Wechsler insists, going small will succeed only if other changes are made as well. And as I have suggested, going small is no guarantee that teachers will automatically involve themselves in understanding the nonacademic and personal sides of their students' lives. No matter what size the school is, it is vital for teachers to develop new beliefs that say, "yes, in spite of the school size and student load, my vision and mission require me to know my students more fully, to give it my best shot." It requires teachers to grow new habits that encourage them to be a positive source of everyday student contact, to be open and friendly, accepting and welcoming, accessible in good times and bad, tough and honest when a student needs a confrontation or a wake-up call. I argue that these are things teachers can do no matter how large the school.

As Dr. Robert Blum, director of the University of Minnesota's Center for Adolescent Health and Development and the author of the national *Longitudinal Study of Adolescent Health*, a federally funded survey of 72,000 adolescents in grades seven through twelve, suggests, a sense of connectedness to school is critical to teenagers' well-being.[24] Dr. Blum advises that what goes on in the classroom is the key to keeping kids from becoming disenchanted with school. Dr. Blum says it doesn't matter whether you have twenty or thirty kids in the class. It doesn't matter whether the teacher has a graduate degree. What matters is the environment that a student enters when he or she walks through the classroom door. In Dr. Blum's survey, the effect of school size was minimal, and class size was not found to have any influence on teenagers' sense of attachment to their schools, leaving the authors to suggest that even in large classes and large schools, it is possible for students to form social ties with teachers and classmates.

Expanding the definition of intelligence is a factor.   Daniel Goleman suggests that there are widespread exceptions to the rule that IQ predicts success.[25] He says that, at best, IQ contributes about 20 percent to the factors that determine life success, which leaves 80 percent to other forces. Goleman's concern is with a key set of these "other characteristics." He describes emotional intelligence: abilities such as being able to motivate oneself and persist in the face of frustration; to control impulses and gratification; to regulate one's moods and keep distress from swamping the ability to think, to empathize, and to hope. He advises that academic intelligence offers virtually no preparation for the turmoil, or the opportunity, that life's vicissitudes bring. He says that much evidence testifies that people who are emotionally adept, who know and manage their own feelings well and who reward and deal effectively with other peoples' feelings are at an advantage in any domain of life.

Goleman's push to incorporate emotional intelligence into the ways we assess students is supported by Howard Gardner, the guiding visionary behind Project Spectrum at the Harvard School of Education. Gardner reports that it is time to broaden our notion of talent, that we should spend less time ranking children and more time helping them to identify their natural competencies and gifts and cultivate those.[26] Goleman also enlists the research of Yale psychologist Peter Salovey to make his pitch for educators to be more focused on the emotional intelligence of children. Salovey's definition of emotional intelligence includes five main domains:

1. Knowing one's emotions. Self-awareness, recognizing a feeling as it happens, is the keystone of emotional intelligence. The ability to monitor feelings is crucial to psychological insight and understanding. An inability to notice true feelings leaves us at their mercy. People with greater certainty about their feelings are better pilots of their lives.

2. Managing emotions. Having the capacity to soothe oneself, to shake off rampant anxiety, gloom, or irritability. People who are poor at this ability are constantly battling feelings of distress while those who excel at it can bounce back far more quickly from life's setbacks and upsets.

3. Motivating oneself. Marshaling emotions in the service of a goal is essential for paying attention, for self-motivation and mastery, and for creativity. Emotional self-control, delaying gratification and stifling impulses, underlies accomplishment of every sort. People who have this skill tend to be more highly productive and effective in whatever they undertake.

4. Recognizing emotions in others. Empathy, another ability that builds on emotional self-awareness, is the fundamental "people skill." People who are empathetic are more attuned to the subtle social signals that indicate what others need or want.

5. Handling relationships. The art of relationships is, in large part, skill in managing emotions in others. Social competence, and the special skills involved, undergirds popularity, leadership, and interpersonal effectiveness. People who excel in these skills do well in anything that relies on interacting smoothly with others. They are social starts.[27]

What are the implications of emotional intelligence for teachers? The Carnegie Council on Adolescent Development report *Turning Points 2000: Educating Adolescents in the 21st Century* advises that under current conditions, far too many young people will not make the passage through early adolescence successfully. Their basic human needs, their caring relations with adults, their guidance in facing overwhelming biological and psychological changes, the security of belonging to a constructive peer group, and the perception of future opportunity go unmet in this critical stage of life. Millions of these young adolescents will never reach their full potential. Early adolescence for these young people is a turning point toward a diminished future.[28]

I believe one of the primary goals of every teacher is to help each of his or her students avoid a diminished future. Concerned teachers, acting collectively, can intervene to provide a caring relationship, be a source of credible information and guidance, help students become part of a constructive peer group, and instill in them a sense of hope for the future. These are things teachers can do as part of their daily interactions with students. Their modeling can increase the level of emotional intelligence for students, helping them to learn self-motivation, persistence in the face of frustration, how to control impulses and delay gratification, keep distress from swamping their ability to think, and how to empathize and hope. Teachers can teach students habits, as John Dewey suggests, that will give them some control over their ever-changing environment and success and hope in navigating through life's challenges.

As Anthony W. Jackson and Gayle A. Davis remind us, the trajectory of a young adolescent's life is not wholly determined by social and economic circumstances.[29] The soundness of choices he or she makes and the guidance available to make good decisions are critically important. It is not a mystery to say that students need ongoing, informed, and caring teachers to help them make good decisions, decisions that provide a way to open doors to academic and personal opportunity and success. Increasingly, teachers need to be the key providers of such support. As Goleman suggests, because family life no longer offers growing numbers of children a sure footing in life, schools are left as the one place communities can turn to to correct children's deficiencies in emotional and social competence.[30] In terms of teaching students skills to build their emotional intelligence, there is perhaps no subject where the quality of the teacher matters so much, because how a teacher handles his or her class is itself a model, a de facto lesson in emotional competence or the lack thereof. Whenever a teacher responds to one student, twenty or thirty others learn the lesson.

As I have suggested, like it or not, schools and teachers are being thrust into this role. While it is understandable that many teachers may be reluctant to take on this role because of their historic subject-mastery role, Goleman believes that there are new and exciting opportunities that come with this new landscape. For example, in this new expanded mission for schools, teachers are encouraged to use opportunities in and out of class to help students turn moments of personal crisis into lessons in emotional competence. As any experienced teacher or administrator knows, every school has more than its share each day of students in personal crisis. It comes with the adolescent territory, a given that requires respect, understanding, and a positive response. It cannot be hidden away and glossed over by district public relations that suggest "we have no student problems here."

I believe that one does not need a "program," a program coordinator, a special curriculum, an expensive training program, or increased funding to carry out such interventions. It can be done and, in fact, is being done already by many teachers as a natural part of their everyday work with students. Intervening and helping students in the ways described above are instinctively done by concerned teachers. They know from their own personal development and real-life experiences about motivation, persistence in the face of frustration, gaining control over impulses and delaying gratification, and keeping distress from swamping their ability to think and how to empathize and be hopeful. They didn't arrive at the classroom door without a high degree of emotional intelligence and experience based on many failures, setbacks, and bouts with loss of hope.

A direct correlation can exist between health and the ability to learn. According to Valerie Ebbes, associate professor of health at Miami University in Ohio and facilitator of the American Society of Curriculum Development in Health Education Network, health has "physical, mental, emotional and social dimensions. People are holistic and wellness is determined by those dimensions interacting in your life." Ebbes suggests that a direct correlation can exist between health and ability. She advises that new brain research shows that a person must have food, water, sleep, and other factors for optimum learning.[31] We cannot learn if we are not healthy. If a student cannot come to school with all those tools, the school must provide them. For example, Sue Maguire, principal of Molly Stark Elementary School in Bennington, Vermont, believes that "the school's job is academic, but we can't ignore that the physical and mental well-being of kids is tied to academics"[32]

Just what is the health and well-being picture of youth in America? The Children's Defense Fund report *The State of Children in America's Union, A 2002 Action Guide to Leave No Child Behind* indicates the following:

- An American child is reported abused or neglected every 11 seconds; 581,000 children are in our foster care systems, 127,000 of them waiting for adoptive families.
- An American child is born into poverty every 43 seconds; 1 in 5 children is poor during the first 3 years of life, the time of greatest brain development. One in every 5 children under 3 is poor.
- An American child is born without health insurance every minute; 90 percent of our 9 million uninsured children live in working families.
- An American child or teen is killed by gunfire every 2 hours and 40 minutes—9 every day; 87,000 children have been killed by guns since 1979.
- Millions of American children start school not ready to learn and millions more lack safe, affordable, quality child care and early childhood education when their parents work.
- A majority of America's fourth graders can't read or do math at a proficient level.
- Seven million children are home alone on a regular basis, without adult supervision, often after school when they are at greatest risk of getting into trouble.
- Nearly twelve million children are poor and millions are hungry, at risk of hunger, living in worst-case housing or homeless. Almost 80 percent of poor children live in working households.[33]

The impact of welfare reform on childrearing and schooling. The Manpower Research Demonstration Project report *How Welfare and Work Policies for Parents Affect Adolescents* indicates that when welfare recipients get jobs, their teenagers tend not to do so well in school.[34] Adolescents of working mothers did worse, on average, than adolescents whose parents continued to receive aid under the old welfare rules. Forcing mothers into work also results in inadequate supervision at home. Teenagers are more likely to get into trouble and take drugs, and are less likely to turn off the television, stop hanging out with friends, and do their homework. The report also suggests that teenagers who have younger siblings have a greater chance of being suspended from school or dropping out before graduation, because when mothers are at work their adolescent children may have to watch their younger siblings and not study.

The impact of violence on the health and well-being of youth. The National Center for Injury Prevention and Control reports that violence is a public health issue because of its tremendous impact on the health and well-being of youth.[35] Violent injury and death disproportionately affect children, adolescents, and young adults in the United States. Homicide is the second leading cause of death for persons fifteen to twenty-four years of age and the leading cause of death for African Americans. In this age group, homicide is the second leading cause of death for Hispanic youths. The Center also reported that in regard to dating violence, the average prevalence rate for nonsexual dating violence is 22 percent among male and female high school students and that eighth- and ninth-grade male and female students indicated that 25 percent had been victims of sexual dating violence.[36] Not surprisingly, the Center reports that as the consumption of alcohol by either the victim or the perpetrator increases, the rate of serious injuries associated with dating violence also increases.

The impact of the increase of discipline problems and violence in the schools. The Principal/School Disciplinarian Survey on School Violence indicates that more than half of the U.S. public schools reported experiencing at least one crime incident in the school year 1996–97.[37] One in ten schools reported at least one serious crime during the school year. Physical attacks or fights without a weapon led the list of reported crimes in public schools with about 190,000 such incidents reported for 1996–97. The report also indicated that schools that reported serious discipline problems were more likely to have experienced one or more incidents of crime or violence. In both 1990–91 and 1996–97 the three discipline issues most frequently rated as serious or moderate problems by principals were student tardiness, student absenteeism or class cutting, and physical conflicts among students.

The impact of the lack of vigorous physical activity on the health and well-being of American youth.   The National Center for Chronic Disease Prevention and Health Promotion (CDC) data indicate that nearly half of American youth aged twelve to twenty-one years are not vigorously active on a regular basis. About 14 per cent of young people report no recent physical activity.[38] About 14 percent of young people report no recent physical activity. Inactivity is more common among females (14 percent) than males (7 percent) and among black females (21 percent) than white females (12 percent). CDC also reports that participating in all types of physical activity declines strikingly as age or grade in school increases. Only 19 percent of all high school students are physically active for 20 minutes or more, 5 days a week, in physical education classes. A *New England Journal of Medicine* study reported that teenage girls are less and less active and that physical exertion among teen girls drops sharply with age.[39] The average decline in exercise time from age 6–9 to age 15–16 was 100 percent among black girls and 64 percent among white girls. By the time the girls were 16–17, 56 percent of the black girls and 31 percent of the white girls reported that they did no leisure time physical activity. The study suggested that lack of exercise is a risk factor for becoming overweight and subsequently developing diabetes and heart disease.

The impact of being overweight or obese on the health and well-being of American youth.   In terms of young Americans being overweight, CDC data indicates that about 13 percent of children and adolescents are overweight or obese, more than double the number two decades ago.[40] Experts blame TV, computer games, lack of safe playgrounds, and other factors that encourage kids to be sedentary, plus more access to super-sized portions of high-calorie food. Overweight children are at risk for cardiovascular disease, diabetes, and other health problems. Dr. Jeffrey P. Koplan, director of CDC, says the epidemic of being overweight and obesity must be addressed among children and teens so they can lead healthier lives. As columnist Jane E. Brody suggests, the nation's children, indeed the world's, are fatter than ever, with no end in sight to their increasing girth, and unless something is done now to reverse this trend, the health costs, already too high, will be astronomical in the not-too-distant future. David Ludwig, director of the obesity program at Children's Hospital in Boston, has found that one additional can of soda a day can raise a child's risk of being overweight by 60 percent. Ludwig says, "We are seeing a takeover of our diet by the fast food industry."[41] And as Associated Press medical writer Lindsey Tanner reports, the nation's surging population of Hispanic children has a disproportionate share of obesity and other health problems that are not being adequately treated. Tanner reports that Hispanic children are much more likely to have no health insurance, have no regular doctor, have cavities, attempt suicide if they're girls, or be obese if they are boys.[42]

The impact of other eating disorders such as anorexia and bulimia on the health and well-being of American youth. Being overweight and obese are not the only eating disorders plaguing American youth. As *New York Times* writer Daniel Goleman suggests, anorexia and bulimia are a growing health concern for many female teenage students. Here are some of the facts:

- The cases of both anorexia (self-induced starvation) and bulimia (bingeing and purging for weight control) are increasing steadily.
- Women who die from anorexia often end their life by suicide.
- The single most culpable precursor of these eating disorders is the glamorization of diet.
- There is much greater dieting among women than among men.
- Eating disorders are about ten times more common among women than among men.
- The desire to fit the cultural ideal of thinness drives many women to diet severely.
- In some vulnerable young women, severe dieting leads to self-starvation.
- Emotional situations such as arguing with a boyfriend or a bad day in school can trigger binge eating.[43]

One only has to look at a sampling of fashion magazines read by young women to note the powerful impact of the cultural ideal of thinness on the teenage mind-set. As writer Kate Betts reports, models get skinnier and skinnier.[44] The average model in 1985 was a size 8, while today the average model is a size 0 to 2. Reporter Mim Udovitch also says that about 1 in 200 American women suffers from anorexia and 2 or 3 in 100 suffer from bulimia.[45] Arguably, these disorders have the highest fatality rate of any mental illness, through suicide as well as the obvious health problems. But as Udovitch reports, because these diseases are not threatening to passers-by, as psychotic disorders are, or likely to render people unemployable or criminal, as alcoholism and other addictions are, they are not a proportionately imperative social priority. Ellen Davis, clinical director of the Renfrew Center of Philadelphia, says, "So many women who don't have the disorder say to me, 'Well, what's the big deal? It's like a diet gone bad.' And it is so different from that. Women with the vulnerability, they really fall into an abyss, and they can't get out. And it's not about, 'OK, I want to lose the 10 pounds and go on with my life.' It's 'this has consumed my entire existence.'"[46]

The impact of the increase of suicide and suicidal thoughts on the health and well-being of American youth.   The National Household Survey on Drugs Report, sponsored by the Substance Abuse and Mental Health Services Administration indicates that close to three million Americans ages twelve to seventeen considered suicide in 2000 and more than a third of those tried to kill themselves.[47] Girls were almost twice as likely as boys to have thought about or tried to commit suicide. According to CDC, from 1952 to 1995, the incidence of suicide among adolescents and young adults nearly tripled.[48] From 1980 to 1997, the rate of suicide among persons ages 10 to 14 increased by 109 percent. From 1980 to 1996, the rate increased by 105 percent for African American males ages 15 to 19. For young people 15 to 24 years old, suicide is the third leading cause of death, behind unintentional injury and homicide. Let's put a real face on these numbers. As we all know numbers don't carry with them the pain that comes with a teenager's suicide, particularly with a student like Scott, who was among the best and brightest students in his school, a gifted athlete and respectful and caring with his peers, family, and teachers. In a way, he seemed the perfect student, headed for Harvard or some other elite school. His is a real-life story of a suicide that might have been prevented. The clues were there but no one seemed to notice, as is often true in the seemingly perfect high school careers of the Scotts of this world. As educators, we often look only to acting-out or withdrawn students to be troubled and ignore those successful, I-cause-no-trouble students.

As the *New York Times* reported on October 1, 1995, under the front-page headline, "At 17, A Star and Suicide Victim: An Athlete Dies Young, But by His Own Hand," Scott was an A student.[49] He was also a star football player and a popular but modest teenager who carried note cards scribbled with phrases to push himself farther. On September 8, 1995, he was just as driven to commit suicide. He was found hanging from a tree with a bullet wound in his head. His death was diagnosed as a suicide. Even though suicide is currently the third leading cause of death among teenagers, the people who knew Scott had a difficult time believing he killed himself. As the story suggests, there seem to have been some clues that Scott was becoming unwound. When Scott walked to a nearby wood on September 8 with a rope and revolver in hand, he may have done all he could to signal that he was going over the edge.

- He carried note cards with phrases to "push himself farther."
- He appeared to have "no enemies."
- Scott's older brother Brian said, "No one's perfect, but Scott was as close to it as anyone in the world. He was the All-American boy."
- Scott's father, Ron, echoed the same theme: "He was a straight arrow; he was not street smart. He was nonconfrontational. As far as I know he never got into a fight in his life. But he could play football hard because the rules were there, and they were clear. The other stuff in his life was not so clear."
- Scott had a troubled family life. His parents were divorced in 1981. It was apparently a messy divorce. Scott's mother twice sought protection-from-abuse orders against her husband.
- In the divorce judgment the judge ordered psychological counseling for Scott, his brother, and his mother. There was no evidence that he ever got the counseling.
- The gun that Scott used to kill himself was purchased by his father in 1986 to protect himself, he said, against threats by his ex-wife and her boyfriend.
- After the divorce, Scott lived with his father. He succeeded in

school. He was described by teachers as compulsive, nice, and modest to a fault. One teacher said, "He liked everybody."
* His mother described Scott as looking "sad" before his death.
* Some classmates, in retrospect, thought he seemed "depressed."
* He was applying to Harvard and hoped to play football there. The Harvard application was found on his desk.

The impact of alcohol, tobacco, and drug use on the health and well-being of American youth.   According to Carol Falkowski[33], director of research communications at the Hazelden Foundation, coming of age in the twenty-first century presents new challenges and choices about drugs and alcohol.[50] The adolescent drug abuse landscape has changed considerably. Just as the types of available drugs have expanded, so too have the risks associated with their use. Kids today are exposed to drugs and alcohol at a younger age. In 2002, half of eighth graders had tried alcohol, and one out of four have been drunk. By eighth grade, 27 percent of students have tried illegal drugs at least once and by tenth grade, almost half of them have. By tenth grade, over three-fourths of students report that marijuana, alcohol, and cigarettes are fairly easy or "very easy" to get. According to the CDC, alcohol is involved in about 35 percent of adolescent (15–20 years old) driver fatalities and in about 40 percent of adolescent drownings. The CDC also reports that more than one-third (34.8 percent) of high school students reported using some form of tobacco in the past month.[51] More than a quarter (29.4 percent) of high school students were current cigarette smokers, with male and female students smoking at equal rates. What kinds of risks is Falkowski talking about?

Here again it may be helpful for readers to move beyond these statistics and describe some of the real-life issues of students who suddenly get caught up in risky behavior related to alcohol. Here are two examples of the kinds of situations we are facing in some schools that appear to be pressure cookers for high-achieving students looking for relief from alcohol. One example involves a school dance that begins and ends with a number of students intoxicated, some requiring hospitalization. The other example describes risky behavior that leads to a student's unnecessary death and the self and community scorn of his seemingly irresponsible peers. Let's begin with the age-old high school ritual of the homecoming dance and see how this ritual has changed. According to *New York Times* staff writers, twenty-eight students at Scarsdale High School in Scarsdale, New York, were suspended for arriving drunk at the dance and four students were treated at a hospital.[52] According to parents, students, school administrators, and police, a large number of the six hundred students who attended the dance were intoxicated. Some students were seen vomiting into trash receptacles and one was taken unconscious in a cab to the hospital. Many in Scarsdale, a bastion of high income and test scores, were asking whether the scope of teenage drinking had taken a more dangerous turn. Dr. Alan Tepp, an adolescent psychologist, said the problem is deeply rooted. "We hold our children to these demands and standards that have raised the bar to a world-class level, but at the same time, we're putting less restraint on them, watching them less. We push them out, and then allow them out."[53]

Geraldine Greene, executive director of the Scarsdale Family Counseling Service, in an interview with reporter Jane Gross points a finger at Scarsdale families, almost half of whom earn more than $200,000 a year. "What do affluent families not have a lot of?" she asked. "Time. And it takes a lot of time to raise a teenager. Underage drinking," she added, "is an adult failure. In every case an adult has let the child down. Somewhere along the way they haven't exercised due care. This community has high academic expectations for its children. Why can't it have behavioral expectations as well?"[54] Gross suggests that children in competitive communities like Scarsdale are under enormous pressure to succeed. The measuring stick is admission to brand-name colleges, which leave many destined to disappoint themselves or their parents and inclined to take refuge in alcohol and drugs.

In my second example, sometimes the risks involved in abusing alcohol lead to sudden injury, even death, and irresponsible (some say reprehensible) teenage behavior. Things get out of hand quickly. Teens, suddenly grasping the reality and perhaps negative consequences of their situation, fail to act. They freeze under pressure. Take the case of Rob Viscome, a Harrison, New York, high school student. Rob died as a result of injuries suffered in a fistfight at a house party held after an early school dismissal. He died a week after the party of head injuries received when he fell onto a concrete patio after being struck by a classmate, Patrick Rukaj. As reporter Matthew Purdy revealed, Rob was attending an impromptu and parentless beer party after the high school canceled afternoon classes due to a power failure.[55] The dispute started small, witnesses said, escalating when Mr. Viscome, who had been drinking heavily, taunted Mr. Rukaj about his father, a millionaire lottery winner now in prison for murder. "Don't ever talk about my dad," a witness said Mr. Rukaj warned before the punch. But as Purdy says, a thornier question is what happened after the punch, with more than a dozen teenagers caught between the unimaginable prospect of a friend dying and the utterly imaginable anxiety of being caught partying. "I was screaming, 'Call 911, call 911.' They were, 'No, no, no, no,'" Mr. Rukaj told the police. Asked why, he said, "They don't want any cops coming there and seeing all the alcohol." Police witness statements show panicked teenagers trying to revive their friend for up to twenty minutes instead of calling 911 and then, some witnesses say, dropping him on his head while carrying him to a car. Mr. Rukaj and others screamed for someone to call for help. A girl told police she asked for a cell phone to call 911 but "nobody moved." When they decided to drive Mr. Viscome to the hospital, she said, "I just remember people saying, 'No, not me.'" Another girl said someone asked that his car not be used because he "did not want it to get dirty," according to police reports. Before the ride to the hospital in a BMW, one witness told police, someone said, "Just say it happened at a park." According to reporter Lisa W. Foderaro, the police initially charged Mr. Rukaj with second degree assault and charged six other teenagers at the party with misdemeanors, saying they had lied at first and told investigators that the fight took place in a park.[56]

The impact of teenage pregnancy on the health and well-being of American youth. According to the CDC, the United States has the highest teenage pregnancy rate of all developed countries.[57] About 1 million teenagers become pregnant each year; 95 percent of those pregnancies are unplanned and almost one-third end in abortion. And yet, as a study by researchers at the University of Minnesota demonstrates, half of all mothers of sexually active teenagers mistakenly believe that their children are still virgins.[58] Robert Blum, director of the Adolescent Health Center at the university and one of the authors of the study, described the results as stunning. Dr. Blum said the study did not examine why so many mothers were unaware of the children's sexual activity. "Perhaps it is because they don't want to know," he said. "Perhaps they're not involved in the lives of their teens. We just don't know." Blum labels these mothers "clueless moms" and says his data suggests that less than 4 percent of mothers are actually comfortable talking about sexual relations with kids.[59]

The impact of the increase in use of prescription drugs to medicate acting-out students. There is an increase in the use of prescription drugs to medicate acting-out students. According to researcher Neil Munro, the use of Ritalin and similar drugs grew threefold in the early 1990s, partly because it was being prescribed for boys diagnosed with Attention Deficit/Hyperactivity Disorder.[60] In children, the disorder's symptoms are "fidgetiness or squirming in one's seat, excessive running and climbing, difficulty playing or engaging quietly in leisurely activity, or talking excessively." The sudden rise of Ritalin prescriptions has fueled criticism by experts such as Dr. Peter Breggins, who runs the International Center for the Study of Psychiatry and Psychology, and Dr. Lawrence Diller, a behavioral pediatrician. They say drugs are promoted by school officials and harried parents to pacify unruly schoolboys. "The use of drugs is cheaper and faster" than other approaches says Diller, author of the book *Running on Ritalin.* "But is it the moral equivalent of better parenting or schools?" Breggin says, "The emphasis on 'brain disorders' in people who are in conflict with society or their families or schools is a scam."[61]

The impact of sexual abuse on the health and well-being of American youth. Thelma Bear, Sherry Schenk, and Lisa Buckner, educators and psychologists involved in programs to help sexually abused children, report that although the statistics are overwhelming, professionals in the mental health field generally accept that the incidence of child abuse is much greater than reported.[62] They indicate that in its newsletter, the National Organization for Victims' Assistance reported that 2.2 million children are reported physically or sexually abused each year. Many cases are closed after a cursory investigation; many cases remain unreported.

The increasing pressure of the college admission process on the health and well-being of American youth. There has been an increasing pressure on students to achieve and be accepted at select colleges and universities. The pressure on our best and brightest students appears to be veering out of control. Here is an extreme, painful example of where this pressure sometimes leads. As newspaper columnist Erica Goode reports, Justin Chapman was the smartest little boy in the world.[63] There were documents to prove it. An IQ test given when Justin was 6 recorded his score at 298 plus, the highest on record. He scored a perfect 800 on the math portion of the SAT. Based on such achievements, Justin enrolled in an online high school at the age of five, and at six he took courses at the University of Rochester. He met with Governor George Pataki of New York. He was featured in a BBC documentary about child geniuses. He spoke at conferences about the special needs of highly gifted children. His mother, Elizabeth Chapman, told reporters how her son walked and talked precociously, evidenced a relentless hunger for learning and needed only two to five hours of sleep each night.

But in an interview with the *New York Times* after a newspaper raised some doubts about Justin's accomplishments, Ms. Chapman admitted that many of the records attesting to his superior intelligence were a sham. Ms. Chapman said she falsified the records of the IQ test and the SAT score belonged to a former neighbor's son. She said that Justin was unusually bright and that she was trying to open doors for him that would otherwise have remained closed. "I didn't plan it," she said. "It just happened and I let things get out of control."

After the release of the story Justin was hospitalized for psychiatric problems and taken away from his mother and put in foster care. Ms. Chapman was charged with neglect. The story evoked passionate letters to the *New York Times* by Jay S. Kwawer, director of clinical education at the William Alanson White Institute in New York City, and Miriam Arond, editor-in-chief of *Child Magazine*. Here is what Mr. Kwawer had to say about the Chapman article: "The sad indictment of Justin Chapman's mother for neglect, for falsifying test records, sidesteps the role of an educational system that encourages the 'packaging' of children. The story caricatures a deeper, more widespread problem in educational admissions. In our own city, thousands of families seek entrance into independent schools and public school 'gifted' programs, subjecting children to intelligence testing administered in a fashion psychologists say is of dubious validity and which has no demonstrable predictive power."[64]

Arond adds that "the effort of Elizabeth Chapman to falsify her son's IQ is admittedly an extreme example, yet it underscores the extraordinary competitiveness parents are feeling today and the burden many are imposing on their children by applying such pressure. As parents we all want to provide our children with as much enrichment and opportunity as possible, both in and outside the academic arena. Yet there is no benefit, and potentially a great deal of harm, in not recognizing and not appreciating childhood. If we trust that each child is special, and appreciate him for the person he is and the stage he is in, his gifts will grow and glow."[65]

Arond's sensitive and wise plea concerning our children's development may be drowned out in our increasingly competitive school world. Reporter Nancy Ann Jeffrey suggests that more and more teens are being taught to run their lives like CEOs.[66] She reports that if it looks like kids are growing up even faster than usual lately, one of the reasons is that they're getting a big push today from parents and teachers seemingly intent on raising a new generation of Organization Kids. They're getting help from an industry that is deluging kids with MBA-style strategies for success, from books (a teen-tailored version of the blockbuster *Who Moved My Cheese?*) and $400 palm organizers to workshops to tapes that push go-getter mantras like "sharpen the saw." Schools across the country are buying into the idea big time, shelling out thousands on journals, workbooks, and other classroom materials intended to teach organizational skills. As Jeffrey indicates, critics, of course, say all the time management tricks in the world can't make up for the real problem, which is that kids are just too busy these days. No less an expert than Marilyn Benoit, president of the American Academy of Child and Adolescent Psychiatry, goes so far as to call the efficiency push "dehumanizing."[67] And then there's the question of how some kids will do once they get to collect and they're no longer being spoon fed with organizational tips. "They lose their way and take a huge nose dive," says Carl Thum, academic skills director at Dartmouth College.[68] But the pressure is on. As Jeffrey notes, the $3.6 billion organization industry sees a whole new market, pimply future CEOs out there, and is churning out products to cater to them. For example, Spencer Johnson, author of the bestseller *Who Moved My Cheese?*, says coming out with his new version for teens was a no-brainer. "Parents want their kids to win, to get into good colleges, to be well-liked, to be good in sports."[69]

But increasing pressure on parents and their children has, as Miriam Arond, Marilyn Benoit, and Carl Thum suggest, has its costs. A worst-case scenario can be seen in the suicide of Massachusetts Institute of Technology student Elizabeth Shin, who burned herself to death in her dorm room. As reported by Deborah Sontag, Elizabeth's parents, Cho and Kisuk Shin, are strivers, but it's not only classic immigrant striving.[70] They lived in upper-middle-class America, where many parents believe in giving their children every opportunity to enrich themselves, to excel, to become superkids. It's a culture of ambition but also one of high anxiety that is having a kind of Generation Stress. And colleges, whose ever-increasing selectivity fosters this phenomenon, reap the good and ill effects. As Sontag suggests, administrators, especially at elite schools, worry about students who start college ready to do graduate level research and yet are unprepared to be one among thousands of other "perfect" children. They talk about kids who seem to have been bred in a hothouse and who, after a high school experience packed with electives, college level courses, test preparation classes, internships, and after-school activities, are simply burned out by the time they arrive for freshman year. Thomas A. Dingman, an associate dean at Harvard College, said, "More and more kids want to position themselves to get into college early admissions. You have high school juniors feeling right from the get-go that they can't make mistakes. Everything is too costly. Ultimately, this makes some of them less resilient and less equipped to handle college."[71]

William Doherty, a sociologist, calls our frenzied rush to capitalize on, or nurture, our children's potential not parenting so much as "product development."[72] The education researcher Gerald W. Bracey gives us a dark picture of where it could all end when he describes the run up to national examination day in Korea, a day that seals the fates of high school seniors.[73] Many mothers go to the temple for a few hours for ninety-nine consecutive days to pray for their children's success. On the hundredth day, they arrive around 8:00 P.M. and pray all night— hands up, clasp hands in prayer, bow, down on one's knees, head to floor, clasp hands in prayer. Repeat three thousand times. Many stores and kiosks sell chocolate axes and forks to help students "spear" the right answers. Bands and cheering throngs meet the seniors as they approach the test sites. Workers report an hour later for work, to ensure that rush hour traffic jams don't prevent the seniors' timely arrival. In Seoul, takeoffs and landings at Kimpo International Airport are banned for certain periods. The U.S. military halts training at all ninety Korean bases for nine hours. The students are not exactly happy. "I've been preparing for college since elementary school, and it all comes down to just one day that will decide my future," said one. Stakes are indeed high. The people who end up with the most prestigious jobs and who hold public office are those whose test scores admit them to one of the three most prestigious universities. These three institutions will enroll 15,000 of the 873,000 applicants. That's 1.9 percent!

The increased pressure of standardized testing on the health and well-being of American youth. Pressure on students is exacerbated because of the increase in high stakes standardized testing. As writer James Traub says, in Scarsdales and Mamaronecks all over this great land, educators, parents, and kids are fulminating over a regime of state administered tests that have become nearly universal.[74] They believe, of course, in "standards," the very essence of their culture is high achievement, but they do not like the contents of the tests, the number of tests, the way the tests have distorted the curriculum, the way they are scored, the way they are used to judge students, teachers, schools, and real estate value. And they feel life is pressured enough as it is. Why, now, this?

As educator Donald B. Gratz suggests, many states have decided that their assessments must be high stakes ones, tests that significantly determine opportunities and outcomes for the test takers.[75] Today, radically more difficult (and sometimes poorly designed) tests are being used to determine who will graduate, who will be licensed to teach, and which schools will get rewards and sanctions. As Gratz says, in a recent study of high stakes testing the National Research Council concluded that educational decisions "that will have a major impact on test takers should not be made solely or automatically on the basis of a single test score, even if the test is a good one."[76] A 1998 study of Chicago schools reached a similar conclusion, that the district's much-vaunted improvement should not be judged solely on standardized test scores. Yes, I do believe that's a hope of many concerned educators who are aware of the downside of high stakes testing. But in the real world, school test results are being used in many schools to make decisions about teachers, students, and parents, the downside that many educators fear is happening. That this is happening should come as no surprise to savvy educators who understand numbers do not carry with them any emotional quality, human component, nor faces of children affected by low test scores. The assessment of these numbers is often made by well-intentioned district level administrators in offices that are often far removed from the emotional impact of high stakes testing on students. Administrators are under great pressure from state and national political and education reform groups to produce higher test scores. I believe this is a striking, negative, dilemma indeed when we observe that *every* member of the school community—students, parents, teachers, principals, and district administrators—is at risk from the pressures being placed at their doors.

Here is an example of the kind of pressure many well-intentioned and caring administrators are resorting to. Gratz says schools are employing such strategies as piling on homework, abolishing recess and free play, cheating on tests, transferring pressure to students, flunking more students, teaching to the test and seeking ways to rid themselves of low performers. He indicates one of the unintended consequences of high stakes testing is stress on students. He refers to David Elkind's book, *The Hurried Child*, in which Elkind suggests, "Today's child has become the unwilling, unintended victim of overwhelming stress. Stress born of rapid, bewildering social change and constantly rising expectations. Tests are now determining school curriculum and the conduct of teaching is beginning to look more and more like that of a factory foreman than that of a teacher."[77] Gratz indicates that in 1981, the year *The Hurried Child* was published, the average time that grade school students spent on homework was 85 minutes a week; by 1997 it had grown to 134 minutes, an increase of nearly 60 percent. He also indicates that child advocates estimate that as many as 40 percent of the nation's 16,000 school districts, including large districts such as Atlanta and Orlando, have either curtailed or eliminated recess.[78]

Gratz concludes that in a high stress world, greater pressure on schools is creating greater pressure on children and families. Policies governing homework, recess, retention, and testing are ignoring research on student learning and motivation in favor of conventional wisdom and political expediency. Inconsistent, hurried, thoughtless, mean-spirited, and politically motivated implementation of standards and accountability is leading to negative consequences for children. Writer Richard Rothstein supports many of Gratz's findings by indicating that in 1990, 26 percent of American adolescents failed to graduate from high school.[79] By 2000 the figure had risen to 30 percent. Rothstein suggests there has been too little discussion about why the rate apparently climbed. One worrisome possibility is that as the states required students to pass tests for promotion, more pupils who were held back now leave school when they are old enough to do so. States are beginning to require students to pass graduation exams that are tougher than the high school equivalency test. California, Florida, Massachusetts, and New York are among these. If the modestly higher standards of the last decade were themselves enough to cause dropout rates to rise, the new exit exams could produce even more failure. Rothstein also says the big increase in the dropout rate was not foreseen. Although some students were inspired to reach for a higher standard, too many others either have not had the opportunity to succeed at the higher level or have been unable to do so. Rothstein concludes that without academic policies that are more realistically calibrated to students' abilities and to the opportunities, the dropout rate could continue to climb.[80]

The impact of the increased use of computers, television, and electronic toys on the health and well-being of American youth. There has been a negative impact because of the increased use of computers, television watching, and use of electronic toys. Patricia Greenfield, a cultural psychologist at UCLA, points out that as a culture we increasingly esteem technological intelligence and devalue the social and emotional.[81] Professor Linda Pogue of York University in Toronto observes in describing the impact of computers, "This machine is so cognitive, we're forgetting the emotional development. I find children and university students too much into their heads. They're not experiencing life, they're thinking about life."[82] Physicist Fritjof Capra sees the information technology as totalitarian, demanding even more of our time and priorities, distorting peoples' relationships to the world, and to each other. Capra believes we are too worried about our youngster's store of information; we should be more concerned with the kind of aesthetically sensitive human beings they are becoming.[83] And as author Healy indicates, electronic "environments" entice children to spend hours playing with popular product characters, such as talking animals or hero figures. Healy says children feel a more personal relationship to these characters and may fail to distinguish the fantasy and may take serious exhortations to use particular products. Some companies even encourage children to e-mail messages to characters, implying that the reply they receive is actually written by the icon itself.[84]

Healy suggests that many parents believe that children are learning more when they are at the computer than they would if they were in gym or playing in the back yard. But health experts join developmental psychologists in expressing grave concern about this dangerous trend. Not only is physical activity, preferably outdoors, vital for health, good sleep patterns, dissipation of excess energy, and socialization, but the subtle learning and problem solving that takes place in spontaneous play are important in mental development as well. Healy says we seem to care more about how fast our children can learn than how deeply they feel. Instead of offering children our thoughtful companionship, we saturate them with noise and temporary self-satisfying objects of the electronic world, hooking them on artificial stimulation and self-gratification.[85] Therefore, as the Associated Press reports, it should come as no surprise that a new study by a team of researchers at Columbia University led by Jeffrey G. Johnson found a correlation between adolescents wanting to watch more than one hour of TV daily and higher rates of assault, fights, robberies, and other aggressive acts in later years.[86] But the connection of kids with their ever-increasing electronic world is not going away. In fact, that electronic world is challenging the way our culture views schools and schooling. Writer Martha Woodall reports that there are 1,200 Pennsylvania students enrolled in the Western Pennsylvania Cyber Charter School. It's one of seven online schools in Pennsylvania. The online school, which is based in Pittsburgh, provides families with two computers, Internet service, textbooks, and other educational materials they receive by mail or by e-mail. The children are supervised by parents and contact their cyber-school teachers via e-mail, chat rooms, and phone calls. Cyber students take all their classes at home. The cyber schools are charter schools funded by taxpayers' money and are considered alternatives to public schools because they are exempt from many state regulations. Woodall says critics of the program, such as Glenn Snelbecker, an educational psychology professor at Temple University in Philadelphia, worry that cyber students will miss out on important opportunities to learn to get along with other students and to form bonds with teachers.[87]

The impact of 9/11 on the health and well-being of American youth. The World Trade Center disaster on 9/11 has had a tremendous impact on students throughout America. Students in New York City appeared to have been hit the hardest. As writer Joyce Purnick reports, a New York City Board of Education study indicates that about 75,000 of the more than 710,000 public school students in grades 4 through 12 are suffering symptoms of posttraumatic stress disorder and as many as 190,000 have mental problems, both related and unrelated to 9/11.[88] Dr. Spencer Eth, professor of psychiatry at New York Medical College, suggests "those kids affected and untreated will go on to have potentially lifelong disabilities directly related to 9/11 in the form of educational handicaps, substance abuse and antisocial behavior."[89] Yet, as writer N. R. Kleinfield reports, "eight months after 9/11, children in New York seem to have bounced back and returned to rooting for the Yankees or Mets, flocking to *Spider Man* movies, or playing in their soccer league with the same childhood zeal they showed in living their lives prior to 9/11. However, many others continue to struggle to find their old bearings. Sometimes they are seemingly carefree children. Sometimes they are living children's lives with adult worries."[90] Anna Switzer, principal of PS 234 in Brooklyn, New York City, brings this reality home when, as reported by Erica Goode, she told a congressional hearing on children's mental health needs in the wake of the terrorist attack, "merely wanting the normalcy of our lives and our feelings before September 11 is not enough to make it happen."[91]

I believe that 9/11 has had other harmful aspects in addition to posttraumatic stress disorders for America's youth. The increase in adult animosity, bigotry, even hatred, toward Muslims and Middle Eastern immigrants after 9/11 has been carried over to some vulnerable stu-dents, encouraging them to unleash their hostility toward Muslim peers and creating new barriers to inclusion. The destructive age-old process of targeting and excluding a minority group for problems not of their own doing again revisits our schools and communities.

What are the implications of these health and well-being issues for teachers? Clearly, teachers can't prevent their students from experienc-ing many of the health and well-being issues I describe here. But they can offer their students what Healy calls "thoughtful companionship" when these issues become troublesome and impact negatively on their academic and personal development. They can offer adult guidance and wisdom that has been hard-earned through their own real-life expe-riences. The issues of health and well-being affecting America's youth are no strangers to teachers. Not all, but many of them have experi-enced first-hand the world of poverty, little adult supervision and guid-ance, abuse, eating disorders, risky behavior with drugs, tobacco, alcohol, or sex, pressure to succeed, high stakes testing and the nega-tive impact of computers, TV, and the like. They have lived a life that for the most part hasn't been all success, safety, hope, and joy. You might say they've been down some of the bad roads with health and well-being issues their students are experiencing today. Many can relate also to the suggestion by Dr. Larry Aber, one of the chief investi-gators of the research project commissioned by the New York City Board of Education to learn the impact of 9/11 on the mental health of city school children, who suggested that there are a lot of psychological problems among city students and it would be a very good idea to deal with them every day rather than reacting to an emergency situation.

Dr. Aber, like many teachers, speaks with knowledge gained from his own adolescent experience. As writer Anemona Hartocollis reports, Dr. Aber's own childhood was not without hardship. "My family's economic status changes frequently. At various times they were com-fortable, lived on welfare, were working poor or lived on social secur-ity." Dr. Aber was the eldest of six children. Born in Memphis, he went to eight grade schools in eight cities. It is a story that Dr. Aber, mild-mannered and somewhat timid, tells reluctantly. "I told you only because I wanted you to know that I feel like I come by this interest honestly."[92]

I would suggest that many teachers come by their interest in strengthening the health and well-being of their students honestly. Hard-earned experiences from their own academic and personal battles, like Dr. Aber, may have taken them to eight schools in eight states. But, like Dr. Aber, many teachers have survived these rough times and made a mark for themselves. A lesson, if shared with their students, even reluctantly, as Dr. Aber says, can help them to feel they too can survive, have hopes and dreams, find their place in the community, and become contenders.

The daily presence of caring and concerned teachers brings with it unlimited opportunities to provide our students with support, hope, and advice on how to turn their lives around. As I have suggested earlier in this chapter, we are not talking rocket science here. Simply put, we are asking teachers to be aware of each student, understand the particulars in their students' lives, compile data about their academic and personal lives, and intervene when they observe a change in students' behavior; hear their stories and not look the other way or run for cover when real-life troubles intrude. Encourage them to shine their light, be known; teachers should do the same, telling their students, as Dr. Aber did, "I told you because I wanted you to know. I feel like I came by this honestly."

No, I am not suggesting that teachers have to have personally experienced every problem their students are going through. Fortunately, many of us have not experienced their closeness to the 9/11 disaster. Yes, it is helpful to have walked the walk. Be like Dr. Aber and know what the journey is really like, from moving from a world of poverty, being on welfare and constantly moving and changing schools, to becoming a successful adult. Sometimes we have not walked in their shoes and shared the kinds of experiences our students are going through. But that shouldn't stop us from intervening when we see, hear, and feel the struggles of our students. As teachers we need to remember that maybe we haven't had the same trauma and difficulties that our students are experiencing but we've had our share of family, professional, personal, and health crises. What we need to be about is continuing to connect with these students on a regular basis by being empathetic, interested, and available. I believe this process enhances our teaching careers by giving our work meaning, and gives us dignity and the opportunity to share our wisdom and knowledge with our students.

As psychologists and educators Bear, Schenk, and Buckner suggest, when talking about child abuse there is probably no adult who is more trusted by children who have been abused than a beloved and caring teacher. They say that teachers have an opportunity afforded few adults to identify abused children and to start a process that will restore safety in the child's world. There is no escape for children caught in a world where silence seems the only way to survive. And, I would suggest, the same goes for students who are experiencing other health and well-being issues. Teachers who model care and concern and can connect with students on personal and health as well as academic issues will find many opportunities to support children as they seek a safe and secure path to new lives.

We have only to look to the recent sniper shootings in the Maryland, Virginia, and Washington, D.C., areas for an example. As writer Jean Schemo reports, the October 2002 sniper shootings in the suburbs of Washington, D.C., that killed ten people and wounded three forced school officials to bolt school doors, keep all the shades down, cease after-school extracurricular activities, and hold children inside until school closed. They lived daily with the contents of a note from the snipers that said, "Your children are not safe anywhere, at any time."[93] As Schemo reports, one principal of a Montgomery County, Maryland, school said of the sniper's threats to children, "There is a lot of pressure in the atmosphere, but I think students can find refuge in having a routine. Parents are pitching in with suggestions and praise and teachers are being understanding about children who are late or absent." The sniper story, ending with the arrest of forty-one-year-old John Allen Muhammad and seventeen-year-old John Lee Malvo on October 24, highlights the importance of the guidance and guardian aspect of teachers' work, illustrating, I believe, why their nonacademic and personal intervention is so needed when parents and children are daily buffeted by fears beyond their control. Daily routines, as our Montgomery County principal suggested, accompanied by understanding teachers who care and provide safety, hope, and encouragement.

I believe this tragic event had some important positive outcomes and lessons to be learned. One of these lessons is that we need to be about helping teachers to be aware of the gift they have each day to be a source of guidance, hope, and encouragement that things can change for the better and a reminder that maybe along the line, the life of seventeen-year-old murderer John Lee Malvo might have been changed for the better by a chance connection with a savvy and caring teacher. As reporter Lynette Clemetson suggests, here was a child who led a chaotic life in a swirl of ever-changing schools and addresses in the Caribbean and the United States; his participation in the murders may have been a search for parental guidance.[94] Clemetson says in Malvo's early years in Jamaica, he appeared to his teachers to be well adjusted and studious. "As I look through his file, I have to wonder if he is the same boy," said Delcy Williams, principal of Spalding High School in Jamaica. But by the time he showed up at Bellingham High School in Bellingham, Washington, he arrived with no transcript, his address a homeless shelter where he lived with Mr. Muhammad. Mrs. James, John's mother, appeared at the school, alarmed. Mr. Muhammad, she tried to convince school officials, had a dangerous grip on her son. Mary Haycox, whose daughter Devyn attended Bellingham High School with Mr. Malvo, said neither her daughter nor any of her friends remembered a thing about him. "I guess nobody paid much attention to him." Nobody except John Allen Muhammad.

Clemetson also reports that Dr. Alvin Poussaint, a professor of psychiatry at Harvard Medical School, believes that John's involvement in the murders "may have become a twisted way of developing self-esteem and earning validation. If he got the message that this was the way to please Mr. Muhammad, this was the way to show him he had what it took to be a man, that may have pushed him forward."[95] Yes, like the story of our successful student, Scott, who committed suicide, the clues were probably there to show that John Lee Malvo was at great risk and pressing at the margins. Something bad was probably going to happen. His chaotic life, ever-changing schools and addresses, and a search for parental guidance present a painful picture of a well-adjusted, studious little boy turned homeless and parentless. The clues were there. And I suggest that responding to clues is an important part of the work of teachers. Most kids will send a signal and let a concerned adult know when they are heading into deep water. And I believe for every John Lee Malvo there are literally thousands of other would-be Johns in our schools who have been deterred from violence by teachers who did not look the other way, who accept that this is an important part of their role, when clues are left by students.

The issues I have identified in this chapter—the increase in family mobility and immigration bringing a constant flow of newcomers into our schools, changing family and community connections, the continued existence of large comprehensive secondary schools, and the relationship between health and well-being and achievement—all are having a major impact on schools, administrators, teachers, students, and parents. For students, many of these issues are having a negative impact on their school achievement and well-being and causing multiple problems for them to resolve. For example, while we know many teenagers are increasingly leading passive lives in front of computers, not participating in physical activities, and becoming overweight, some schools are curtailing physical education classes, recess, and play time. Other students, under the pressure of finding a brand-name college, are turning to alcohol, drugs, and tobacco for temporary relief. Still other students crack under the pressure of trying to be model students and sadly choose to commit suicide as a way out. And then there are the low-performing students who are headed toward the margins and dropping out because they cannot meet the demands of high stakes testing. Meanwhile, a huge wave of legal and illegal immigrants is flowing into our schools, many unwelcomed and victims of a new kind of racial conflict. And there is the ongoing issue of teenage sex. As Goodman suggests, everyone who deals with teens seems to agree that the most important and toughest job is staying in touch and conversation—not delivering a lecture but saying what we think. But as Ms. Goodman reports, Sarah Brown of the National Campaign to Prevent Teen Pregnancy says, "A lot of parents tell me, 'I hardly ever see my children. When I do I don't know whether to talk to them about the sniper, safe driving or sex.'" Ms. Brown's comments crystallize what's going on in the lives of many teens—parents who hardly ever see them and when they do, not knowing how to provide straight talk about all the complicated well-being issues the world is bringing into their home and school lives.[96]

I believe many of these issues spell trouble for schools and need a strong response. As I have suggested, we can't wait for smaller schools and smaller student loads to respond effectively. I believe these issues are creating an urgent need for teachers to develop habits that offer thoughtful companionship, guidance, hope, and direction to their students, creating a school climate in which *every teacher* is a potential advisor for students seeking a connection, as well as for those students who, while resisting a connection, leave clues that they indeed need help with their poor academic performance and troubled personal lives, who want to be involved but don't know the drill. The good news is, as the Public Agenda study states, there is a national resolve to help youngsters get a good start in life and that the most troubled students can be saved.[97] As the research of Daniel Goleman demonstrates, we are beginning to see that the teaching and modeling of emotional intelligence can be an effective way to ready our students for the ever-changing world they are entering.

I believe that in establishing this kind of school climate where every teacher wears an advisor hat, we will be able to direct our attention not only to our most needy and acting-out students but also to students like Patrick Rukaj, his teenaged peers involved in the unsettling death of Rob Viscome, and friends of Rob, left dealing with their lives. Let's face it. As every secondary-school teacher knows, kid go down wrong roads. They screw themselves up and sometimes take their peers with them. No, we shouldn't absolve students' irresponsible behavior when it results in a frightening situation such as the death of Rob Viscome. But we don't have to ignore their plight and let them drift without support and become victims themselves of community scorn. I am sure there are many readers of this book who, in their teenage experience, drank some beers, got into an argument, punched or got punched by a taunting peer and tried to extricate themselves from a volatile situation. In a sense Rob Viscome, Patrick Rukaj, and their peers at the party are all victims. There is plenty of hurt and pain to go around.

In the kind of school climate I am calling for, teachers would be there to offer support for Rob's family and friends and for the other students and parents affected by this sad event. There are no winners in a situation like this. Helping doesn't take sides. Things change. We all make mistakes, sometimes big-time mistakes. Students need to be helped to find the way out of this awful mess and learn important lessons about living and dying, to be able to look forward to better days.

But students can't learn these lessons on their own. Rob Viscome's friends will need trusted advisors to help them get beyond feeling guilty and irresponsible.

As author William Damon suggests, "guardians" of all sorts can interact with children in high-quality ways that establish excellent interactional and communicational settings for their growth.[98] Children need relationships that they can benefit from and that they can count on over time. Through these relationships and guidance, children learn to find their own voices. Damon wisely says that if children are to acquire competence and character, they need to have sustained relationships with people who care about their intellectual and moral growth. Any improvement in our schools must begin by making sure these kinds of relationships are available to all students, relationships that build bridges that can provide guidance for the legions of disaffected, demoralized, and directionless young people growing up in today's world, relationships that help students to develop real skills for getting along with others, acquiring respect for social rules and legitimate authority, caring for those in need, and assuming personal and social responsibility in a host of ways. Sometimes an event like Rob Viscome's death creates an opportunity for self-centered, disaffected students living in a pressured and high stakes world, the opportunity to question the value of the road they are on and begin to assume personal and social responsibility and care for those in need. As every reader of this book knows, we all get hit by life's hurts. No one escapes, not even the most affluent and protected.

As Maurice J. Elias suggests, students need teachers in their lives to help them find answers to the following questions:

1. How can I understand who I am now and who I will be in the future?
2. How can I nurture and build positive relationships?
3. How can I develop skills to handle everyday challenges, problems, decisions, and choices?
4. How can I become a moral, ethical, active, committed human being?
5. How can I develop a positive, constructive identity?[99]

Caring, concerned, and easily accessible teachers are ideally positioned to help students answer these questions. What other institution, as Damon asks, other than the public schools, has access to all children in a society? What other institution is in the position to offer every child nurturance, support, guidance, and a chance for a successful future? Only public schools have this kind of universal reach and are able to offer adult guidance, one of the priceless commodities that have become rarer with each passing year.

What is keeping educators from expecting all teachers to think of themselves as advisors and get on with the work of making sure every child gets the nurturance, support, guidance, and the chance for a successful future he or she deserves? You've heard the arguments against this kind of role for teachers. Here is the list of "why not's?"

1. This kind of advisor role can't happen in large schools.
2. This kind of advisor role can't happen with high student loads.
3. This kind of advisor role can't happen when the school's focus needs to be on academic achievement.
4. Teachers are not qualified to advise and have close helping relationships with students. This role should be left to school counselors, social workers, and psychologists, professionals who can offer nurturance, support and guidance, and the chance for a successful future.
5. Teachers can become advisors only when there is a formal advisory created in which each advisor meets each day with a small number of students.

These are the arguments educators present when asked why they don't become more closely involved with their students. And, yes, there is some credibility to these arguments. However, I believe these arguments pale in light of the present needs of teenagers. In fact, these arguments serve as a powerful counterproductive force as they send a signal to teachers that their advisor role cannot really be accomplished because of the ways schools are currently organized. They represent calls for action. Furthermore, most of these arguments call for a structural change in the schools rather than an examination of how to enhance the personal contact between teachers and students in our present educational delivery system.

Most importantly, I believe these arguments for structural change mask other more critical reasons as to why teachers do not become more personally connected with their students. I believe we need to help educators become more aware of these reasons if we are going to succeed in helping teachers alter their one-dimensional subject-mastery role. There are formidable barriers to changing teachers' behaviors that go beyond the historical themes I identified in chapter 2. In order to overcome these barriers we need to shed some light on how these barriers operate in our teachers' psyches and the school climate and consider ways for teachers to form new habits in relating to students. Clearly educators cannot hope to succeed in their mandate to help each child get off to a good start in life, even the most troubled students, unless they understand what is holding them back from more positive student–teacher interactions. Here is a list of the complex issues and barriers we need to focus on:

How do we proceed to remove the barriers to caring and attention to our students.   Damon suggests that our society abounds with children whom teachers have given up on, part of the reason being that many teachers no longer see it as part of their job to devote extra attention to children who need it.[100] In a sense, our focus on only the subject-matter mastery role of teachers has minimized the important place of caring in their daily work. Caring is as vital and necessary an ingredient in the teacher–student relationship as it is in all other relationships. As Gay suggests, caring binds individuals to their society, to their communities, and to each other. Teachers who really care about students honor their humanity, hold them in high esteem, expect high performance from them, and use strategies to fulfill their expectations. They also model academic, social, personal, and moral behaviors and values for students. Gay says that students, in kind, feel obligated to be worthy of being so honored. They rise to the occasion by producing high levels of performance in many different areas—academic, social, moral, and cultural.

But to be honest, caring between teachers and students doesn't always come easily. As I have suggested, some students are difficult to deal with and would prefer the anonymity that Horace offers. Some students welcome ongoing confrontations with teachers, using the teacher as a target to get even for the pain and insults inflicted upon them by other abusive adults, parents, or family members.

Removing the barriers caused by student–teacher personal and cultural issues. Educators George and Louise Spindler wisely suggest that teachers carry into the classroom their personal cultural background.[101] They perceive students, all of whom are cultural agents, with their inevitable prejudices and preconceptions. Students likewise come to school with personal cultural backgrounds that influence their perceptions of teachers, other students, and the school itself. Together, students and teachers construct, mostly without being conscious of doing it, an environment of meaning enacted in individual and group behaviors, of conflict and accommodation, rejection and acceptance, alienation and withdrawal.

Here are some examples of how this "differentness" phenomenon plays out in the schools. As Valerie Ooka Pang and Velma A. Sablan report, research has indicated that most teachers are middle-class European Americans and the majority of students from the twenty-five largest school districts in the United States are children of color who may be linguistically different and from low-income families.[102] In addition, many teachers often have limited contact with persons from underrepresented groups and the experience gap between teachers and their students may be large. Teachers have demonstrated uncomfortable feelings with racial and ethnic differences and perceived cultural diversity as an obstacle rather than a resource. Pang and Sablan indicate that teachers have little knowledge of the cultural orientation of African American males and teachers often misinterpret the behaviors of their students. Students may be highly verbal, using language to maintain identity, acquire status, and develop leadership in the community. This style of communication can be in direct conflict with classrooms where teachers are the primary speaker and the students are expected to remain quiet and attentive to the teacher's words. Perhaps this kind of conflict is part of the reason that discipline is the area in which most significant inequities occur. As Martha R. Bireda, race and gender coordinator for the southeastern Equity Center, reports, black students represent 17 percent of enrollment nationally but 32 percent of out-of-school suspensions.[103] Black children, particularly black males, are disciplined more often and more severely than any other minority group. Almost 25 percent of all black males were suspended at least once over a four-year period.

John I. Goodlad adds another dimension to the "differentness" between teachers and students when he observes that as educators we believe Asian students to be well taken care of in schools to which they have adapted well.[104] They are often referred to as "model students" because of their consistently high levels of academic achievement and obedient behavior. However, as Goodlad suggests, research is showing that many Asian students pay a price; academic achievement may mask unhealthy levels of anxiety. Japanese and Chinese American college students, compared in a study with mainstream students, exhibited some somatic complaints and family conflicts. Similar results have been reported for third-generation Japanese American high school students. Goodlad's data suggest that teachers have difficulty perceiving anxiety in children (of any race) who perform well on what achievement tests measure, and they often fail to realize that the creative potential of these strong achievers may be underutilized.[105] The problem is accentuated for Asian children, whose parents expect much. The suicide of MIT student Elizabeth Shin is a painful reminder that the best and brightest of our students, the standard bearers, can also be troubled. In fact, the Elizabeth Shins of the world may be more at risk than acting-out students because they are achievers, bring credit to their schools and teachers, and are not supposed to have a dark side or to be troubled. Schools and teachers who are focused only on academic achievement may miss their cries for help. Kids who do well, don't make noise, and are off to MIT and Harvard may be our most at-risk group in today's highly competitive world.

Removing the barriers that suggest only the most problematic students are at risk. I believe the research of educators Robert L. Sinclair and Ward J. Ghory about marginal students can help us move from a global conversation about school reform into a more concrete analysis on how to create conditions for each student to improve academically, socially, and in their well-being.[106] As Sinclair and Ghory suggest, it is sobering to realize that anyone is at risk of becoming at least temporarily disconnected from full and productive involvement in classrooms and schools—the well-adjusted cheerleader whose parent dies, the merit scholar whose first romance ends, the legions of young people whose family life is strained, the children who become seriously ill or injured. Anyone can be quickly knocked out of a pattern of productivity and go unattended to at school for long periods. Experiencing even greater odds against success are those learners whose ways of handling information and developing skills are not favored by relatively monolithic school environments—learners who like to work with their hands, for example; the extroverts who prefer to work in groups and have to verbalize continually to stay on task; or the intuitive thinker impatient with step-by-step processes. Precious little is done to draw out the quick minds with special aptitudes, the linguistically different, the learning disabled, and the culturally distinct, into exciting school learning. Sinclair and Ghory suggest that when students are seen moving to the margins of a classroom or school, it is necessary to question what conditions in the school–student relationship are not working.

Sinclair and Ghory advance the term "marginal" to move away from the potentially negative and divisive connotations connected with most labels used to describe young people who have difficult relations with the school. Use of marginal to explain student-learning shifts the perspective from deeply seated problems rooted in the individual to problematic relationships between individuals and the school environment. They suggest the term "at risk" tends to isolate and stereotype youngsters. The at-risk language focuses on a population of students considered unlikely to succeed, those who are black or Hispanic and from low-income households. The term marginal makes the shift to any student who is seen moving toward the margins of a classroom or school, thus drawing our attention to the progress or lack of progress of each student and beginning the work of creating conditions that correct their difficulties.

Clearly, as Sinclair and Ghory suggest, when students are seen moving to the margins of a classroom or school, it is necessary to question what conditions in the school–student relationships are not working. To be marginal is to experience a strained, difficult relationship with the school environment. They advise that rather than providing a means to separate individuals and their behaviors neatly into two categories, normal and "at risk," the marginal perspective highlights the fact that any individual's action is always relative and changeable, a matter of degree. The degree of school marginality depends not only on the char-acteristics of the student actor or action, but also even more on the way in which the person or the behavior is interpreted and related to by educators. They cite Dewey, who emphasized that teachers and other educators inherit a perpetual responsibility to shape and reshape envi-ronments to promote constructive behaviors. Problematic behaviors are not an individuals total personality and behavioral repertoire; in part, they are responses to how a person is being treated. Marginal learners can change even deep-seated, unproductive habits, just as constructive adjustments can be made in relatively static educational environments. There is no single point at which an individual becomes marginal or nonmarginal once and for all. It is necessary, therefore, to understand the path to becoming marginal and the ways in which educators can collaborate to reintegrate individuals with an improved and responsive school environment.

Removing the barriers of increased social distance from the teacher–student relationship so that teachers can grow professionally and students can grow academically and socially. Gary Fenster-macher suggests that teachers, like physicians, may at times wish for social distance from the complex, tangled, and sometimes destructive lives of their students, but they cannot both teach well and ignore the many dimensions of the lives of their students.[107] Teaching well requires a broad and deep understanding of the learner, a concern for how what is taught relates to the life experience of the learner and a willingness to engage the learner in the context of the learner's own intentions, interests, and desires. Social distance of the variety favored by many physicians inhibits the capacity of teachers to do their jobs well. Creating increased social distance between students and teachers also has a professional and personal cost for teachers, a cost that comes when the school climate allows teachers, even encourages them, to voice demeaning and critical comments about some of their students. The creation of social distance in the teacher–student relationship, like all other relationships, allows discontent and mistrust to fester. As Par-ker Palmer observes, the lenses through which many teachers view the young these days tend to distort who, and how, students really are.[108] As Parker reports, "When I ask teachers to name the biggest obstacle to good teaching, the answer I most hear is 'my students.' When I ask why this is so, I hear a litany of complaints: my students are silent sullen, withdrawn; they have little capacity for conversation; they have short attention spans; they do not engage well with ideas; they cling to narrow notions of 'relevance' and 'usefulness' and dismiss world ideas. Whatever tidbits of truth these student stereotypes contain, they grossly distort reality and they widen the disconnection between students and their teachers. Criticizing the client is the conventional defense in an embattled profession and these stereotypes conveniently relieve us of any responsibility for our students' problems or their resolution."

As Parker suggests, behind their fearful silence, our students want to find their voices, speak their voices, have their voices heard. A good teacher is one who can listen to those voices even before they are spoken, so that someday they can speak with truth and confidence. What does it mean to listen to a voice before it is spoken? It means making space for the other, being aware of the other, paying attention to the other, honoring the other. It means not rushing to fill our students' silences with fearful speech of our own and not trying to coerce them into saying the things we want to hear. It means entering empathetically into the student's world so that he or she perceives you as someone who has the promise of being able to hear another person's truth.

Removing the barriers created by some school administrators to limit teachers' interaction with students on nonacademic issues. Although the major focus of this book is on encouraging teachers to understand the personal sides of their students' lives, an important backdrop to the process is the response of school administrators to this process. It is no secret that administrators need to listen to teachers if we expect them to do the same for students. Teachers' voices have to be heard and their ongoing needs for support, affirmation, and inclusion addressed. That means hearing their hopes and dreams as well as their fears, failures, and disappointments. It means being aware of and honoring their contributions, highlighting their skills, and hearing, observing, where they need help and support. Like their students, teachers want to find their voices, hear their voices, and have their voices heard by others, to be a significant part of a community of educators, be contenders and be respected for their work.

Anyone who has worked in a school knows that caring and concern for students doesn't go far if teachers themselves don't feel the care and concern for their work. Like their students, teachers can become marginal, disconnected, and experience a strained, difficult relationship with the school environment. Like their students, teachers can become testers, coasters, resisters, and rebels. I am suggesting that any teacher is at risk of becoming at least temporarily disconnected from full and productive involvement in their classrooms and the schools. I am not talking solely about the teachers who constantly whine, cry burnout, take the path of least resistance, and look the other way when they see a student or a colleague in trouble. I am talking about any teacher being vulnerable to life's blows. It might be, for example, the star teacher who speaks at national conferences, authors many professional articles and books, whose wife suddenly dies, the new teacher who finds himself in a painful divorce; the department chair who discovers she has a life-threatening disease; the language teacher whose daughter dies in the World Trade Center disaster. What Sinclair and Ghory say about students can be said for teachers as well. Anyone can be quickly knocked out of a pattern of productivity and go unattended at school for long periods.

When teachers are seen moving to the margins it is necessary to act. I believe if teachers are part of a school climate in which they are left alone to sink or swim, chances are they will act the same toward their students. If teachers are expected to be advisors, confidants, role models, thoughtful companions, and mentors for their students, then administrators and teacher leaders have to offer them the same ongoing interventions. Isn't that what a supportive school climate is all about? It should be a setting in which the stories of every member of the community, whether it be a student, parent, teacher, or even an administrator, can be heard and his or her needs addressed before they become disconnected. In this supportive school climate it is important to keep in mind that when teachers, like students, disconnect, it doesn't have to lead to failure. Marginal teachers, like students, can change even deepseated, unproductive habits. Any teacher's action is always relative and changeable. One should not be doomed to failure when one stumbles. Instead, we need to encourage administrators, teacher leaders, and concerned colleagues to use their observations, as we do with our students, to gather data and assess what conditions in the teacher's relationships are not working, whether they are school, personal, or family based.

In a sense what I am suggesting is that administrators, like teachers, need to be concerned with more than subject-matter mastery. They, too, need to understand the personal sides of their teachers' lives and their impact on the teachers' performance. That means having ongoing contact, personal contact, with every teacher, knowing his or her hopes and dreams, fears of failure, areas of strength, and areas that need attention and improvement. That means, as educator Roland S. Barth, founder of the Harvard University Principal's Center advocates, encouraging teachers to talk about "nondiscussables," subjects sufficiently important that they are talked about frequently but are so laden with anxiety and fearfulness that these conversations take place only in the parking lot, the rest room, the playground, the car pool, or at dinner time at home.[109] In other words, I advocate for school administrators to be open to the domain of silence among teachers, professional and personal topics that find their place only in rumors. That means being present to observe changes in the teacher's performance that may spell trouble and lead to being marginal, to develop a sense of each teacher and be able to anticipate problems and to listen to their voices before they are spoken.

However, I believe these kinds of new behaviors, habits, and responses I am advocating for will not come easily. Administrators, like teachers, come into the profession with a set of biases, judgments, and prejudices. They, too, have a dark side. Being human, they may have difficulty relating to teachers who are "different" from them, different in culture, color, appearance, ability, behaviors, motivation, gender, age, and so on. As I pointed out in my book *An Administrator's Guide to Better Teacher Mentoring*, in order for administrators to relate to every teacher and hear his or her voice, they have to become aware of what teachers they prefer to relate to and feel comfortable with and those they push away and prefer to remain anonymous.[110] They must take notice, if you will, of those teachers with whom they have created great social distance because they resist, challenge, continuously question decisions or simply are not tuned in to the administrator's overtures. They must cease being hypocritical and not pretend they care for each teacher equally.

Some administrators may be caught in the same dilemma as Horace. Without ongoing self-awareness and the hard work to change behaviors and form new habits, they remain trapped, unable to connect with the majority of teachers who, like Horace's students, remain a genial blur and anonymous. Administrators, too, have to shine the spotlight on their dark side, face their demons and fears, recognize and accept them as a part of their administrative persona, and set out to free themselves from these self-imposed barriers that keep them from connecting with all their teachers. This process requires administrators to quiet and control the voice inside them when it shouts, "Run! You can't work with these teachers, they don't care, they're not motivated, they're complainers"; to cease and control the bad habits and negative behavior of blaming teachers for what they are not rather than focusing on what they can be. I argue that this process opens up new ways for administrators to be models of inclusion for even the most disgruntled teachers and be a major stimulus in helping teachers accept and include the variety of "different" students they encounter each day.

When caring and concerned administrators intervene, listen, and help teachers who are headed for the margins, that lesson will not be lost on the part of other teachers, students, and parents in the school community. They will learn that if they have setbacks, it will not go unnoticed or unattended. They will not be brushed aside, left on their own or labeled at risk and a problem case. This kind of caring behavior by administrators can serve as a model for students to help and support their peers and not look the other way when they see them headed for trouble, not let them end up like Rob Viscome or Patrick Rukaj. Helping teachers to understand the personal sides of their students' lives is just one part of the work we need to be about. What I am advocating is a whole school support process, with every member of the school community—students, teachers, administrators, and parents—set and ready to act when they see school community members heading toward the margins.

Yes, that's a big order for busy administrators, but we can't expect our teachers to be advisors, confidants, and role models if their leaders distance themselves from those roles. As Parker Palmer advises, leadership means looking behind the masks we wear and perceiving our true condition.[111] It means seeing more in teachers than teachers sometimes see in themselves, just as good teachers see in their students more than the students realize they have. It means being available to col-

leagues who seek help with their teaching, whether in developing a syl-
labus, dealing with an immediate crisis, or wanting a classroom
observer who can reflect with them on practice. I would also add to
this being available to hear the personal and well-being issues of other
teachers, perhaps Roland Barth's "nondiscussable" issues that are
impacting on their performance, fears of failure, hopes, dreams, and
emotional and physical health. That does not mean that administrators
have to be friends, counselors, or therapists for their teachers. It means,
as teachers with their students, being an advisor who has learned valuable lessons from his or her own personal experience and is willing to
share that knowledge gained from these experiences.

Finally, Parker also suggests that good talk about good teaching can
take many forms and involve many conversation partners and it can
transform teaching and learning. But it will happen only if leaders
expect it, invite it and provide hospitable space for it to take place.[112]

Removing the barriers erected by failed school reforms.   Sinclair
and Ghory call attention to why many school reform efforts have been
doomed to failure because of their focus on creating new structures
rather than on assessing how to improve the ways in which teachers
relate to their students.[113] They suggest that leaders of past reform
efforts were too easily satisfied with proposing adjustments in school
structures, from self-contained classrooms to team teaching; from set
schedules to flexible scheduling; from A, B, C report cards to check-
lists. However, the well-intentioned changes in school structure did not
result in changes in how educators thought about or acted toward students who were struggling with learning. Past reforms also focused on
"tightening" the standards for scholarship. Attempts to establish higher
standards translated into new textbooks, strict attendance policies,
stringent discipline policies, competency tests for graduation, more
advanced classes, and so on. The impact here was a tendency to inten-
sify the school conditions that already existed.

By starting with the problems of students who are not successful in
school, it may be possible to link reform initiatives to creating necessary roles and responsibilities for educators in order to help marginal
students increase their learning. As Sinclair and Ghory say, the students in the margins are a crucial problem that must be addressed in
the next phase of school reform.[114] If American public schools are to

become even more effective, it is necessary to reach and teach those young people who are not realizing their potential.

Goodlad agrees with Sinclair and Ghory's analysis when he, too, suggests that education reformers need not dismantle the system to set them free to design the human elements of the schools' ecosystem.[115] I would suggest that we do not need massive school reform to foster a climate of care, concern, and understanding of each student and the ripple effect of such a process on boosting the overall performance of teachers and administrators. School climate, class climate, and human connections do matter. As Goodlad strongly advises, these are the elements that school reformers need to leave intact. These are the elements of schooling that are prescribed and carried forward in the imagining of the public and school personnel alike. These are the elements most resistant to change when school reform initiatives are proclaimed, largely because they seek to rearrange or reconstruct the system rather than change the circumstances of learning and teaching that shape our images of what schools are and what they should be.

Goodlad's research with a group of eighteen schools over a period of six years convinced him that schools can become good places without radically disturbing the educational delivery system we have.[116] However, as he suggests, this delivery system cannot be detached from purpose. I believe educators have lost some of their purpose and necessary human connections to students by buying into arguments that say our hands are tied until school and class size become smaller. We are being led to believe, as Goodlad derides, that the sought-after model of good schools is the model offered by homogeneous groups who create little enclaves of schooling led by nationally recognized patrons. Small classes and formal teacher advisory that propose to decrease student–teacher anonymity and increase students' academic achievement are often the hallmark of such good schools. However, I believe these individual schools, backed by ample resources, patrons, academic networks, and powerful research and communication capabilities that allow them to report their successes nationally do not represent the vast number of schools in America. They represent a vision of good schooling that is unattainable for the vast majority of secondary schools in America. In a sense, these little enclaves of schooling are problem creating for educators in mainstream schools as they say, "You can be like us; have smaller schools, less student load and formal advisory systems." The result? Teachers wait for these structural changes and ignore or water down the education delivery system that offers human connection and purpose for both themselves and their students.

I have had first-hand experience with this negative and illusory process. Part of my education experience has been in a leadership position in the development of the Louis Armstrong-Queens College Intermediate School in New York City and the Shoreham-Wading River Middle School on Long Island's north shore, both nationally recognized middle level schools. They are good schools that were supported by ample resources, nationally recognized patrons, academic research networks, and powerful communication capabilities that allowed them to tell their stories on a national level. Both schools had small class size, many specialized services including summer camps, before school tutoring, Project Adventure, and ongoing opportunities for administrators and teachers to report on their schools at international, national, and state conferences. Shoreham had a formal teacher advisory program in which each educator served as an advisor to a small group of students. Louis Armstrong had an informal teacher advisory system in which teachers were trained to be advocates for their students.

These schools attracted nationwide—even international—interest. Educators from schools far and wide routinely visited and praised these schools. Yet as I continually observed, these educators left saying, "We can never have this kind of school. We don't have the money or your resources." The visiting experience was deflating for even the most dedicated and inspired educators. What was disturbing to me was not only the fact that these educators left the schools without real hope for change but that they weren't told, or missed being told or maybe didn't want to hear, that these ample resources—small class size, formal advisory systems, academic research networks, and the like—did not guarantee a high level of human connection between teachers and students, teachers and teachers, teachers and administrators, and administrators and parents. It appeared to me, an educator who was in the school each day, that the hype about the school clouded over what was really happening in the day-to-day operation. There were leading educators in both schools to present the school as a perfect setting with few, if any, flaws, a selling process that I believe was a disservice to the visitors as they only observed and heard the hype and good news about the schools, not the problems and the "nondiscussable" issues that were festering. I suggest it was also a disservice to educators in the schools, who began to believe the public relations releases directed at attracting a steady base of support among parents and national education groups. The driving force behind the education delivery system was selling the school as an outstanding model for middle level education, telling the good news and listing the accomplishments. I believe that this process had the direct result of overlooking the problems and flaws in the school climate or putting them on the back burner.

The school climate in the daily operation of the schools was very different from what was touted in publications and public relations brochures. The creation of a smaller school and smaller classes did not magically change the way some teachers interacted with students. I observed teachers who were subject-mastery teachers only and paid little attention to the personal sides of their students' lives, even with the built-in advisory structure to make this kind of informal contact flow easily. They were no different from Horace in that the students they chose to interact with were students that interested them or who pressed themselves on them. They made a conscious choice to create great social distance between them and the majority of their students. The schools were no different from Horace's in that while they stressed close teacher–student relations in the publicity to parents that was not happening with some teachers. The administration, while extolling the close student–teacher connections, often chose to ignore teachers who regularly failed to act as advisors and advocate for their students. In my observations these well-intentioned administrators were under great pressure to tell and sell the good news about the school, a subtle but powerful force driving the daily school operation. The reality I observed in both schools was that some teachers and administrators, while extolling the philosophy of close student–teacher interaction, had in fact not bought into that philosophy or incorporated it into their daily work. Remember for a moment De Witt Clinton High School principal Norman Wechsler's comment that "small will only succeed if other changes take place as well." As I have suggested earlier in this chapter, in talking about the problems with high stakes testing, depending on numbers only for assessment doesn't always reveal the real impact on the lives of students. The smaller student numbers that come with smaller schools and smaller classes don't in themselves, as Wechsler implies, shift the school climate in favor of closer student–teacher interactions.

I believe it is not always helpful to buy into self-promoting models of good schools that may be (a) unattainable for the vast majority of schools; (b) not delivering the kinds of human connections they espouse; and (c) causing educators in the so-called have not schools to give up on forming close connections with their students because of large numbers and lack of formal advisory programs. I would suggest that this is an ill-conceived argument for school reform, an argument that allows educators to abdicate their professional responsibility to care for their students and claim that our present education delivery system doesn't work. What we need to be about is telling educators that they don't have to aspire to the Shoreham-Wading River or the Louis Armstrong school delivery model as the only way to proceed. I don't negate the fact that these are good schools and the structures they have instituted are helpful, but these structures are not a panacea or a guarantee for change in reducing student–teacher social distance.

I believe a much more effective and life-giving approach is to encourage educators in mainstream schools to focus on their own education delivery systems, assess how to foster more human connections and increase teachers' understanding of the personal sides of their students' lives. Encourage and expect every teacher to become an advisor, a confidant, and an adult model for students. One does not need a formal advisory system to connect with students. Rich human connections can come about between students and teachers without a formal structure and time set aside for such interactions. Simple teacher overtures to students work best, overtures that take only a minute and send a caring message, that encourage students to tell their stories about family life, friends, successes, failures, fears, well-being, hopes, and dreams, stories told in passing. A one-minute conversation with a student can help a teacher gain a great deal of insight. Caring minutes can pack a huge wallop in making a dent in student anonymity.

As Goodlad suggests, "Schools with trusting, caring relationships among the teachers and between the principal and the teachers in our research sample tended to have such relationships between teachers and pupils in their classroom, between parents and teachers and between school and home."[117] Ongoing, schoolwide caring minutes can add up to a nourishing school climate in which the barriers are removed and the following practices are part of the daily education delivery system:

1. Teachers care about and attend to their students and each other.
2. There is an increased understanding of personal and cultural differences for both teachers and students.
3. The problematic academic and social needs of all students are recognized and addressed, not just the students designated "at risk."
4. There is a lessening of the social distance between students and teachers.
5. Administrators are models for personal understanding and inclusion.
6. There is an ongoing reassessment of the school's education delivery system, rather than looking to other illusory models that offer no clear road to education reform.

Removing the barriers that keep counselors locked in roles where they are unable to successfully respond to the growing needs of students, parents, and teachers.   Reduced funding, austerity budgets, and counseling positions left vacant after retirements have resulted in staff cutbacks in many counseling programs. This situation is further complicated by the growing numbers of school districts that are increasingly contracting for outside agencies to provide counseling services for the growing number of at-risk teens now in the schools. Student assistance counselors are now in many schools offering individual and group counseling to teens affected by tobacco, alcohol, and drug abuse, family violence, and school failure. The school counseling movement, which has provided leadership since the 1950s in helping open up doors of opportunity for teens and make schools more child centered, is in danger of losing its vital position in the schools. There are new players in the schools, such as student assistance counselors who are competing for funding, student clients, and administrative support. Many superintendents and principals, already under the gun to reduce costs and at the same time come up with new ways to effectively help troubled teens, are looking for new approaches. Their jobs are on the line. They are turning to whatever resource they can to develop "can do" programs that work. Put simply, secondary-school counselors are no longer the only source of counseling help in many schools. School counselors are going to have to develop "can do" programs to help troubled teens if they are to remain vital players in the helping process in schools. The issues are clear. Unless school counselors can restructure and mount an effective intervention program for counseling at-risk teens and training significant others (teachers, student peer leaders, school support staff, parents) to help at-risk teens, their role in our secondary schools will be reduced to academic, vocational, and college counseling. While these roles are important, the advent of computerized programs to assist teens, parents, and school administrators with course, occupational, and college selection will rapidly diminish even these roles over the next ten years. Put grimly, the proposed informational highway will provide a quick exit for many counselors whose main role is providing information. But many teens, their parents, and teachers will continue to need personal counseling and training in the helping process. The world is growing more complicated and new skills are needed. Can a new breed of counselors be developed to seize the opportunity to help our growing number of teens? Can secondary guidance and counseling programs restructure their services so that both personal and academic/occupational/college counseling go on under the same umbrella? Separate but equal.

In my conversations with counselors, their responses to reduced support and the growing number of student assistance counselors in the schools usually falls into three categories:

1. Give school counselors more time to do personal counseling and the problem will be solved.
2. Hire more well trained counselors.
3. Require noncertified student assistance counselors to become certified.

For example, in January 1990 the New York State School Counselor Association (NYSSCA) drafted a position paper that stated:

NYSSCA is prepared to initiate a Commissioner's Appeal for the protection of public school students from exposure to "counseling services" delivered by non-certified counselors and pupil services personnel. It is our belief that the initiation of the appeal will bring attention to the scope and practice throughout the State of New York and ensure that counseling services for students be delivered by the appropriately licensed and certified personnel.[118]

The problem with this kind of a response is that it is based on the notion of expanding resources rather than on an examination of how to use the existing counseling resources to meet the current needs of at-risk teens. Many counselors are still looking to the federal government, state, and local boards for more resources and legal guarantees. But federal, state, and local politicians are fighting for every cent. Let's face facts; hiring student assistance counselors is a win-win situation for local boards. The costs are often lower and drug and alcohol grants are available to further reduce funding. The programs are cheaper and look effective. Local school boards will continue to be after the biggest bang for the fewest bucks. Schools no longer operate in a world of unlimited resources such as in the 1960s. In the 1960s, many schools and other institutions operated in a culture that said the nation had ever-expanding resources and, if these resources were applied correctly, all our problems could be solved. Those days are over.

Many counselors I talked to agree with the above responses, however. They say give counselors more time, hire more well-trained counselors, and require noncertified counselors to be certified and all will be well again. Many of these counselors are well-trained professionals who have devoted their professional lives to helping kids. But either they do not see the slow but sure encroachment of their helping roles or throw up their hands and say nothing can be done. They develop a "circle the wagons" mentality. In some respects many counselors can't be blamed for this attitude. They have seen coworkers let go and both psychological and funding support dwindle. No one wants to work in a system headed for trouble. They are looking for a lifeline, not retrenchment. How can we involve them in defining their resources in another way so they can compete in the modern schoolhouse? How can we help them develop new structures that do not throw out the old, but integrate new life-giving components into the school counseling delivery system?

I believe we need to look at this age of diminishing resources and the advent of the student assistance counseling movement as a wake-up call for the guidance and counseling professionals. The key words for counselors in the twenty-first century should be, "How can we compete?" in my view; counselors cannot compete without offering an effective personal counseling component that helps teens at risk. Teens, parents, teachers, and school leaders are looking for help. Can counselors help them and in the process, help themselves?

One approach to the problem is utilizing differentiated staffing patterns to restructure secondary-school counseling programs. I believe the problem confronting counselors in our schools is not simply one of more time, hiring more counselors, and requiring noncertified counselors to be certified. In fact, both the problem and solution come out of the same source—the way counselors organize guidance and counseling services and assign counselors. The major problem confronting counselors is the way they define their resources. For example, I believe assigning counselors by grade or alphabet is not an effective organizational strategy. Instead, counselors should be assigned to lead intervention efforts based on the current needs of the students and the skills of the counseling staff. If there is a need in the school for group counseling, then which counselors are best suited and skilled to offer this service? Which counselors are best suited and skilled to offer academic counseling? We have to look at the entire gamut of students' needs—not just the academic needs—and bring our resources to bear on problems such as teens at risk.

How can counselors proceed to begin assessing how best to utilize their resources to meet the needs of today's students, parents, and teachers? There are two key factors in this assessment. First, any new plan for counselors to address the present needs of students must place teachers-as-advisors at the top of the agenda. A small number of counselors can never expect to meet the growing academic and personal needs of students. Teacher-advisors on the front lines need to be our primary source of intervention and prevention. Second, counselors' assignments need to be based on the skills of counseling staff to meet the varying needs, such as academic, college/career, and personal/

social development, not on the outdated system of assigning counselors by grade or alphabet. Simply put, cease the flawed practice that says, "All counselors will perform the same service regardless of their training, skills, and the needs of students, parents, and teachers." It's a practice that has led to counselors' personal counseling skills being overshadowed by the organizational demands of their role.

Unfortunately, the American School Counselors' Association National Model for School Counseling, developed in 2002, makes no reference to this issue. In my reading, the model clings to the out-of-date and vague role definition of counselors that says, "In ASCA's National Model for School Counseling Programs the school counselor is described as a program leader. In this leadership role, the school counselors serve as change agents, collaborators and advocates. School counselors must be proficient in retrieving school data, analyzing it to improve student success and using it to ensure educational equity for all students. Through collaboration with other professionals in the school building, school counselors influence systemic change and advocate for students by using strong communication, consultation and leadership skills."[119] There is no recognition that many secondary-school guidance departments are experiencing staff cuts or having the personal counseling aspect of their role being taken over by part-time student assistance counselors because they haven't been able to deliver on their promise to provide personal counseling for all their students.

And in the introduction to the National Model there is a failure to understand that the efforts by counselors trained at institutes sponsored by the National Defense Education Act in the 1960s may have been onto a solution to eliminate role confusion of counselors when they suggested a differentiated staffing pattern that would encourage some counselors to offer individual and group counseling to students and train teachers to be respected colleagues (i.e., advisors) in the helping process while other counselors carried out the scheduling, testing, college, and career placement tasks required in the large comprehensive secondary schools. In fact, in the introduction of the model school counselor leaders Judy L. Bowers and Patricia A. Hatch inadvertently crystallize the problems afflicting the school counseling profession when they say, "The school mission of 2002 is not altogether different than in the 1960's. Today, in a world enriched by diversity and technology, school counselors' chief mission is still supporting the academic achievement of all students so they are prepared for the ever-changing world of the 21st century."[120] Bowers and Hatch go on to say that in the 1960s, "Counselors trained in programs rooted in psychological and clinical paradigms differed greatly from those rooted in educational paradigms. These changes and varying perspectives confused and caused role confusion among school counselors, school administrators, teachers, parents and guardians. In an effort to unify the profession, comprehensive guidance and counseling programs emerged in the 1980's."[121]

But the reality is, as I have suggested throughout this book, the school mission of 2003 is very different than it was in the 1960s. In order to support the academic needs of all students, attention needs to be paid to their personal, social, and well-being issues. In spite of what Bowers and Hatch say, I would suggest that the guidance programs developed in the 1980s still maintained that counselors were the professionals best able to deliver these services. I believe the time is long overdue for counselors to begin developing counseling services using the helping and advising skills of teachers, administrators, students, and parents. A shared approach that calls on every member of the school community to be his or her brother's helper is desperately needed in our increasingly anonymous schools.

I believe that removing these barriers will help teachers take their rightful place as the primary source of help and advice for their students. In chapter 4 I would like to add some real faces, and needs, to my argument for educators to understand the personal sides of their students' lives. Let's listen to a sample of student voices, in stories that will hopefully encourage teachers to spend caring minutes with students. These vignettes offer educators an opportunity to hear stories that are often hidden by students because they feel their own experience is somehow different, even abnormal. These stories are locked in the domain of silence because no one ever asked, "How's it going?" But things can change dramatically with the ongoing intervention and straightforward queries of a sensitive and observing teacher. Students like the ones found in the next chapter will find their voice and a path that shows them how to solve personal problems and become successful achievers.

The psychiatrist and writer Robert Coles describes the kind of teachers' behavior I am talking about when he recalls a conversation with psychoanalyst Anna Freud on how to connect with teenagers. Although Freud is talking about a psychoanalytical relationship, I believe her advice is very appropriate for the teacher–student relationship I am promoting. Here is what she had to say:

> We are here to listen and learn. We may have to reach out the best we can. You are afraid that we won't succeed; the suspicious, sullen, resentful adolescent might clam up, or refuse to come back. That has happened and that will happen! We are not miracle workers who can say something and presto! the trouble in life has vanished. But I have noticed that in most adolescents that I see that in most of them a real effort at understanding on my part, a gesture that shows that I'm at least trying to understand, and that I've been in some of the distress they're experiencing, hard as it might be for them to believe (or for some of my colleagues, or at certain times of the day, for me!), all of that can go a long way. The adolescent will be interested long enough to want to continue our meetings; and as you know, that is all-important. We have another chance, and another still, to sort out some of these difficulties and figure out what is happening.[122]

I believe Freud is right on target when she suggests that as part of our teaching role we are here to listen to teenagers and learn from these experiences. This process requires a genuine effort to understand what is going on in our students' lives and a sharing on our part that we are human and have experienced some of the problems they are going through. Our lives have more in common than different, in spite of our age differences, educational level, and so on. But as Freud rightfully warns, we are not miracle workers. Many teenagers are suspicious of efforts by teachers to know their stories, the secrets that keep them locked in a failing mode. Sometimes, as Patsy Walker suggests, it seems like "teachers knew they were in a losing battle right down the line. But like, what they did was plant those little time capsules of theirs, kind of like they were saying, 'Hey, you might like to see what's inside you one of these days, might like to find out there's more than one way to go about this . . .' Damn strange, somebody seeing inside you to where you keep your secrets, where they know you keep your secrets."[123] Freud wisely observes, "Whenever I hear teenagers being especially scornful of their elders, I know they are in need of exactly what, of whom, they are most scorning. If they can find that person, well, there's a possible second chance: to try to work things out once more."[124]

Hopefully these vignettes, composites of voices I have heard in secondary schools, will help teachers understand that their own life experiences are not very different from those of their students and they are ideally positioned to provide care, concern, advice, and help for their students to regain their academic footing. Hopefully these vignettes will help those education reformers who seek to change the schools to avoid the assumption that adjusting the balance of attention to the several domains of the school's instructional program is all that need concern them. As Goodlad indicates, his data suggest that the caring way in which the school conducts this educational function is a major factor in determining client satisfaction paralleling in importance perceived attention to intellectual matters in the instructional program. In the view of parents surveyed by Goodlad, "Teach my child with tender loving care," might well be posted on the bulletin board side by side with, "Knowledge sets the human spirit free."[125]

Now, let's hear what's on the minds of high school students as they pass in the hallway and learn why it is important to treat our children with that tender, loving care. Often these students are heading toward the margins because of failure. Others are academic successes but heading toward the margins because of pressure from parents, the school community, their peers, or themselves. Still others have health and well-being problems that are increasingly affecting their academic performance and in some cases are life threatening. There are seven themes in chapter 4:

1. The reality of teenage life.
2. The pain that sometimes comes with relationships.
3. Schooling and adolescence—what it's really like.
4. Drinking and drugging—the need to get away from it all.
5. Death and loss; you know you're growing up when people start to die.
6. Divorce and other endings that are never simple for kids.
7. Setting a new course in life after a setback.

NOTES

1. Arthur Levine, "Rookies in the Schools," *New York Times*, 29 June 2002, 15 (A).

2. Theodore R. Sizer, *Horace's School: Redesigning the American High School* (Boston: Houghton Mifflin, 1992), 40.

3. Gene I. Maeroff, *Don't Blame the Kids* (New York: McGraw-Hill, 1982), 113.

4. Lilian Katz, "Some Generic Principles of Teaching," in *Essays on Teachers' Centers*, ed. Kathleen Devaney (San Francisco: Teachers' Center Exchange, 1977), 30.

5. Jane M. Healy, *How Computers Affect Our Children's Minds: For Better or Worse* (New York: Simon & Schuster, 1998), 28–29, 84, 121, 199–200.

6. *Webster's*, 3rd edition, 20, 340, 848.

7. John I. Goodlad, *A Place Called School* (New York: McGraw-Hill, 1984), 88–89.

8. Goodlad, *A Place Called School*, 89.

9. Steve Farkas and Jean Johnson, *Kids These Days: What Americans Really Think about the Next Generation*, (New York: Public Agenda, 1997), 8, 9, 11, 13, 16–19, 25–26.

10. Farkas and Johnson, *Kids These Days*, 19.

11. E. D. Hirsch, *The Schools We Need* (New York: Doubleday, 1996), 33–35.

12. Geneva Gay, *Culturally Responsive Teaching* (New York: Teachers College Press, 2000), vii, 17–19, 45–46.

13. Gay, *Culturally Responsive Teaching*.

14. Gay, *Culturally Responsive Teaching*.

15. Robert D. Putnam, *Bowling Alone* (New York: Simon & Schuster, 2000), 277, 283–84, 298, 302.

16. Thomas H. Sanders and Robert D. Putnam, "Rebuilding the Stock of Social Capital," *School Administrator* 1999, http://www.assa.org/publications/sa/1999_09/sander.htm (accessed 14 March 2002).

17. Sanders and Putnam, "Rebuilding the Stock of Social Capital."

18. Rick Allen, "Big Schools: The Way We Are," *Education Leadership* 59, no. 5 (February 2002): 36–41.

19. Allen, "Big Schools."

20. Allen, "Big Schools," 39.

21. Allen, "Big Schools," 39.

22. Allen, "Big Schools," 39.

23. Kirk A. Johnson, "The Downside to Small Class Policies," *Education Leadership* 59, no. 5 (February 2002): 27–29.

24. Darcia Harris Bowman, "School 'Connectedness' Makes for Healthier Students, Study Suggests," *Education Week*, 24 April 2002 http://www.edweek.org/ew/newstroy.cfm?slug = 32health.h21 (accessed 7 July 2002).

25. Daniel Goleman, *Emotional Intelligence* (New York: Bantam Books, 1997), 34, 37, 42–44.

26. Goleman, *Emotional Intelligence.*

27. Goleman, *Emotional Intelligence.*

28. Anthony W. Jackson and Gayle A. Davis, *Turning Points 2000: Educating Adolescents in the 21st Century* (New York: Teachers College Press, 2000), 8.

29. Jackson and Davis, *Turning Points.*

30. Goleman, *Emotional Intelligence.*

31. Karen Rasmussen, "Schools and Social Service," *ASCD Curriculum Update* (Fall 1999): 6.

32. Rasmussen, "Schools and Social Service."

33. Children's Defense Fund, *The State of Children in America's Union, A 2002 Action Guide to Leave No Child Behind* (Washington, D.C.: Children's Defense Fund, 2002), iv–v.

34. Richard Rothstein, "Schoolchildren of Welfare Parents," *New York Times*, 5 June 2002, 8 (B).

35. National Center for Injury Prevention and Control, "Youth Violence in the United States," Center for Disease Control (CDC), 2002, http://www.ede.gov/ncipc/factsheets/yvfacts.htm (accessed 3 July, 2002).

36. National Center for Injury Prevention and Control, "Dating Violence," Center for Disease Control (CDC), 2002, http://www.ede.gov/ncipc/factsheets/datviol.htm (accessed 3 July 2002).

37. National Center for Education Statistics (NCES), "The Principal/School Disciplinarian Survey on School Violence, 1996–97," NCES, 1998, http://nces.ed.gov/pubs98/violence/9803001.html (accessed 3 August 2002).

38. National Center for Chronic Disease Prevention and Health Promotion, "Adolescents and Young Adults," Center for Disease Control (CDC), 2002, http://cdc.gov/nccdphp/sgr/adoles.htm (accessed 3 July 2002).

39. Ridgely Ochs, "They're Not Getting Physical: Girls Too Inactive, Study Finds," *Newsday*, 5 September 2002, 20 (A).

40. National Center for Health Statistics, "More American Children and Teens are Overweight," Center for Disease Control (CDC), 2001, http://www.cdc.gov/nchs/releases/01news/overwght99.htm (accessed 3 July 2002).

41. Michael Waldholz, "To Tame Kids' Junk Food Urges: Fewer Speeches, More Fruit Bowls," *Wall Street Journal*, 25 July 2002, 4 (D).

42. Lindsey Tanner, "Hispanic Kids Face Health Crisis," *Associated Press*, 2003, http://detnews.com/2002/health/0207/03–529270.htm (accessed 7 July 2002).

43. Daniel Goleman, "Eating Disorder Rates Surprise the Experts," *New York Times*, 4 October 1995, 11.

44. Kate Betts, "The Tyranny of Skinny, Fashion's Insider Secret," *New York Times*, 31 March 2002, 1, 8 (9).

45. Mim Udovitch, "A Secret Society for Starving," *New York Times*, 9 September 2002, 18, 20 (6).

46. Udovitch, "A Secret Society for Starving," 20.

47. Substance Abuse and Mental Health Services Administration, "3 Million Youth Are Suicide Risks," *Newsday*, 15 July 2002, 14 (A).

48. National Center for Injury Prevention and Control, "Suicide in the United States," Center for Disease Control (CDC), 2002, http://www.cdc.gov/ncipc/factsheets.suifacts.htm (accessed 7 July 2002).

49. *New York Times* Staff, "At 17, A Star and Suicide Victim: An Athlete Dies Young, But by His Own Hand," *New York Times*, 1 October 1995, 1 (6).

50. Carol Falkowski, "What's New in Youth Substance Abuse," *Hazelden Voice*, (Winter 2002): 11.

51. Tobacco Information and Prevention Sources (TIPS), "Tobacco Use among Middle and High School Students—National Youth Tobacco Survey 1999," Center for Disease Control (CDC), 2000, http://www.cdc.gov/tobacco/research_data/survey/mmmwr4903fas.htm (accessed 3 July 2002).

52. *New York Times* Staff, "Scarsdale School Suspends 28 Students for Drunkenness," *New York Times,* 27 September 2002, 6 (B).

53. *New York Times* Staff, "Scarsdale School Suspends 28 Students."

54. Jane Gross, "Teenagers' Binges Lead Scarsdale to Painful Self-Reflection," *New York Times*, 8 October 2002, 1, 7 (B).

55. Matthew Purdy, "A Teenage Party, a Punch, and a Choice That Can't Be Reversed," *New York Times*, 1 September 2002, 29 (B).

56. Lisa W. Foderaro, "Suburb's Residents Not Pacified by Charges in Students' Death," *New York Times*, 24 August 2002, 4 (B).

57. Center for Disease Control & Chronic Disease Prevention, "Teen Pregnancy," Center for Disease Control (CDC), 1999, http://www.cdc.gov/nccdphp/teen.htm (accessed 3 July 2002).

58. Diana Jean Schemo, "Mothers of Sex-Active Youths Often Think They're Virgins," *New York Times*, 5 September 2002, 20 (A).

59. Ellen Goodman, "Sex—Is There Joy in Not Knowing?" *Newsday*, 27 October 2002, 30 (A).

60. Neil Munro, "Brain Politics," *National Journal*, 3 February 2001, http://www.pbs.org/wgbh/pages/frontline/shows/medicating.readings/brain politic s/html (accessed 4 February 2002).

61. Munro, "Brain Politics."

62. Thelma Bear, Sherry Schenk, and Lisa Buckner, "Supporting Victims of Child Abuse," *Education Leadership* 50, no. 4 (December 1992–January 1993); ASCD Online http://www.ascd.org/readingroom/edlead/9212/bear .html (accessed 7 July 2002).

63. Erica Goode, "Boy Genius? Mother Says She Faked Tests," *New York Times*, 2 March 2002, 1, 12 (A).

64. Jay S. Kwawer and Miriam Arond, Letters to the Editor, "Is the Boy a Genius, or a Victim," *New York Times*, 8 March 2002, 20 (A).

65. Kwawer and Arond, Letters to the Editor

66. Nancy Ann Jeffrey, "The Organization Kid," *Wall Street Journal*, 6 September 2002, 1, 4 (W).

67. Jeffrey, "The Organization Kid."

68. Jeffrey, "The Organization Kid."

69. Jeffrey, "The Organization Kid."

70. Deborah Sontag, "Who Was Responsible for Elizabeth Shin?" *New York Times*, 28 April 2002, 58 (6).

71. Sontag, "Who Was Responsible for Elizabeth Shin?"

72. Austin Bunn, "Terribly Smart," *New York Times*, 3 March 2002, 17 (6).

73. Gerald Bracey, "11th Bracey Report on the Conditions in Public Education," *Kappan Online*, http://www.pdkintl.org.kappan/k0110bra.htm (accessed 28 May 2002).

74. James Traub, "The Test Mess," *New York Times*, 7 April 2002, 48 (6).

75. Donald B. Gratz, "High Standards for Whom?" *Kappan Online*, May 2000, http://www.pdkintl.org/kappan/kgra0005.htm (accessed 14 March 2002).

76. Gratz, "High Standards for Whom?"

77. David Elkind, *The Hurried Child* (Reading, Mass.: Addison-Wesley, 1981), 3, 53.

78. Gratz, "High Standards for Whom?"

79. Richard Rothstein, "Dropout Rate Is Climbing and Likely to Go Higher, *New York Times*, 9 October 2002, 8 (B).

80. Rothstein, "Dropout Rate Is Climbing."

81. Healy, *How Computers Affect Our Children's Minds.*

82. Healy, *How Computers Affect Our Children's Minds,* 29.

83. Healy, *How Computers Affect Our Children's Minds,* 29.

84. Healy, *How Computers Affect Our Children's Minds,* 29.

85. Healy, *How Computers Affect Our Children's Minds,* 199, 200.

86. Associated Press, "Study Links TV to Teen Aggression," *Newsday,* 29 March 2002, 4 (A).

87. Martha Woodall, "There's No More Teachers' Dirty Looks," *Newsday,* 12 March 2002, 25 (A).

88. Joyce Purnick, "In Schools, A Hidden Toll of Sept. 11," *New York Times,* 13 May 2002, 1 (B).

89. Purnick, "In Schools, A Hidden Toll of Sept. 11."

90. N. R. Kleinfield, "In Nightmares and Anger, Children Pay Hidden Cost of 9/11," *New York Times,* 14 May 2002, 1, 4 (B).

91. Erica Goode, "Progress Can Be Fragile for the Young Witnesses of Sept. 11," *New York Times,* 18 June 2002, F1.

92. Anemona Hartocollis, "For City School Children, the Healing Starts Here," *New York Times,* 9 May 2002, 2 (B).

93. Diana Jean Schemo, "For Schools, No Shutdown But Spread of Lockdown," *New York Times,* 23 October 2002, 18 (A).

94. Lynette Clemetson, "For Teenager, Troubling Bond in Chaotic Life," *New York Times,* 27 October 2002, 1, 36 (A).

95. Clemetson, "For Teenager, Troubling Bond," 1, 36 (A).

96. Goodman "Sex—Is There Joy in Not Knowing?"

97. Farkas and Johnson, *Kids These Days.*

98. William Damon, *Greater Expectations* (New York: Free Press, 1995), 113, 199, 202.

99. Maurice J. Elias, "Easing Transitions with Social-Emotional Learning," *NASSP Principal Leadership Online* 1, no 7 (March 2001), http://www.nassp.org/news/pl_soc_emo_lrng_301.htm (accessed 7 June 2002).

100. Damon, *Greater Expectations.*

101. George Spindler and Louise Spindler, eds., *Pathways to Cultural Awareness* (Thousand Oaks, Calif.: Corwin Press, 1994), xii.

102. Valerie Ooka Pang and Velma A. Sablan, "Teacher Efficacy," in *Being Responsive to Cultural Differences,* ed. Mary E. Dilworth (Thousand Oaks, Calif.: Corwin Press, 1997), 43.

103. Martha R. Bireda. "Education for All," *NASSP Principal Leadership Online* 1, no. 4 (December 2000), http://www.nassp.org/news/pl_ed4all_1200.htm (accessed 6 June 2002).

104. John I. Goodlad, *Teachers for Our Nation's Schools* (San Francisco: Jossey-Bass, 1990), 8–9.

105. Goodlad, *Teachers for Our Nation's Schools.*

106. Robert L. Sinclair and Ward J. Ghory, "Last Things First: Realizing Equality by Improving Conditions for Marginal Students," in *Access to Knowledge*, eds. John I. Goodlad and Pamela Keating (New York: College Entrance Board, 1990), 129–30, 137.

107. Gary D. Fenstermacher, "Some Moral Considerations on Teaching as a Profession," in *The Moral Dimensions of Teaching*, eds. John I. Goodlad, Roger Soder, and Kenneth A. Sirotnik (San Francisco: Jossey-Bass, 1990), 137 .

108. Parker Palmer, *The Courage to Teach* (San Francisco: Jossey-Bass, 1998), 40–41, 46, 158–59.

109. Roland S. Barth, "The Culture Builder," *Education Leadership* 59, no. 8 (May 2002): 8.

110. William L. Fibkins, *An Administrator's Guide to Better Teacher Mentoring* (Lanham, Md.: Scarecrow Press, 2002), 76–77.

111. Palmer, *The Courage to Teach.*

112. Palmer, *The Courage to Teach.*

113. Sinclair and Ghory, "Last Things First."

114. Sinclair and Ghory, "Last Things First."

115. John I. Goodlad, *In Praise of Education* (New York: Teachers College Press, 1997), 110–11, 135–36.

116. John I. Goodlad, *Education Renewal* (San Francisco: Jossey-Bass, 1994), 211.

117. Goodlad, *In Praise of Education.*

118. New York State School Counselor Association, Position Paper (Leicester, NY: New York State School Counselor Association, January 1990).

119. Judy L. Bowers and Patricia A. Hatch, *The ASCA National Model: A Framework for School Counseling Programs* (Alexandria, Va.: American School Counselor Association, 2002), 7–9.

120. Bowers and Hatch, *The National Model,* 7–9.

121. Bowers and Hatch, *The National Model,* 7–9.

122. Robert Coles, *The Moral Intelligence of Children* (New York: Random House, 1997), 148–49, 159.

123. Thomas J. Cottle, *Children's Secrets* (Garden City, NY: Anchor Press, 1980), 265.

124. Coles, *The Moral Intelligence of Children.*

125. Goodlad, *A Place Called School.*

CHAPTER 4

The Reality of Teenage Life

When a child is born, he or she should be a symbol of hope and new growth for the family. This is how it *should* be. It doesn't always happen that way. A newborn child is full of hope and wonderment. Some families, some homes, provide the necessary nourishment and support that help to keep that hope and wonderment alive in that child's soul and mind. That's the way it *should* be. That's the kind of family we want for our children. But it doesn't always happen that way. In all families things go wrong: kids fail, parents lose their jobs, illness and death are regular visitors. Families have a lot to deal with in modern America. Some families have a more difficult time than others. In these homes the families often appear "together" but the daily lives of the children are filled with a quiet chaos and disorder. It's a different kind of chaos—you don't see it unless you really look and listen. There is food in the fridge and the lawn is cut. On the surface, things look all right, but the family has lost its way. Things don't fit; things don't work out.

As Beverly Lowry reports,

"You get so used to scaling down," she recalls. "OK, so he won't go to college; OK, so maybe he won't graduate from high school this year, maybe never; so he has a juvenile record; so he smokes dope, OK; but—I used to think—do I scale down as low as prison? . . . To this day I have no idea what I did for my two boys that was constructive and useful and right and good and what damaged them, none. It is a puzzle the whole way."[1]

How is it that for some families "it is a puzzle the whole way" while in others things work out? The following stories about high school kids growing up in families tell us a lot. In Beware of the Parent Who

Appears Too Good, we hear about the parent who is trying to do everything for the child, to help the child avoid all the pains of life. But in doing so, she puts the child at great risk, the risk of becoming an emotional invalid, a child who has not learned how to deal with the demands and consequences of life. Is raising a child unprepared for life a form of child abuse, as deadly a blow as physical abuse? Should a child in a family like this flee as soon as possible? But where would she go? Could, would, the school help? The church? There are no bruises, at least none you can see.

In Holding Your Own Mother as a Hostage, the reverse is true—a child who bullies, lies, and manipulates her parents. Here is a child who finally uses the ultimate threat of suicide to stay in control of her parents. There is no puzzle here. Good intentions on the part of the parent spill over into a world of no limits, no restraint. The child becomes the bully. Is this abuse? The parents have no bruises, none you can see.

In My Mother Chose Him over Me, the child has bruises. He shows them to his mother and asks why she allows her boyfriends and husbands, one after the other, to beat up on him. She begs him not to tell the school, the police; she fears she will lose her man if he is found out. She will be alone again. The mother won't—can't—help her child. She needs her man too much. The boy is looking for safety, care, love. He is in the wrong place, a danger zone. How long can he survive in this home with being badly hurt? He is fair game to the bullies in his mother's life but he can't flee. Even if he had a place to be safe, he can't bring himself, not yet, to believe his mother has chosen these bullies over him.

In The Bad Parent, things are clear. The parents have a child they don't want. The child knows it. He is stuck in a home where he knows he is not the child the parents wanted. It shows in all the simple ways of everyday family life. It is clear to others—the school, the child's friends—but what can be done? He needs a roof over his head, a bed to sleep in. He cannot flee; where would he go? He longs for his real mother; he is adopted. But the call, the knock at the door, never comes. He bides his time. Is he better off than the child of the "too good" parent? At least he knows the truth; there is no making believe about his life.

In I Had Become My Father's Son, the bully of a father shows the way for the son to become like him. The son, at first repulsed and iso-lated by his father's attacks on the school, adopts his father's tactics to save himself. In the process he finds a power that excites and attracts him, an evil spirit out of the bottle. The father has taught his son about life with his own practices. Is this what he wanted or will the father say he is puzzled by his son's behavior if it is turned against him in the future? Will he be surprised?

In All I Want Is to Buy Combat Boots and a Black Leather Jacket, the boy struggles to define himself through his clothes—boots and jacket. It's simple. He is not in the bars or hanging out. He just wants the world to know that he, like the newborn child, is unique. But the parents resist. Boots and a jacket mean trouble. What will be next, drugs, booze, smoking, wild parties, DWIs? Better to put your foot down now before things get out of hand. But he is a good child, not asking for much. Why do the parents fear so much? They read too many newspaper and magazine stories about teenagers out of control. They vow that it will not happen with their child. They have family values. But they have little real control over their child and to realize that would frighten them. The child no longer needs them in the same way he did in the past. So the child tells white lies to spare himself and spare his parents. The parents don't see that he can handle life. If they did, they would have to let go and do other things with their lives. That is not easy for parents who want to be good parents. Sometimes they don't know when their job is done. Sometimes they don't want to know.

I'm Giving up That Part of My Life, Mom and Dad speaks to us about children who one day give up the piano, the baseball team, that part of their life, whatever it was, that was so consuming and so much defined their identity for the world. One day, in a conversation between child and parent, the child puts down a part of his or her life around which all conversations and family activities flowed. The child moves on. For the parents it is difficult to give up the dreams of the child becoming a major leaguer, a concert pianist, a rock drummer. The cer-tificates, awards, newspaper clippings describing the child's talent must now be put away, the drums or piano sold or given away. But can the parents give up that part of their child's life and, like the child, move on to new things? It seems easy for the child, not a puzzle. For the parents it may bring uneasiness and fear of the future. The evenness of our lives as parents often depends on the child we know and can count on for routine. If the child changes, who are we? Can we get out of the way of the child?

Finally, No Place Like Home challenges the notion that home is a place to return for nourishment and support. The child knows that things don't work that way for her. But she hangs on. Her teachers tell her good things are possible, that she can make it out. They tell her that her experiences can help others. She can be a teacher. She has potential, possibilities. She walks a fine line. Will she make it? The child has one thing going for her—she looks outside her home for help and support. She knows what other doors she can knock on.

When family life goes bad, when things aren't what they should be, kids need doors to knock on, people to listen, people to help them. And parents need the same support. They can go down a lot of wrong roads with good intentions, roads that bring hurt to themselves and to their children. Things can get out of control in family life. But not all abuse, not all the struggles of family life, show up in these numbers. As these stories tell us, the line between abuse and either too much or too little caring is often hard to see.

It's a Different Kind of Chaos

Beware of the Parent Who Appears Too Good.   My mother screwed up my older brother and sister. I know people always say that about their parents but in this case it's true. I saw just how she did it. She didn't physically or mentally abuse them like you read about in the papers. Instead, she hovered over them all the time, making every small problem they had into a big deal that she had to solve for them. She made weaklings out of both of them. They never learned how to fight their own battles. My mother would always tell them they shouldn't fight back. Her credo was, "Better to turn the other cheek; only bullies fight." By the time my brother and sister got to high school, they were helpless wimps. They would whine and carry on about all the things that were wrong with the teachers and other kids. And my mother would agree with them, never telling them to stop complaining. She treated each word they said like gospel, like they were gods. Even as a little kid—I was still in middle school when they were in high school—I went to my room when they came home. It made me sick just to be around the three of them. And now my mother is trying to do the same thing to me. It makes me crazy. She always has to be doing something to "help" her kids. I keep telling her, "I don't need your help," but she doesn't listen. I want out of the house! I'm graduating this year and I can hardly wait to leave. I feel like I'm always walking on quicksand or a minefield; there's always a problem or something wrong. It's like a disease—she can't let things alone—always involved in one of her kid's business when she shouldn't be.

Like when my older brother got this girl pregnant, my parents insisted that she have the baby and come live with us. Christ, my brother wasn't even out of high school—he was a senior—and here he has this baby and he's not even married. It was a nightmare. The girl should have had an abortion, period. When they came to live with us, the kid would scream all the time and my brother and his girl would fight. And then one day she moves out and leaves the baby with us. Guess who gets stuck taking care of the kid? You got it—my mother. My mother—oh, she's so good—said we were doing the right thing in helping out and that having my brother's girl have an abortion would have been a sin. So here we are, stuck with this kid, while my mother carries on about what a good thing we are doing. Meanwhile my brother goes on his merry way, out with friends partying all the time. My mother is taking care of "his" baby while he's not working, out drinking and drugging. Meanwhile, she's still slipping him twenty bucks every time he goes out! Twenty years old, with a baby, no job, still living at home and my mom loves it. It's like she wants to keep my brother a baby all his life. It's almost as if my mother planned it that way just to keep things crazy around our house. The baby is even calling her "mommy" now. My mother will be sixty years old and still raising a kid.

And what does my father do about this? He does his usual thing—nothing. He's either working or at the Knights of Columbus and the firehouse, drinking it up with his buddies. All he says is, "Your mom is just trying to do the right thing." Hell, what does he know about it or how crazy it is here? Maybe he does know and that's why he's out all the time. I can't remember him ever being home. I think that's why he joined the fire department. It's ridiculous. Who ever heard of grown men "volunteering" to put out fires? They just do it to get away from their wives and kids. I know.

But that wasn't enough. My older sister, who is a sophomore in college, decides she wants to come home because she's developed this disease like mononucleosis that makes her tired all the time. She's such a fake. Ever since she was a kid, she had some kind of sickness. My mom was always making excuses for her and searching out some doctor who would treat her. We must have gone through at least ten family doctors; they just got sick of my mother bringing my sister in. First it was asthma, then ulcers, then migraine headaches, then a learning disability—on and on. Lucky my dad had insurance or we would be broke now. There wasn't a disease my sister didn't try to get and my mother was always right there with her little baby saying, "Once we find the right doctor, you'll be fine." It makes me so angry to think about it. My sister got all the attention. I used to tell my mother that she was making her an invalid but she never listened. You see, that's my mom. She never tells people to cut it out or take responsibility, like with my brother or sister. It's always taking care of them or picking up the pieces for them after they screw up.

My mom was always the one going to the school and filling out the SAT applications for my brother and sister, or writing their reports because they were too sick or too busy. Even as a kid, I could see how she was doing things for them that they should be doing for themselves. I would tell her that they were using her, always expecting her to do for them. But she didn't care. She seemed to like it, always doing for them, making them weaker and weaker. I guess she was using them, too. And she was always trying the same stuff with me. Sometimes it was treating me like I was sick: "You don't look good. You better take some of Mommy's medicine." I knew she took tranquilizers and I didn't want that stuff. Or she would say, "We have to get you a good physical. You don't look well to me." There was always, every day, some comment about my not looking well or going to the doctor. When I started playing sports in junior high, she almost didn't let me play because, as she said, "You could get seriously hurt for life. I never let your brother or sister play. Why don't you just come home after school?"

I've had to battle them all the way—really, battle my mother—not to become a hypochondriac like my sister or irresponsible like my brother. She made them what they are today and I feel bad for them. I've tried to talk to my sister about it but it's too late; she doesn't see the danger. I worry about her and bet she ends up never leaving home until my parents die. Why should she? She's doted over and watched all the time. And my brother? He's stuck—no job, no money, on unemployment, and no one cares. They keep feeding him and they don't charge him for rent or food. They even got a car for him and paid the insurance. He acts like a high school kid. I don't see him making it out either. My brother and sister and my mom and the baby, they're all stuck together. It's some kind of abuse my mom is pulling but I don't know the name for it. It's just not right.

So I'm trying to get out of here before all of this "care" gets to me. The neighbors and people in school are always saying what "caring" parents I have. They're always at the workshops on parenting and talking about how they raise their children. Other people don't see what really goes on. They don't see that too much care, overkill, can ruin a kid's life. I hope I can get out of here before it catches up with me. Sometimes I worry that something bad will happen to me and I'll need my parents' help. I worry that I'll become dependent on them and I'll be like my sister, not doing for myself. I can't let that happen.

Holding Your Own Mother as a Hostage.   It was true from the beginning—my mother always trying to do everything for me, give me everything. I guess when you think about the whole thing, it was abnormal from the start. I was the one in charge. My mother was my servant. She was always asking me what I wanted—breakfast, clothes, toys, furniture for my room, TV, VCR, where to go on vacations, what clothes she should wear; whatever I wanted, she got for me. My dad was always complaining that we ate what I wanted and watched the TV shows I liked. He was forever telling my mother that she was raising a little tyrant. After awhile he gave up. He had no power in the house. When I think about it now, it was a bizarre situation. Even before I went to kindergarten, I was in charge. If my mother didn't do what I wanted her to do, I would scream and throw things around the house until she relented. At first she did things for me because I was her "little baby" but by the time I got to school, she had become afraid of me and my tantrums. She was a slave, hostage to her own kid, and she had created it. By middle school I had become a manipulative, selfish, irresponsible liar; no one could pin me down. If the teachers or school accused me of lying or cheating, which I did a lot, my mother was there to defend me. After awhile they gave up, like my father; no sense wasting their time on some kid whose parent didn't see what was really going on. I guess they thought, why should they try to change this destructive kid if her own mother lied and fronted for her at every turn.

But when I went to high school, things started to get out of hand. I started having parties, nonstop parties, at my house after school and on weekends. At first my mother liked the idea of me having so many "friends" and kids over to the house. In middle school I was a loner; the other kids were afraid of me. They knew I was capable of anything in order to get my way. If other kids crossed me, I would make up stories about them or their parents and spread it all around the school. I would break into kids' lockers and take their stuff, particularly in gym. I would take their clothes and flush them down the toilet. When they came back after class, their clothes would be gone. No one ever caught me, although the kids knew it was me. So the kids stayed away from me. I never got invited to parties or to sleepovers. I had burned them too many times. Even the parents were afraid of me. I had seen the way they looked at me when I gave my mother a hard time in public. They probably knew it was me who made the prank calls to their kids in the middle of the night. I used to love that. I'd get up at three o'clock at night and call some kid I really hated and when they answered, I'd hang up. Then I would call again and again. At school the next day I would smile at these kids. They knew it was me, but they couldn't do anything. One time a parent called my mother and complained that I was making obscene phone calls. My mother told her that "my daughter would never do that." My mother knew enough not to mention it to me.

So my mother liked having the kids over to the house—at first. She said she was glad that I was making so many friends and had become so popular. What she didn't know was that these kids weren't really my friends. I was buying them off, using my house as a place where they could come and drink and smoke. Suddenly I was the most popular kid in the high school. Kids I didn't even know would come up to me and ask if they could "stop by" with some beer or pot. Even those kids I had put down in middle school were kissing up to me. I guess you could say I was a whore, letting them do whatever they wanted. But I didn't care; I liked being in charge—letting in those kids I liked and telling other kids that the party was full. At first my mother didn't catch on; she worked every day. But after a while she started noticing that the windows were always open (to get rid of the beer and pot smell) and that a lot of food was missing. The kids would come over right after school or on Friday and Saturday nights when my parents were out and start right in raiding the fridge. I guess the final straw came when I had a big party after the homecoming dance. A lot of kids had signed up to go to a "Safe Homes" (no alcohol was served) party at school, but I wasn't about to become one of those "Safe Homes" kids. My parents were going away for the weekend. I was into partying.

But things got out of hand. I had invited over a hundred kids. Too many. A fight started between two gangs. A lot of my mother's good furniture got broken and the fight spilled over into the street and the neighbors' yards. During the fight someone ripped off my parents' new stereo and the VCR. One of the neighbors called the police. They showed up and told everyone they had to go home and issued a summons to me for allowing liquor to be served to minors in our house. When my parents got home on Sunday, a bunch of the neighbors came over to complain. And when my parents found out about the summons, they couldn't believe it. My dad started saying that I was irresponsible and a liar. But my mother said that there must be something bothering me; her "little girl wouldn't do something like this." She asked me if I was having any "personal problems" that would lead me to do something like this.

And that's how the suicide thing started. It was perfect. An easy out. It just came to me. I started telling my mother that I was so depressed that I was thinking about suicide. I couldn't get it out of my mind. I told her that I had even tried it a few times by taking a lot of pills. I had even thought about taking a gun and putting it to my head. I told them that's why I had the party, to have some fun and forget things. My mother and dad just sat there. Finally my mother said, "I knew there had to be a reason. You would never lie or be irresponsible. We'll have to get you help." I knew then I was home free. The suicide threat worked. From that day on I used it a lot. Whenever I didn't get my way I would just pop it into our conversations, saying things like, "I don't want to live any more," or leave a note saying, "I won't be back." It would drive my mother crazy. I had her where I wanted her. There was nothing she could do to me now. The suicide threat is the ultimate weapon against parents. She was my slave, my hostage. Party time!

My Mother Chose Him over Me.   My mom was putting me second again. I couldn't believe it. She knew that Lenny hit me on the face and left a big bruise. She knew I hadn't done anything. All I was doing was playing my radio loud. He just came in and said, "Ever since I moved in with your mom, I could see that you've got no rules. You do what you want, like blasting the radio. Well, I talked to your mom and she's giving me control of your discipline. So you little s——, turn down that f——ing box before I belt you one. You're going to start shaping up around here, Buddy." I thought to myself, "What right does this guy have to tell me what to do? He's not even my father. Christ, he just moved in with my mother last month. Another loser!" So I told him to get off my back; "You're not my father; you can't tell me what to do."

And then he came at me with both fists flying. He knocked me down and smashed my radio. I couldn't believe my mom was allowing this guy to do this to me. I was her kid, her son, and she hadn't known this guy more than two months. I ran out of my room crying, blood all over me, into the kitchen where she was sitting. I yelled at her, "How can you let this guy beat me up and break my radio? I didn't do anything. Besides, he's drunk again. He's not my father and he's got no legal rights over me. This is the same stuff that happened with Joey. You let him beat me up all the time, before he started abusing you. When you divorced him you said it would never happen again, that you'd never let anyone beat me up again. And just when we're getting everything back together again, you go and bring this sleazy worm home. Why are you doing this to me again? I'm not taking it any more. I'm calling the cops or the child abuse number. And I'm going to tell them at school. They have records that you let Joey beat me up. My teachers told me to tell them if it happened again and they would call the 800 child abuse number."

But I didn't call the police or the child abuse number. And I didn't tell my teachers, even though they asked me about the bruises on my face. I told them I had fallen down. Why? Because my mother pleaded with me not to call or tell anyone. She said she was trying to start a new life and Lenny was a good man. She said he just wasn't used to having a high school kid around and he was sorry that he hit me. Sure, she said, he did drink too much but maybe living with us would help him to be a family man. My mom said, "If you call and report this, he's going to move out and I'll have no one. I beg you not to do this. Please, for me. I'll make sure he doesn't come near you any more. Please, honey, do this for your mom."

So I didn't call. I loved my mom and I wanted her to be happy. But this was the third guy that had moved in with us since my father left when I was five! They had all been losers and loose with their fists. She seemed to attract these guys who were macho and heavy drinkers. She would meet them at a bar or Parents Without Partners and before long, they would move in. I always hoped she would bring home someone who would be a real father to me but that never happened. Usually the first couple of months were OK. They would take me to a ball game or go fishing or teach me how to drive. But then the arguing and hitting would start. Like with Tommy, the guy that moved in with my mom after my dad left. He used to hit my mother so much she would cry. When I tried to help her, he would throw me against the wall. I pleaded with her to throw him out but it took him breaking her wrist to finally wake her up. It was so awful. The police were always at our house. The same thing happened with Joey. At first it was great. He seemed like such a nice guy. My mom and he got married in the back yard and I was the best man. But then he started drinking and coming home late. Then he stopped coming home for weeks at a time and when he did show up, he'd yell at my mom and call her awful names. One day he left and we never saw him again.

So Lenny's the new man, but I don't trust him. I don't believe my mom, either. She's got some crazy sickness about guys that lets them take over her life and her own kid. I know she loves me but she can't protect me. She always chooses them over me, even when they're beating me up and abusing me. I put a new lock on my door and I'm thinking about getting a gun. I'd like nothing better than to put a big hole right through Lenny's head. Then my mom and I could have some peace again, at least until the next guy shows up. All I know is I have to protect myself. I made up my mind that I'm not going to be a punching bag any more. But I just can't bring myself to call the police or tell the school. Maybe the next guy will be different, a real father. But I'm running out of time. In the meantime, I'm lifting weights and working out. I'm getting bigger and stronger. Maybe Lenny will get what's coming to him if he comes at me again.

The Bad Parent.   I sometimes think to myself, what's better? To have one of those good parents who's always doing everything for their kids in public but when they get home, they are mean and abusive to the kids? No one ever knows but the kids themselves and who can they tell? No one would believe them. Or is it better to have parents like mine, who are bad parents—at least to me. They don't mince any words. They like my sister better than me. We're both adopted, but I'm the kid they don't want. Don't get me wrong; they don't beat me up with a bat or anything like that. They just beat me up with words. Let me give you an example. If I need a ride to or from school, they will never do it. Even if I'm sick in school, my mother won't come and pick me up. The high school nurse knows better than to call her. She always says, "I shouldn't be telling you this but I feel so sorry for you. Is your mother always so unpleasant? I hate calling her on the phone. I can feel the hostility. I know you're adopted but she has no right treating you like that. Here you are, running a fever, and I can't send you home. I really should call the Child Protective Services but what are they going to do? They're already over their heads with real abuse cases. They'll just make a house visit and things will probably end up being worse for you. How come she doesn't treat your sister that way? If I call about your sister, she or your dad is right here within minutes. Does your mother know how abusive she is being to you?"

I thought a lot about what the school nurse said, the Child Protective Services already being "over their heads with real abuse cases." Wasn't my situation abusive? It felt like that to me. Sure, I lived in a nice home, had my own room, plenty of food, decent clothes, but that wasn't enough. I felt like my parents were watching my every move. Every time I took the car, they asked where I was going and would check the mileage when I got home. I wasn't allowed to have anyone else, particularly a girl, in the car. My father always checked the car to see that it wasn't scratched. Most of the time I just rode my bike because it wasn't worth the hassle. I was the only junior in the high school who still had a bike. It seemed to me that every time I wanted to do something, the answer was "no." When my sister and I went to high school, I was the one who had to take Industrial Technology courses, because my parents said that they couldn't afford two college tuitions at the same time. So my sister got to take the academic classes while I got stuck with all the losers in the blow-off curriculum—losers' heaven, they called it. I had as good grades as my sister in junior high, so why was I shoved off with the rejects? I hate saying that but it's true. None of the kids in my program want to be there. They want out of school. Each day is the same. The kids fool around and try to get the teacher to throw them out. Besides, I hate all the technology stuff. Who needs auto mechanics, carpentry, electricity, and mechanical drawing? I taught myself all the stuff on my own. Why should I be going to school to learn things I know already? And the other courses are garbage; the Introduction to the Business World class is taught by a guy who has been there forever. They just keep moving him around, from program to program, hoping he drops dead. All he does is read from the book and ask us to take notes. It's all in the book so why should we be taking notes? Half the time he falls asleep and the kids sneak out the door. Or the kids will ask for a pass at the beginning of the period and never come back. He never asks them where they were. He doesn't care; he just pretends not to notice. And the math class I'm taking is so easy. It's called Math in the Business World. It's all about learning how to keep a checkbook and do a budget. I've had a job on my own since seventh grade; I know all about that stuff. And why am I taking this blow-off course when I passed the state exam in junior high with a 95 and got an A for the course? I was recommended for all academic courses with honors in math and science and where am I? In the bottom track. I keep telling my parents that I don't belong in these courses, but they say I have to learn something that I can use to make a living when I get out of school. Again, the same old line:—"We can't afford two college tuitions. We'll be on a fixed income by then. Remember, we were older when we adopted you and your sister. We've tried to give you a good home but we can't be expected to do everything. We just feel you're better suited to the work world, that's all. There will be no more discussion. You're never grateful for all we've done for you.

Where would you be if we had not come along, in some foster home or back with your real mother? You should be down on your knees thanking God for finding you a good Christian home with your dad and me. Never satisfied, that's you, mister. The reason we're letting your sister go to college is that she's a girl; she'll never be able just to leave high school and find a trade like you can. Besides, you can always go to college on your own if it's that important to you. I don't know what the big deal is about college anyway. Neither your dad nor I went and we did OK."

It was always the same conversation, almost word for word. Why did I continue to ask? It hurt my ears. It was like hearing a tape on the wrong speed—and not being able to turn it off. And my dad was just as bad. They both had the same party line: fixed income, good Christian home, they made it without college, boys can make it without an education but girls can't. It all came down to the fact that I was in the wrong place at the wrong time. I wasn't the kid they wanted and they surely were not the parents I wanted. I didn't fit. I thought about what my mother said: "You should be down on your knees thanking God for finding a good Christian home." Maybe I should, but all I thought about was being with my real mother. I always had this dream in which she came to the door and told my parents that she was taking me back. She was tall and beautiful, with a good education and a big job. She took me home and let me take all the college prep courses. After high school, I got a scholarship to Princeton.

But that day never comes. Sometimes when I hear a knock at the door or an unfamiliar voice on the phone, I actually think that she has come for me. Where is she? Why has she abandoned me to these people, Mr. and Mrs. No? Maybe she had to. Maybe she couldn't support me and felt that I would have a better chance being adopted. Sometimes I would even talk to her, telling her how unhappy I was and asking her to please come and take me "home." Once in a while, when I get up enough guts, I ask my adopted mother who my real mother was. But she always avoids the question, saying she doesn't know and to stop asking her. But I know she knows something. There must be papers somewhere. When I get to be twenty-one, I'm going to find out. A part of me, though, is afraid to find out who she really is. What if she's in jail or a prostitute? What if she is not nice and is worse than my adopted parents? But I know she's not; I know she's a good parent and a good person. She would have come for me if she only knew how unhappy I am. I know she thinks I'm being well taken care of. She'd be here in a minute if she only knew. She's a good parent. She'd pick me up at school if I was sick. She's a good parent. I know.

I Had Become My Father's Son. I knew the teachers, administration, and some of the kids were leery of me. It wasn't anything that was said. It was just there. They knew that my parents had sued the school district when I was in elementary school and won. The word was passed from teacher to teacher to watch out for me and my parents. It could cost them their job. The gossip around town was that the Johnsons were "suit happy" and they shouldn't be messed with. I remember when my dad sued the school all too well. It changed my whole school life. I was in the sixth grade. One day during recess I fell off the slide and hurt my knee. I didn't think it was anything until I got home. My mom asked me how the day was and I showed her my knee. It was bruised but nothing bad. When my dad came home, my mom told him about my knee. He just exploded, calling my teachers "irresponsible" and "overpaid incompetents." I still remember how afraid I was. I couldn't understand why he was acting that way. The next thing he said was, "We're going to get that examined by a doctor and if there is anything wrong, I'm suing them for plenty. Was there a teacher there when you fell?" I couldn't remember; I was shaking all over. Why was my father doing this?

So we went to the doctor. He said I had a sprain and should stay off of it for a few days. But my dad made me stay home for two weeks. In the meantime Dad went to the school and told the principal and my teacher that they were irresponsible and that he was bringing a lawsuit. He even called the parents of the kids who were on the playground to check out what had happened. I was so embarrassed. My father said he was bringing the lawsuit to teach them a lesson. By the time I got back to school everyone, including me, was on edge. I could sense that teachers and kids were treating me differently. Every time I went out to play there was always a teacher near me. I was never left alone. It made me feel ashamed. Why was my father making all of this happen? Didn't he know that this whole thing was making people avoid me? Suddenly I was a loner, a kid to be watched, "that Johnson kid" with the father who sues. To make matters worse, my father won the lawsuit. He said he had done the right thing and the school would be more careful now. He didn't know what it had done to me. I was the victim, literally.

So I went along grade by grade with that whole episode hanging over me. I thought by the time I got to high school that people would have forgotten. But no one did. It showed up in small ways. Like when the teachers gave papers back after an exam, they always made a point to hand my paper directly to me. It was as if they were making sure there was no problem. And my parents were never called to school. It wasn't that I got into a lot of trouble, but whenever I did I was always given warnings. And the other kids never pushed me around. In fact, they left me alone. It was as if they all—the kids, teachers, and administrators—were afraid of me. I hated it, yet in a strange way it gave me a power that no one else had. I remember the day when I first felt this power. I had a major term paper due for social studies but I put it off and put it off. When the paper was due I told the teacher that I had put it in her mailbox and I didn't have a copy. The next day she told me she couldn't find it and I would have to submit a new paper. Suddenly I found myself yelling at her, saying, "Are you calling me a liar? I'm going to get my father up here and he'll sue you for this." I couldn't believe the words that were coming out of my mouth. I was the liar, not her, and I was wrong. But I could see that my words had made her think. She backed up and said, "Well, give me some time to think about this." The next week she said that she must have "misplaced" the paper and she would give me a "B" if that was all right. I couldn't believe it; because I had cried "lawsuit" it had worked. I was in the clear and I hadn't done any work. I hated what I had done but there was something I liked about this power. If people were afraid to deal with me and my parents, why not push them into a corner if it fit my needs? I had become my father's son. I knew now why the school was afraid of the Johnsons. I never told my father what happened but I think he would have been proud of me. He would do anything to stick it to the—what did he call the teachers?—"overpaid incompetents."

All I Want Is to Buy Combat Boots and a Black Leather Jacket. All I want to do is buy combat boots, a black leather jacket, wear a ponytail, and go into Manhattan to the clubs. That's all—that's no big deal, is it? But my parents won't let me do any of that. They say I'll "create the wrong image" if I get the boots and jacket. As for going to the city, they say, "Someone will mug you. You look too much like a kid from a small town." My dad says, "You'll get in with the wrong crowd if you keep going like this. I never should have let you get into this art and music stuff. I should have seen it coming and put a stop to it right then when you were in elementary school." They want me to be in sports and school things like the National Honor Society, but I've never been into that stuff. I've always wanted to be my own person. Music and art have been my passion. Since I was a little kid I've always wanted to paint and write music. In elementary school I would write these plays with a musical score about good and evil. My teachers were amazed that I had so much talent. But I still did the things that "normal" kids did, like playing Little League and being in the Boy Scouts. I was still "one of the boys."

But in high school that all changed. In grades nine and ten I won a prize to attend a summer creative arts school sponsored by New York State. It was held at this big college campus on Long Island and we lived there for six weeks. It was great! We would sit around and write plays and stories and then act out the plays ourselves. I would write the music for the plays and play the piano or guitar in the background. The other kids loved it and said that I was a genius. The kids were so much fun, not like most of the kids I went to school with who were more interested in sports. And I really didn't miss my parents. They would visit every weekend and ask if I was homesick. I wasn't; I was having a great time. I think that bothered them, that I was so happy being away from home. I tried to explain to them that it wasn't them, I was just doing something that I loved doing. In some ways it was peculiar, even to me. I knew I had found something that I wanted to do with the rest of my life, and I was only in high school. The teachers at the summer program said I was gifted and should pursue a career in the arts. I think my parents were caught off guard with all of this. They wanted me to be like a regular kid, play sports and be involved with the family. You know, go on trips and do family things. Here I was, off on my own, and I wasn't even in college yet. I think it scared them, that they were losing their kid to some kind of avant-garde world. I was already letting my hair grow longer and dressing in clothes they called "arty." When they came to visit, they would always make comments about the way the teachers and kids looked. I must admit that some of them seemed a little weird with their colored hair and different styles. But I think the thing that bothered them the most was that so many of the kids were kids of color—blacks, Asians, Indians. I came from a school that was 100 percent white. My parents, with their traditional middle-class look, stood out among the dashikis and colorful headbands. It wasn't that my parents were racists. We lived in such a white world that this sudden burst of colors seemed to frighten them. It was almost like when I was a little kid and we took the subway in Manhattan. My mother would say to me, "Hold my hand." The noise and the different people seemed to scare her. I felt that when she visited me at school, she was saying and feeling the same things. I entered a new world that was scary for my parents. The difference was that I loved it while my parents saw only a threat. On one visit my mother just let it out: "Maybe this is too much. You're losing all your old friends at home. You'll have no one to come home to. And what if you get involved with some girl here from some other place? How will you handle that? You know some of these people are different and they have different cultures. You're a white kid from a small town. I don't like the way this is going and your father agrees with me." I felt bad for them. I loved my parents and they were good parents. But it was too late. In looking back to that day, that conversation, I had, even at that young age, left home.

When I got back to school in September, I was different. My old friends were into sports and getting ready for college. I wasn't interested in the same things. School just became a place where I went because I had to. I had left there, too! My parents kept asking, "How was school?" and "When are your friends coming over?" I felt so bad for them. They wanted me to like school and be happy there. It was as if they blamed themselves for what was happening to me. My father said, "I told you this would happen. You've burned your bridges. We never should have let you go to that art school. All of this could have been avoided. I hope you don't live to regret this." But I had my own life. I was still seeing the kids from the summer program. Each Saturday I would tell my parents that I was going to visit a friend. I guess you would call that a white lie. But I couldn't tell my parents the truth. They couldn't handle it. They were upset enough with me already.

So I would take the train to Manhattan where I would go to my friend's apartment. She let me keep my combat boots and leather jacket there. It had taken me months to get up the courage to buy them. When I finally did, I was shaking all over when I paid the bill. I'd never done anything my parents opposed until then. So that was my routine. When I got to the apartment I would change into what I called my "me" clothes and then we would go down to the Village and just watch people. This is where I wanted to go to college and live. I was applying to an art institute and NYU and someday I wanted my own loft with a big piano and beautiful pictures. My heart raced with all the sounds and excitement. I felt more at home there than I did in my own home. I didn't want my parents to know about the boots and jacket and where I went on Saturdays. I knew it would break their hearts and I didn't want to hurt them. Better to tell a white lie. But when I got home on Saturday night, I knew they knew. It wasn't something that was ever said out loud; it was just there. They would ask me about my day. I would make up some story about going to the beach and that was it. I knew they knew I was lying but it was beyond them. I was eighteen; what could they do? At least I wasn't shoving the truth in their faces. I didn't want to hurt them. Maybe when I went to college they would come into the Village and I could wear my boots and jacket and even have a ponytail. I wouldn't have to lie any more and they wouldn't have to pretend. Sometimes parents don't have to know everything about a kid. It's less painful.

I'm Giving up That Part of My Life, Mom and Dad. My parents want to know everything; I can't move. "What time will you be home?" "Where are you going?" "Make sure you wear your jacket." It goes on and on. My father says it's their responsibility to be involved with my life. Well, who says? I tell them, "Where is it written that you guys have to know everything about my life?" And then my mother starts crying and my dad starts all this nonsense that I don't appreciate what they've done for me. I try to tell them that I do, but it never gets through. They want me to be like I was in middle school. I was always on the honor roll and into sports; I was involved all the time and they were there at all the games. Even on weekends I belonged to traveling teams in football, basketball, and baseball. You get the picture. My parents and I were always together and I loved it. They were the only parents who would drive to all the games. Most of the other kids' parents never showed up, and my father and I were always together, playing and practicing some sport. It wasn't pressured stuff like some other kids' dads. My dad didn't expect me to make the major leagues or play Division I in college; he just wanted to be there and see me have a good time. I guess they couldn't understand when things began to change. I didn't even know myself. All I know is that by the time I was in tenth grade, I was changing real fast. I wasn't the kid they knew in middle school. Hell, I wasn't the kid I knew.

The changes came in both big and subtle ways. First I lost interest in sports. That came as a big blow to my father, I mean, that was our life together, playing, going to games, watching sports on TV. That was all we talked about every night at the dinner table. It was something my father looked forward to. When I told him that I didn't want to spend all my time after school involved in sports—I was playing football, basketball, and baseball—that I had no time for myself, he just sat there. "What are you going to do with your time?" he asked. I told him that I just wanted to come home and relax, play my piano and guitar and hang out with my friends. I told him that I was sick of coming home every night at 7:00 and having to rush my dinner and go through three hours of homework. I was taking an honors program and the work was piled on. I had no time to relax or hang out. I didn't want to be like some of the other kids who just did schoolwork and sports. They were like zombies going from one activity to the next plus more teams on the weekends and in the summer. Most of my friends went away to sports camps in the summer and never stopped. I didn't want to be like that. Besides, I was getting into music and loved just coming home and playing the piano and guitar. It helped me relax after a tense day at school. I had also met this girl and I wanted to hang out with her. When my dad heard me, he started to cry. It was like I was shattering his whole life. My mother heard him crying and came in and asked what was the matter. I told my mother and she started crying, too. God, what was happening? I was ruining our whole family. But I didn't want to go on with my life like it had been. My mother started saying things like, "It won't look good on your school record to have no sports. It might stop you from getting into a good college. Besides, you're not going to just come home and hang out or be a couch potato. There's going to be some rules around here if this happens." I could see they were both upset, my mom angry and my dad sad. My dad then said, "You never gave us any problems, not a one. I just figured it would always be like this, going to your games in high school and then when you went to college we'd be doing the same things. I never thought it would change. It's just such a shock. It's something I never had as a kid; my father didn't care about sports. And (laughing), what will your mom and I do now? Our whole lives have been planned around your sports; even the people we know socially, we've met through the teams. And just think, we bought those new chairs and cooler so we'd be comfortable at the games. And what will the coaches say? You're so good at sports. I mean, they have you groomed to be All County in three sports. We haven't had anyone do that in this town for years. I don't understand what happened. Why don't you think about this for a while before you decide?"

I looked at him and said, "Dad, please understand, I don't want to hurt you and Mom but I'm different now. I don't understand it either but I am. You taught me to trust my decisions. It's true with school, too. I want to take the courses that I have to but I don't want to take so much that I have no life. I need to have a life besides school and sports. Look for yourself. What do we talk about as a family? Sports, school, what exams I have, what am I going to take for courses next year— that's the stuff we've been talking about for years but it doesn't interest me any more. I don't want to hurt you; you've both been great parents and I love you so much. I appreciate all you've done for me; you've always been there. But I've never taken any time for myself. It's been go, go, go and I'm beginning to feel it. I'm just a kid. If I don't learn to relax and have fun now, I'll never learn. I can't keep this pace up all through high school and college; I'll be a basket case!"

So I stopped the sports. My dad was right; the coaches couldn't understand. They put all kinds of pressure on me, with comments about scholarships. They even had the other kids, parents, and teachers trying to talk me out of dropping. Wherever I went, someone was bugging me. They couldn't understand how I could give up something I was so good at. When I tried to explain my reasons, it didn't seem to make any sense to them; I could see it on their faces. For the first time in my life I felt like a loner. But it was something I had to do, doing something that was good for me even though it didn't feel right. I got really good at the piano and guitar and got my own band going. At the pep rallies I'm just a nobody now. Sometimes it bothers me; I could be up there getting the cheers. But I like coming home and playing the piano and my parents are even getting into it. My dad comes in now and we talk music. But I have to keep reminding him that I'm just doing it for fun. He's not going to see me at Carnegie Hall, I don't think. It's hard for a kid to do something just for fun, without having to use it for the school record, college, or resume. It seems, in looking back, that everything I did in sports or school was just to get ready for next year, the next level. No one ever stops and says, "Let's just enjoy things for now." It's always next year, next course, next season. I'm trying not to let that happen to me or my parents with the piano. It's just for now.

No Place Like Home.   I'm living downstairs in the basement with my boyfriend. My older brother is living upstairs with his girlfriend and her little kid and my other brother is living out in the back room with his girlfriend and her kid. And guess what. My grandparents are coming up from Florida to spend the winter with us. Great, huh? And what are my parents doing about it? Squat, that's what. You'd think they would get fed up with all these kids. For Christ's sake, my brothers are in their twenties and they still don't have a job or a place to live. And my parents put up with it. They should throw the bums out, but do they? No! Besides, my parents are never home. They both work two jobs. What a marriage! Even my boyfriend is a loser. He's another one who's got no job or place to live. He doesn't even have a GED from high school. How I ended up with the creep is beyond me, but I don't have the heart to throw him out. I mean, I'm just a kid, a high school junior, and I've got all this crap floating around me. It's like a zoo. I can't study or concentrate on anything with these little kids screaming and carrying on. Hell, they're not even members of my family. My brothers are suckers just like me. We were always bringing home stray dogs and cats. But now it's people. And this whole thing with the school makes me laugh. Whenever I miss a day or cut out, they call home but they never can get my parents. My parents don't want to be bothered with that BS. Then they call me in and tell me I better shape up. Hell, they don't have any idea about my life or what goes on in my house. They'd crap if they did. I look at all these nerd kids with their

Mercedes and designer clothes and I laugh. Their life, with their moms making them breakfast and taking them shopping to Fortunoff's, is so phony. Those kids would fold if they had half the problems I've had.

You see, I had to be tough even when I was in middle school. I was the one who was always blamed and sent to the office. There was something about me that always made me stick up for the underdog. I was forever getting into fights that had nothing to do with me so I could help some kid who was being bullied. It goes back to taking in those stray dogs and cats. I never wanted to see anyone hurt. I was the only one in my class in elementary school that used to give gifts to all the kids who seemed poor. I still can't stand the idea of a kid going without a present for Christmas. That's why I want to become an elementary school teacher. I want to help all those kids who have troubles at home that no one knows about. You see, I can tell. I just look at a kid who has trouble and I know. It's like a magic power I have. I know I would have trouble with those smart kids with the pushy parents but maybe I could help them to see that other kids don't have what they have, like money, homes, two parents. Maybe there's something good about my parents; at least they taught us not to turn our backs on people. Sometimes it's hard because you can't deal with all the pain in the world, even here in this small town. You think I'm happy every time I see an animal or person in trouble and I stop to help out? Well I'm not. I wish sometimes that I could just drive by and ignore what's happening, look the other way. My life would be a lot easier and so would my brothers' and parents'. We're all the same way. But I don't want to end up like my brothers; they're too good. They're both suckers for any hard luck story and look where it got them. My teachers tell me I have a gift to help people but I'm not much good at helping myself. They're right, but if they really knew my family, they would see why. How do I go from being my parents' daughter to someone who takes care of herself and helps other people?

The Pain of Sexuality and Relationships for Adolescents

These stories are about the pain and fleeting joy that come with sexual awakening. Welcome to the Pain of Adolescence is about a young woman's awakening, the joy and love in the beginning, and the heartaches that followed. Learning about relationships can be painful, particularly for a high school student who didn't see trouble coming. When trouble did come, she felt she had no one to talk to, parents, priest, or friends. She had never been in this kind of trouble before; it was all so painful, so new. She was so unprepared. Like all of us who go through pain, she wished that she could go back to the days before it all happened, but she couldn't. This wasn't the sexuality they talked about in health class. It was something she had to go through on her own or so she thought. Maybe she was right. Maybe her parents could never understand. Why hurt them by telling them, especially with graduation coming up? God had let her down. She had to get through this on her own. No, she wasn't pregnant. In some ways that might be easier to handle. You could have an abortion or have the child; the choices were clear. This pain was different and it was hers alone.

In I'm Not Keeping It a Secret Any More—I'm Gay the need for this young man to tell others who he is is tempered by the advice of friends and teachers who tell him not to be self-destructive. They tell him not everyone will understand—kids, teachers, parents. They urge him to go slow. It's a tough spot for a kid. What's the line between being open and being self-destructive? Where do you draw it? In this story the child wishes he could tell his mother. He leaves pamphlets and articles around about being gay, hoping she will catch on. Maybe she does but she doesn't say anything except wonder where he is all the time. His teacher's advice and contact are important.

She Would Never Make It to the Junior Prom is a different look at sexuality and relationships. It's about a girl who is a victim. She is attacked verbally by students in school and called a lesbian, even though they have no real idea of her sexual preference. Every day she wants to stay home but home is no better. She is attacked because she wears masculine clothes, that's all she has, and is covered up with sweaters and coats, trying not to let the other kids see how overweight she is. Because she looks different, they attack her sexuality. Our enemies can always see our vulnerable parts, especially school kids. At home she is a slave, a throwback to the old days when girls in the family did all the chores and the boys did nothing. She has no privacy, no room of her own, no clothes except the hand-me-downs of her brothers. There is nothing feminine in the home, no model to follow. Her mother has gotten out by working. The running of the house is left to her, the daughter. She is there to wait on her father and brothers, cook the meals, do the laundry, make the beds, empty the garbage, mow the lawn. How can she develop her sexuality in such a place? What the other kids said bothered her. She has never had a dress. She has never had a date. She knows she has no chance of going to the junior prom. Every day is spent dodging verbal bullets at school and home. She wonders if the kids are right about her. Is she a lesbian? She doesn't know. All she knows is that everyone, even the teachers, avoid her. She doesn't know who she is.

So much of adolescence is spent thinking about sexuality, alone. That's not new. What is new is that kids are more sexually active or they think they should be. The girl in the junior prom story knows she is different, that she is missing out. Her experience leaves her wondering who she is. Her sexuality is being defined by others, by the mob. Yet talking to the wrong people about yourself can lead to trouble. Parents, friends, and teachers can betray the confidence of the adolescent. The pressure for increased sexual behavior is leaving its share of victims among adolescents. How can we bring about the right conditions for kids to talk and learn from their experience?

Welcome to the Pain of Adolescence.   The months before graduation are a special time for seniors—ordering limos for the senior prom, getting the prom table together, mailing graduation invitations to relatives and friends. It's a time to remember your first date, your first love affair, your first beer at the beach keg parties, the long summers when you had that gorgeous tan, the fights with your parents over curfew, and the relief you feel when you open the letter from the college of your choice and they want you. The years in high school had seemed endless but now the days are rushing by. Going off to college and leaving the home you lived in for eighteen years is just around the corner. All the seniors fought off the fear of what would happen next by joining in a frenzy of signing yearbooks, partying, and remembering what parents call the "best years of your life." The awards to the most popular, most likely to succeed, best athlete, nicest person, and best academic student filled the air and pushed the future away—for now. The seniors worked hard at hanging on to the "best years" of their lives. It worked for some but not for all.

I had always tried hard. No one could ever say I was a quitter. That's
true no matter what I do—sports, academics, friendships, family, boyfriend or girlfriends, relationships—I give 100 percent!! I've always
done the "right" thing since I was a little kid. I've never missed a
homework assignment and my reports are always turned in a week
early. The teachers and the other kids know I can be counted on. I like
being that way. As for my parents, I never gave them one minute of
worry. That is, not until I met Jim. I had breezed through my first three
years of high school, making the honor roll every report card. I've
played varsity soccer, basketball, and softball since I was in the ninth
grade and had the lead in the Drama Club plays in the tenth and eleventh grades. I excelled at whatever I did without really trying too hard.
My dad always said I had a gift to make hard things look easy.

But in my junior year my life began to change in ways that were
different and exciting but in some strange way, burdensome. That's
when I met Jim. I guess you could say he was my first real love. Up
until that point, school and sports were my life. But when he came
along that's all I could think about. When we started dating my parents
warned me not to get too involved. They felt he was too domineering
and that he never gave me a chance to be with my friends or family.
But I wasn't listening. By then Jim and I were having sex on a regular
basis. It was a hard decision for me because I had been brought up in a
very Catholic environment. We had always gone to church as a family
and I was taught to never lie or criticize anyone. My mother always
talked to me about sex being a very sacred act and encouraged me to
save myself for marriage. But Jim persisted and I couldn't say no. I had
never really said no to anything in my life. I was always the first to
volunteer or to help out. Our family motto was to do for others and put
our own needs second. At first I hated myself for doing it. I felt like I
was letting my parents down, especially my mother. But the bottom
line was that I liked having sex with Jim. I hated to admit it but he was
number one in my life. By April of our senior year we were a couple,
spending all our free time together and even planning to attend colleges
in the same area in Western Massachusetts. If you met me in April
before graduation, you would probably say, "There is one happy kid!"
I had been accepted at one of the toughest colleges in the country and
won a scholarship for basketball. For the first time in my school career

I could let loose for the next few months and relax without having a report or project hanging over my head. I could just hang out with Jim and enjoy. But then it happened. Just when I thought things were perfect in my life, it all fell apart. I never saw it coming. The best time of my life, the time I had been working hard for all my school career, turned out to be a nightmare.

It all began so innocently—the one night that would change my life, probably forever. Jim and I had gone over to my best friend Marsha's house for pizza and beer during April break. After a few beers we got into playing a drinking game with Marsha and her boyfriend. All I remember is that I kept losing and finally passed out. Jim woke me up about two o'clock and took me home. I felt sick but the next morning I forgot about the whole thing. But during the next week Jim seemed distant to me. I wondered if I had pushed him away with my drunken binge. That Friday he called and told me he couldn't take it any more and he had to see me. He said, "You're not going to like me after you hear what I have to say." I thought he was breaking up with me. But that wasn't it; it was a lot worse. We went for a ride to the beach. As we drove along he started to cry and said, "Remember when you got drunk last week at Marsha's? Well, I drank too much, too, and had sex with Marsha after her boyfriend went home. I'm so ashamed of myself. I didn't want to tell you but I can't eat or sleep. I feel so guilty. I want you to know I love you and I'm so sorry it happened. It didn't mean a thing to me and Marsha feels the same way. We don't want to hurt you. She asked me not to tell you but I have to. It was just all the drinking that made us do it." I couldn't believe what I was hearing. My first reaction was to get angry at Marsha. She had been my best friend all through junior high and high school. How could she do this to me? And what was I supposed to do about the prom? Jim and I were supposed to go with Marsha and her boyfriend in the limo and sit together. How could I do that now? I wasn't that mad at Jim but I didn't know why. I wanted to forgive him and go back to where we were before that night but I couldn't. All I could do was cry and ask him to take me home. Things had changed. I felt like I had a knife in my heart.

When I got home my mother was in the kitchen. She could tell I was upset but how could I tell her why? She thought I was still a kid. How could this good Catholic woman understand? It would hurt her too much to tell her. How had my parents put it—put your own needs second? I could do that with my mother but for the first time in my life I didn't know if I could do that with Jim or Marsha. It bothered me to think that they could do what they did and then ask me to just go on and forget about the whole thing, to ride in the limo and drink champagne like nothing had happened. What kind of a sponge did they think I was? Right now I didn't want to turn the other cheek and say things were all right. I was too hurt. I had given up everything for Jim—most of my friends, I had even given up softball because he wanted me to spend more time with him. I wondered if I had been a fool.

And so it went for the next months. I tried to get the whole thing out of my mind. I went to church and to confession and asked God to take away the hurt and anger I felt. But it stayed, like an unwelcome visitor. Each morning I would wake up hoping I would feel like my old self but that day never came. My old self was gone somewhere. In school I tried to avoid Marsha but I couldn't bring myself to change the limo and prom arrangements. I felt dead, unable to do anything. Besides, Jim said that it would look funny to change the arrangements now, so close to the prom. I kept seeing Jim but I was different. No matter how hard I tried, I couldn't get the pain out of my heart. It was funny because Jim thought things were OK, that we had gotten back to our old selves. But he was wrong. I felt like I was in a fog. I had no one to talk to. Before all of this I could talk to Jim and Marsha but those days were all over. I wanted to talk to my parents but why break their bubble? They were so happy for me, especially the scholarship, and couldn't wait to show me off to the relatives at graduation. Besides, they had worked hard to raise me to have good values. Why make them feel like failures now? I tried with all my heart to do what my parents had taught me to do all my life, forgive and forget, but I couldn't. The night of the prom I sat at the table with Jim and Marsha and watched the clock. I wanted to go home. I wanted graduation to come and for my parents to be happy and proud of me. I missed my family! They were all I had right now.

I thought someday, when I'm older, when they're older, I'll tell my parents the real story of graduation, how I saw the dark side of life for the first time. Maybe that was the best graduation gift I got. To forgive and forget and to place your needs second isn't always the best thing. And just when you think your life is perfect, watch out!!

I'm Not Keeping It a Secret Any More—I'm Gay.   For a long time I didn't want to tell anyone, but I can't keep it in any more. Some of my friends at school say I'm stupid for telling so many kids. They tell me that the jocks and the preps will start beating up on me; they hate gays. Even one of the teachers I told cautioned me to go slow. He said, "You don't understand. You're the first kid in the history of the school to come right out. There are a lot of kids, parents, and even teachers who are going to be really threatened. I bet your own mother and that guy she lives with don't even know. What do you think their reaction is going to be?" He was right about my mom and her boyfriend, Marty; I hadn't told them. I would never tell Marty anyway; he's a sleaze. I don't know why my mother keeps him around. He's got a lousy job and he's always hitting my mother up for money for beer and cigarettes. He sits around every night drinking and bossing my little brother and sister. He doesn't dare tangle with me. He knows I hate him for the way he treats my mother. I told him the last time he beat her up that I would kill him if it happened again. And I will. I don't even talk to the guy any more. He's got some hold over my mother that I can't figure out; she just gives him whatever he wants and then stands by while he abuses her and her kids. I guess that she's so lonely that she's willing to put up with anything.

When it comes right down to it, she chose this bum Marty over me and the other kids. But I do want her to know about my life. I feel bad about the way she ended up, living with this creep, but she is my mother and I want her to know about the real me. I got these pamphlets from school on being gay and I leave them around hoping she will read them. She's always saying, "Why are you leaving this stuff around?" But I think she knows. She never asked where I go on weekends. I'm hardly ever home. Sometimes when my lover calls, she asks, "Who is that guy? He sounds like an older guy." I know she knows but I still haven't been able to talk to her. I just don't want Marty involved; if he knew, he'd really go after me. I know he'd make my mother throw me out of the house. He'd like nothing better than to see me gone. Well, he'll have his wish soon. I've got one more year of high school and then I'm getting my own apartment. But right now I have to be careful;

I need a roof over my head. My lover has his own apartment and he wants me to move in with him. But I'd have to change schools if I moved and I don't want to do that. I'm almost out and I need that diploma. I look at it this way: I put up with Marty for ten years, since my parents' divorce. I can make it one more year. Sometimes I laugh about what Marty would do if he saw me with my lover at the gay bars we go to on weekends. I'm sure he would have a heart attack. He knows something's up but I'll keep him wondering.

The only other thing I feel bad about is all the girls at school who want me to go out with them. I try to tell them that I'm different, I like guys better. But they keep coming back, like they don't understand. It's weird, like once they know I'm gay they feel safe and want to tell me all about their problems. Sometimes I wish I was just a normal kid from a normal family, who could have a girlfriend and go to the prom and all that high school stuff. But I'm not. When I see my father at Thanksgiving and the other holidays, he's always asking me about the girls I'm dating. I make up some name—this year it's Maureen—and tell him about all the parties and dances we go to. He keeps asking me to bring her over but I tell him she has a job. I wish I could tell him the truth but he thinks I'm a prep who is involved with girls and school activities. He would die if he knew about the real me.

She Would Never Make It to the Junior Prom.   I'll never make it to the junior prom. It's a sure thing. Bet on it. Hell, I wasn't even going to make it to my junior year. It's just something you know when you come from a family like mine. You see, none of us Gilmartinis ever amount to much. The school secretaries are always saying, "Oh, you're one of the Gilmartinis." That's the code word for saying, "Oh, you're from that family. They never last here. You'll never amount to much." I wasn't on "the list" of ass-kissers that the teachers and secretaries fell all over. No matter what I ever did in school, good or bad, I was forever "just one of those Gilmartinis"—the kind of kid that the school never expected much from—except trouble. No one else in my family had ever gotten their diploma; they had all gotten thrown out or left for work. The big stretch limos never pulled up at our house to take my brothers or me to proms or parties. Hell, I have never even owned a dress. Maybe when I was a little kid I had one, but all I wore from elementary school on was jeans and a jacket. I always kept myself cov-

ered up. I don't know why. Maybe it's because I always had to share a
room with one or more of my brothers. I never had my own room. I've
had no privacy, the only girl in a house with six boys. Plus I'm fat,
obese really. I know for sure that is one reason why I always cover
myself up. I'm ashamed of the way I look with all those rolls of fat.
That's why the kids at school call me "She-man." I dress like a guy,
layers of sweater, jeans and jeans jacket. I hear them calling me "gay
girl" and "lesbian" behind my back. It hurts so much. That's why I
get in so many fights. I just explode when I hear kids calling me gay.
What do they know? They don't even know me and they think they
have the right to call me those things? They don't understand that I
don't have any other clothes. My clothes are my brothers' hand-me-
downs. No one ever buys me anything, not even at Christmas. Someday
I would like to wear something feminine and soft and not look so
tough.

I wonder what it must be like, growing up like a real girl and doing
girl things. And I can't lose any weight at home! All my father wants
me to cook is pasta and more pasta. I tried to tell him about the nutri-
tion stuff I've been learning in health class but he doesn't listen. My
mother says all he wants is his pasta. If I never see another tortellini
again, I'll be ecstatic! If the other kids had to do all the cooking and
eat what I eat, they'd be fat like me. My business teacher says I have
beautiful eyes and would look great if I lost weight. I've tried but it
doesn't work. I know she likes me, but even she doesn't understand
how hard it is for me in my family. No one does. I can't help the way
I look. I don't have a choice.

You see, I'm a slave at home. My mother always said, "It's the girl's
job to clean, cook and do the laundry." She's from what she calls "the
old country"—Italy. She was raised to wait on her father and brothers'
every desire. She was a slave and now she expects the same from me.
She works a double shift at the state hospital so I never see her. She
just leaves me a list of what to do and I've got to do it. If I don't, my
father will give me "the belt." If dinner is not ready and the house
cleaned by the time he gets home from work, he won't hesitate to whip
me. He'll say, "Get in my room." He makes me take down my panties
and hits me with the belt on my buttocks. Sometimes he hits me so
hard that I have big open sores where the buckle hits me. That's why I

never dress for gym. I'm afraid the teacher or the other kids will see the blood or the marks. It's easier to cut the class and take a failure. I'm never going to graduate so what's the difference? I don't want the school finding out and calling my father. He'd really beat me if that happened.

It's always been the same way, since I was a kid. My brothers never had to lift a finger. I had to make their beds, wash their clothes, do their ironing, make dinner, do the dishes, and take out the garbage. If things aren't right—dishes not done right or soup is cold—I'm the one who gets the belt. My father never hit my brothers. Once in a while my mother will stick up for me but my father tells her to shut up or she'll get the belt, too. I know he's hit her before. I think that's why she works a double shift; she doesn't want to be home. She just leaves me to deal with it. I used to think, "Some mother, leaving me to do all this shit." But she can't change things. I guess she's just trying to save herself. And I never get an allowance for all this work. I'm probably the only kid at school who didn't order a class ring. My only hope is knowing that some day I'm going to get out of here. I have to be eighteen before I can sign myself out. I could drop out now but my father would have to OK it. He did it for my brothers. But he would never do it for me. He needs his slave!

At school they think I'm "just another Gilmartini kid" and that I don't care. They don't understand that I need to get out of my house before I can even start to live. I guess other kids will look back at their high school yearbook and talk about the junior prom and the limos. I know I'll look back and feel bad for myself. Now I just want to get out and forget about my life as a teenager. I can hardly wait until the day my father and my brother have to cook their own pasta and clean. Maybe then they'll appreciate and love me.

Schooling and Adolescents: What's It Really Like?

High schools are in trouble. It's hard to find a high school kid, a parent, or even a teacher who speaks with pride about "their" school. Kids, parents, and teachers all battle for the diminishing resources that are available. Every day, in high schools across America, there is a battle over who gets the attention, who gets the rewards, who counts. It's guerrilla warfare among kids, parents, and teachers. For the kids it's the preps and jocks versus the dirt bags. Kids who want to get it all right and move on versus those kids who never seem to get anything right. For the parents it's the "good" parents, the PTA group, against the parents who don't fit, don't belong, the "outsiders." Go to any PTA workshop and, guaranteed, the speaker will say, "I know I'm speaking to the converted here. You probably all know what I am about to say. I really should be talking to all the other people who are home watching TV." It's the converted versus the unconverted. For the teachers the battle has many fronts. It's young versus old, those older teachers feeling the pressure to retire and open their jobs to "new blood" against the young teachers who are losing their jobs. It's academics versus the arts and sports. As one science teacher said, "It's what's important versus the frills." That's the way he sees it in the vicious war of school budget priorities. It's the high school teacher versus the junior high teacher, both fighting off the community attacks for "who's to blame" for the lower test scores, the violence in the schools, the drinking at the dance. You name the problem; any urban or suburban high school has them all. Everyone—kids, parents, teachers—is being pushed to hang onto what they have and survive. Everyone is being torn: the jocks and preps fighting the teachers' union call for a job action that bars teachers from writing college letters of recommendation until the budget crisis is resolved; the "good" parents who are fighting the "dirt bag" parents for not supervising their kids in the ways that the "good" parents want; the older teacher who is fighting for her dignity, the opportunity, the right, to not retire, to remain teaching the high school kids who love her so much. How many kids went through her classes and left with a new view of life? She can't remember. All she can remember is that things seemed easier in 1962 when she started. There was hope and excitement in education. People cared about kids. Now all she sees is disrespect and criticism of the schools. She is caught between wanting to stay in teaching versus the constant pressure to get out of the way and make room for the young teacher. The exit sign is always flashing. It has nothing to do with her ability to teach and reach the kids. It's all about money and forces beyond the school, beyond the kids, the parents, the teachers. They are all caught in the crossfire. It's not much fun. It's a serious business of survival for everyone.

These tensions come through in the stories about schooling. In The Advanced Placement Courses Can Kill You, the bright child does it all. He takes all the difficult courses and he excels. The more he does, the higher the expectations get. He becomes a source of great pride to his family, his school, and his community. He represents good news and success in a time of great difficulty for kids, parents, and teachers. He is the golden boy bound for the Harvards and the Yales. Amid all the bad news about failed school budgets, drug use among kids, and low test scores, parents and teachers can point to him as an example of someone who got it right. He gives them a breather, a reprieve, against the critics who are always attacking kids and the schools. He has a heavy burden and he can't keep up. Who could? He's just a kid, not a machine. He can no longer be the golden boy that everyone else needs. The story is about how he tries to become a kid again, to do less, to enjoy, to stop pushing himself so hard. Better now than when he gets to the Harvards, the Yales, where the pressure to excel will be even greater, where every student is a valedictorian or Merit Scholar, all golden boys and girls, all hometown heroes. But some good can come out of this dilemma. Better now than later. Better to fall near home than in some far away university where the only relief for the gifted and talented who can't go on is to put a bullet through their heart or a razor across their wrist. Some good can also come out of this for the parents, teachers, and other kids. Maybe they can see it's dangerous to expect too much of any kid, whether he's gifted and talented or hits .400 on the baseball team. Kids aren't machines. They can only push and be pushed so far. It's dangerous for parents and schools to build the success of their programs, their families, around the achievements of one kid. Teachers, parents, and schools may need that for their own personal and professional yardstick of success. That's understandable in a world where good news is hard to come by. But kids may not be able to live up to these expectations. The lucky ones may be the ones who can't go on. It gives them time to learn how to be a kid, to hang out, and to approach the adult world knowing their limits, knowing to be careful of the expectations of others, even others who love and care for you. Sometimes expectations are not your friends; they can kill you.

I Was Always in Trouble So They Passed Me Along is a story about a different kid, a kid whose attendance is poor, whose parents seem not to care (they don't attend PTA meetings, they're among the unconverted), a kid who's missed a lot of learning. He gets passed along, as he says, because he can and does cause trouble in school. He knows how to zero in on the teachers' weak points. He is never prepared or ready for school. He has to get to them before they get to him. Naturally, the teachers and principals are glad to get rid of him. You know the type; maybe you were one of them. But in high school his string runs out. The teachers there actually want him to come to school and do schoolwork! They are wise to all his tricks to avoid work and responsibility; they've seen guys and girls like him before. Things get bad, to the point where they want to throw him out or put him in a special school. But he has pride; he doesn't want to be with a bunch of losers like himself. That's the way he puts it. And he has his friends in school, dirt bags, he says, like himself. He doesn't want to leave them. The story is sad, the tale of a child so needy yet so unprepared. He has missed so much caring and nourishment at home and in school, the necessary building blocks of life, as educators say. He knows that he can't compete—can't read, can't write, can't do basic math. But he can't tell anyone that. He has pride. He is like a thief who is caught and surrounded; he weaves and turns and fights to be free but he keeps running into the stone walls of diploma requirements, standardized tests, credits toward graduation. They're everywhere. Other kids graduate and go on with their lives. He's still there. He's one of those kids that the townspeople describe as "he's still in school; he'll be thirty before he gets out!" There is no escape but he won't let them, the school, label him as a retard or a reject. He has his pride. He doesn't know how to ask for help, he only knows how to run. But you can't run too far on just pride—can you?

I'll Start Doing My Schoolwork When She Stops Bugging Me is a story about another kind of a battle. It's a battle about growing up and learning how to do things on your own terms, not your parents'. Some kids are fighters. They have to be in order to learn about themselves. They know if they don't fight back, their entire high school life will be spent doing what their parents want, not what they want. Worse yet, they know their whole life will be like that. Mom and Dad will always be on the phone asking, "Are you prepared?"—even when they're forty! There will be no end to the demands. They instinctively know that the air has to be cleared right now around the basic question: "Who's in charge of my life, me or my parents?" This story is about kids who are called "classic underachievers" by the school shrinks. The more the parents push, the less the kids do. A simple equation, really: the more A pushes, the less B does. But changing this equation is not easy, even when the parents know it's what they should do. The parents anxiously ask, "If A does nothing, who's to guarantee that B will start to take responsibility and do his work?" It's a gamble that most A types won't or can't take. After a while, as this story shows, the battle between the parents and the underachiever, between A and B, stops being about school. It becomes a fight about will, identity, and survival. School is just the battleground. As the child grows older there will be new battlegrounds—religion, sex, marriage, clothes, jobs. The real story of the achieving parent and the underachieving child is which of them knows what is best for the child. Children, the Bs, don't have a lot of firepower to fight back. Think about it; not doing well in school is one of the few weapons a kid has, along with not making the bed, not taking out the garbage, or acting out with drugs or booze. Sometimes, as our story tells us, the child doesn't want to give that up. Neither side can trust the other enough to stop the battle. It is the way life is lived in the home of the "classic underachiever."

There's No Living Down a Bad Reputation is a story about taking sides in school. There are the good guys and gals and there are the dirt bags and troublemakers. Everyone in school has a "reputation" that began somewhere along the line in school. And that reputation stays with you. I guess you could say it's like your identity badge; it lets people know what group you're in, whose side you're on. But sometimes the reputation you have isn't really "you" any more. It's based on some incident, some outrageous thing that you did when you were less mature. You know, being dead drunk at the eighth grade dance, going out with some guy who is a real loser, dying your hair orange, setting off a smoke bomb in school, giving the finger to the assistant principal. You may drink and smoke but you're no druggie or alcoholic as some people say. After a while you get to the point where you know who you are. That's what counts. Screw the other people and what they think. They've got you pegged so why bother? It's too hard to live down a bad reputation. After a while you stop trying. No one cares what you're really like. That wouldn't be any fun.

The story Austerity speaks to the anxiety the child feels when he sees the school he loves so much being destroyed by forces in the community who seem to hate children. For him austerity means paying to play sports, no cafeteria, no bus transportation, fewer books and supplies, no clubs or field trips, and most painful, the firing of young teachers who mean so much to him and his friends. It speaks to the notion of, "I've got mine so to Hell with you, kid," the mentality that many senior citizens and adults display in voting down school budgets and activities for kids. It speaks to the flight of the children of moneyed families from the public schools to private schools. What's left in many communities are school districts offering the bare minimum to poor kids in crumbling buildings with aging teachers. Teachers, parents, and kids are left with only the memories of what used to be good schools. Teachers, parents, and kids are under attack. And for what? These are the schools and communities that opened the doors of opportunity for so many of these same adults and senior citizens who now demand cutback after cutback, tearing the soul and spirit out of once-proud schools. What happened? What went wrong? What's a child to think? Hate and fear replace hope and wonder for the child, the parent, and the teacher.

Please note that a few of these vignettes about schools were previously published in my book *What Schools Should Do to Help Kids Stop Smoking* I want to thank Eye on Education publications for their approval to include this material.[2]

The Advanced Placement Courses Can Kill You.   I was the standard bearer. You know, the one child in the family who is supposed to do well after all your older brothers and sisters have screwed up. I knew my parents were depending on me to get into an Ivy League college and get a scholarship. It had always been that way. It was "the way" that had been chosen for me since I was selected to be in the gifted and talented class in grade 6. It was expected. I remember hating the gifted and talented class. If I hadn't done well on the PSATs I would never have been in there. I hated being taken out of my regular classes, especially gym. The gifted class met on Tuesday and Thursday and those were my gym days. So I hardly played gym in junior high. And I used to hate what the other kids said about me when I left the room for the gifted class. They would say, "There goes the nerd" and "It's just us dumb ones left now." These were kids I had grown up and gone through school with. Now, suddenly, I was different. I was no longer one of the guys. I was being shipped out to a special room where we did these experiments and talked about philosophy. I hated it but I knew my parents were proud of me and it made them feel important. I was the last of four kids and all the others had really screwed up in school. Somehow, when I look back, my being in the gifted class made everything all right with my parents. They weren't failures after all. So I tried to block out all the comments from other kids and do my best. I knew that someday, once I got through all this school stuff, I would be able to do what I wanted to do. But that would have to wait.

So I went along. Each year I won the prize for the highest grades. It came pretty easy, particularly in junior high and in grades nine and ten. Each year I was picked to attend a special gifted and talented program at some ritzy school like Andover. My dad saved all my newspaper clippings and honors; he said, "All of this stuff is going to look great on your college applications. Believe me when I tell you all this work will pay off." The folder with all my stuff grew and grew. I was "somebody" in my town. People were proud of my success. Wherever I went, the parents and townspeople would ask. "What Ivy league school are you going to?" Some schools had winning football teams to be proud of. In our town it seemed to me that people put all their pride in me. I was on my way to something really important and it made my parents, my school, and the town feel better about themselves.

But then it happened! I hadn't wanted to take the four advanced placement (AP) courses in my senior year. It seemed like too much. I wondered why I needed all those courses. I had taken every difficult course offered in the high school and special programs in the summer. Even now I was taking two advanced science courses at the community college at night. I thought enough is enough. But my parents and some of the teachers insisted that these courses would make me a "shoo in" for the Harvards and the Yales. It would put the icing on the cake. There was no saying no because I had never said no before. The words "I would like" and "No, that's not for me" had never come out of my mouth. I was the good child who always took more than I had to. I was the standard bearer who had to do well. So I took the English, math, and two science AP courses. After all, it was my senior year—only nine months to go to graduation. I could handle it.

But before long I realized that I couldn't keep up. I had all the AP courses, college applications and visits, my night courses, and preparing for the SAT exams! It became a nightmare. I had no time to myself and every course was tough. I couldn't cut myself any slack. There was not time in the day to hang out or hear my music. Plus everyone expected me not just to do well but to do very well in each course. It was as if I were a star fullback and was being given the ball on each play. I couldn't keep up. The first sign was that I started shaking; I would literally be twitching twenty-four hours a day. I couldn't stop my eyes and arms and legs from "jumping." And then I began to lose weight. I couldn't relax and I couldn't eat. On top of all that I couldn't sleep and I had awful nightmares. I found myself unable to do my homework. I couldn't believe this was me. It was almost is if I were caught in some crazy plot to keep myself from getting into any Ivy League school. If this kept up, I feared I would end up at a state school or, worse, a community college. I tried to shake it off but instead found myself cutting classes and leaving school early. I was so confused and embarrassed! Everyone was looking at me like I had become a weirdo—I was shaking all the time—and the teachers kept asking me if everything was all right. Even my dad sensed I was in trouble. One night I came home from community college and found my dad in my room writing out "my" college applications. I yelled at him (the first time in my life), "What are you doing? That's my job." He said, "You look under pressure; I was just trying to help you. I didn't know what else to do." I started to cry so hard that I couldn't stop. I remember saying, "Dad, I can't do all of this any more. I'm over my head. I never have time to play or hang out. I've always, always studied and worked at school. I can't do it any more. I don't know why but I know I can't. I can't stop shaking; you've seen me—look at me now! And I can't eat or sleep or do my homework. All the kids and teachers at school look at me like I'm going nuts and I think I am. All I know is that I have to drop the AP courses and the courses at the community college or I'm going to crack. And I don't want to crack. Dad, I'm not asking you, I'm telling you that it has to be this way. I may be letting you and Mom and the school down but I want to have a normal life like the other kids. I've never hung out or had a summer where I had a job and went to the beach. I've never had time to even have a girlfriend. I know other kids and their parents look at me and think 'he's got it made' but look at me, Dad—I can't do it any more!"

Dad sat there, stunned. It must have been twenty minutes before he came over and put his arms around me and said, "Maybe we've made a big mistake. We had so much trouble and pain with the other kids that when you came along and did so well, it made everything easier for us. We didn't have to be ashamed every time we went into the school. We didn't have to worry when we heard the police siren. We didn't have to worry about you coming home drunk or high on the weekends. Because of you, your mom and I became somebody decent in the community after all the years people said things about how terrible our kids are. I knew you'd never be in the DWI column in the paper. But maybe we did put too much pressure on you. God, I'm so sorry for doing it to you. I never thought we were hurting you but now I see it was all too much. Well," he was crying, we were both crying, "it's not too late. We'll go to the school tomorrow and drop those courses. You probably have more credits than anyone in the state anyway. You can take regular English and whatever else is required. And to hell with the night courses. Why the hell did we make you do all of this? It was crazy. As for the applications maybe you should write your essays about all of this. What would we call it? 'Almost Burnt Out by Eighteen'? When your mom gets home we'll tell her that you've decided to make some changes. It looks like you need to do a little less gifted and a little more fun. I love you."

So my life changed. All the kids and teachers were surprised when I dropped the courses but they knew I had had enough. Some people spread the rumor that I had had a "nervous breakdown." Maybe I had. But my life had changed for the better. I still got into some Ivy League schools and that's where I'm heading in September. I know now that I'll be OK. I guess in some way I can thank the AP courses. I wouldn't have had my "problem" if I hadn't let my parents and teachers (and myself) push me into those courses. Maybe now I can make my own decisions because I know what can happen if I don't. I never, never want to feel that way again.

I Was Always in Trouble So They Passed Me Along.   Check my attendance—I usually miss more than forty days a year. Even in the first grade I would get sick on purpose so I wouldn't have to go to school. I hated it from the start. When I was in school I had missed so much book stuff that I had no idea what was going on. So what did I do? Like any other kid who's out of it, I raised hell. Even back then they tried to put me in the resource room and special class, but I wasn't having any of that. My mother was on my side and she came to school and fought them every time. She wasn't having any of this crap of her kid being with those kids. I may not be a prep or a jock but I ain't dumb. So they passed me along. They didn't want me coming back and sure as hell they didn't want to deal with my mother when she gets going. Sometimes I wonder, if those early years had been different, if I would have liked school better. But we were never there. By the time I got to middle school, I didn't know zip, and who wants to go to school when all the other kids know the stuff and you're in la-la land? That's when I started smoking and drinking. We had our own little group that used to smoke out in the field and in the bathrooms. The other kids called us the "dirt bags" of the school. I think the preps and the jocks were sort of envious of us. They had to study, practice, you know, get ready for college, and all we did was have fun, hang out, drink wine coolers and six packs, smoke and have sex. We were all like a family. We didn't do well in school and if there was some trouble in town, we usually had something to do with it. Our parents weren't the PTA type or those who went to open house. Our parents knew that if they set one foot in the school they would be accosted by teachers armed with complaints. You know, in PTA meetings they talk about the "parents who should be here but aren't." They were talking about our parents. We were the outsiders, the misfits, the slackers, the smokers, the dirt bags, and we were proud of it. It was all we had.

It was true that our group was all we had. Most of us were poor. A lot of the kids' parents were divorced or out of work or both. Many of the parents worked two or three jobs to keep things going. Only a few people had medical coverage, so when you got sick or hurt you made the most of it. We weren't the Little League type or those who went to summer camp or SAT camp. We weren't going to college and we knew it. Our parents didn't fit into the yacht club set. They were on the out-side, like us. They were the adult "dirt bags" of the town.

When I got to high school things began to tighten up. They nailed you for everything—coming in late, smoking, cutting class, driving fast in the parking lot. I had more detentions in one year, according to the assistant principal, than any former student. You might say I was setting records. The assistant principal spent more time with my mom than he did with his wife. My mom was there so often the other kids must have thought she had a job there. She was always behind me but things were getting worse. I was smoking so much and was so addicted that I couldn't stay in school for more than two classes. Then I would hang out with my friends or else take off. It was so stupid. Here I was so addicted to cigarettes and they kept busting me because I had to go out and get a smoke. They didn't understand that I had no choice. Hell, the teachers had their own room to smoke. Why were the kids getting busted for a habit they couldn't shake? So when they asked me to leave school and take the GED program, I wasn't surprised. That's what was happening to most of our dirt bag gang. One by one we were knocking ourselves off or the school was doing it to us. I tried to hang on, think-ing if I waited them out that they would pass me to get rid of me. But it didn't work. High school is different. You can't hide. But I wasn't going to any GED with all those morons. I tried joining the Army but they told me I needed a diploma or a GED. So I'm home doing nothing. Maybe I'll go back to school next year or maybe I'll go to Florida or Kuwait to work in construction. I've seen the ads in the papers—"big salaries to help rebuild Florida and Kuwait." I'll come back and show these preps and jocks some day. What do I need their lousy diploma for?

I'll Start Doing My Schoolwork When She Stops Bugging Me.   It was always the same story every year. I never had a choice in anything to do with school. My mother would worm her way in to pick out my teachers and scope out the best classes for me. And then she would bug me and bug me about what homework was due, the reports and all the other assignments. It was endless. And about November I would do the same thing I had done every year before—I would stop doing the work. I told her that I wasn't going to do anything until she stopped bugging me about school. It was that simple! But it never worked. Once the first report card came out, with comments like, "Mark is almost always unprepared with his assignments," "Mark appears lethargic and disinterested," "Mark might do better being in a lower track class," she was up to school for a conference within twenty-four hours. And the outcome was always the same. I could predict the outcome word for word before she came back from the school. It was like a little game I would play with myself. I knew she would come in and yell up to me, "Get down to the kitchen right away."

We would sit at the kitchen table. That was the war room. And she would start in: "I'm up to here (pointing to her throat) with your lack of respect for me and yourself. I'm sick of going down to the school and being humiliated (then why was she going?). It's the same old story—homework and reports not in, poor test grades, cutting classes, appearing half dead to the teachers and on and on. The only good thing they say about you is that you're a perfect gentleman and never cause any trouble. And I'm sick of hearing the same story, that you're a classic underachiever. (She hated hearing that because the therapist she took me to in the ninth grade told my mom that she was the problem and that I would never change until she left my schoolwork to me. Needless to say she pulled me out of therapy the next week.) How are you ever going to survive in the real world? You're a junior already. What college is going to take a student with a C average? You are going to end up in some community college or the army, if they'll take you. I don't know; I throw in the towel. Maybe the therapist was right. It's a lost cause. And to think your IQ is 140. Other kids would give their soul to have your gifts and all you can do is watch TV and eat. Your father and I have worked and saved all our lives to send you to a good college and for what? I'm done. I don't care what happens to your schoolwork. You can graduate in the last decile of your class for all I care. Just remember one thing: you did it to yourself, young man. You can't blame your father or me. From now on it's your life. Don't mention any of this to your father when he comes home. I don't want to burden him with this after he's worked all day. I've got to make dinner. I suggest you go to your room and do some serious thinking about what you want to do with your life."

Wow! Maybe I'd done it. Maybe I've finally done poorly enough to get her to get off my case. Maybe I've won. Wouldn't it be great to have her off my back, not to have to deal with all of this school stuff every day when I came home? Maybe we could have real conversations at the dinner table instead of "how did it go in school?" and "what's for homework tonight?" And maybe we could stop talking about college and who is applying to what school. I hated hearing about all my mother's friends whose kids were getting into Princeton and Dartmouth. I wanted to get to know more about my mother but I couldn't because it was always school, school, school. My dad tried to help out; he could see that her approach was not working with me. But she was too much for him. After a while he would just shut up. My mother always said she was doing what she called this "loving nagging" because she didn't have anyone to help her when she was a kid. She always said she had wanted to go to college but she had no help. I knew I was a big disappointment to her. I wasn't the child she wanted. She never said it but I knew. But she wasn't the mother I wanted, either. The odd couple, for sure. I was leaving home next year, college or no college, and I didn't want to leave home with things like they were. But I didn't think things were going to change. I know my mother. Come Tuesday, she'll be back at her cause, her life's work—nagging me. It always worked that way.

I just hope I never do the same thing with my kids. My mom and I are both trapped in a life about school and neither one of us will give in. I can't and she won't. Or is it that I won't and she can't?

There's No Living Down a Bad Reputation. I can hear the little wimps talking to each other when I come into class: smell the smoke on her, doesn't she know anything about taking care of herself? Sure, I smoke, I drink, and I take some drugs. But what business is it of these little wimps to make fun of me or think they're so healthy? You see, I know what I'm doing. It's not like I'm an alcoholic or a drug addict. I like the taste of beer when I'm having a cigarette. As for grass, I don't do it a lot but it makes me feel really mellow. It's not an everyday thing or something new. I've been smoking and drinking since the sixth grade. I get a kick out of these little nerds hitting on me because I hang out a lot. At least my friends and I don't go overboard like these prissies do every weekend. It's such a joke! A lot of the nerds and jocks that put me down are the same ones who sign the sports pledge not to drink or take drugs while they're on a school team. But you ought to see them at parties on weekends! They're drunk and stoned all over the place—falling down, driving a hundred miles an hour, and vandalizing peoples' lawns and mailboxes. Look at all the torn-up lawns and beer bottles all over the town on Sunday mornings. I can tell you it's not me or my friends pulling that stuff. I mean, if these jocks' mommies and daddies knew what their little babies were doing at the unchaperoned parties, they would die. And these are the same kids who belong to SADD and whose parents are always at those drug and alcohol workshops. In some ways I feel sorry for some of these kids. It's like they're leading a double life. They sign this pledge because the parents and the school put pressure on them to do it. It's like the in thing to do, you know, having a drug-free school or town. That's a laugh. Did you ever see a drug-free school?

Just look at all the parents who booze it up! Then these same kids get thrown into the party world and they can't deal with the pressure. So they break the pledge and feel like liars. How would you feel if they put your picture in the town paper as one of the students who have signed a pledge not to drink and drug and help keep our school a drug-free school, and then you're drinking and drugging all over town? It's sick! They shouldn't have this pledge stuff; it just turns kids into liars. Let's face facts: kids are going to experiment. But these goody kids have to hide it and they go overboard. And for what? So we can have this big lie that our school and town are drug free? These kids don't seem to know any middle ground; like I said, they go overboard. I was at a party last week where this ninth grader drank fifteen—you got me, fifteen—straight shots of vodka and no one stopped her. They were laughing at her, stumbling around and taking her clothes off. She didn't have a clue what was going on. Finally she started vomiting so bad that someone had to call the police. They took her to the hospital and had her stomach pumped. Hell, she could have died. Do you know what it's like for a young kid like that to come back to school on Monday with everyone talking about her? It's sheer terror! It's something she'll never live down. The do-gooders in the PTA will all be buzzing about it and people will knock her parents. No one ever thinks about the poor kid and what she's going through. What a price to pay for one night of craziness! The good thing is that maybe she'll learn her limits and watch out. Better now than later.

You've got to know who you are and what you're doing out there. Thank God I don't buy all of this clean living stuff. The jocks and the nerds have it tough because they're expected to be good, to be smart, to be good athletes—you know, lead the All American life. Believe me, no one expects that of me. I'm just going along and I'll make it. I'll get a good job or go to college. They say there is a college for everyone.

Austerity.   Although it was raining hard the day of the budget vote, the people were turning out in droves, like they were giving something away at the school. Especially the senior citizens—they were coming into the gym to vote in groups of four or five with fire in their eyes. A "NO" vote was written all over them. I was feeling bad because it didn't look good for the school budget or for the sports programs. The senior citizens were out to kill the sports programs. I had heard them talk at the budget meetings about how they were on a fixed income and couldn't afford to pay more taxes. They were out to cut out everything in the program—cafeteria, bus transportation, evening recreation, money for the sports programs, pay for the coaches and firing all the young teachers who were so great. These were the same people who were driving around in new Cadillacs and going on cruises. I couldn't figure out why they were so angry at us kids. They hated us without even knowing us and now they were trying to take away everything in our school that was important to us.

A lot of us kids went to the Board of Education budget meetings and tried to talk about how important sports were to us, how the sports programs kept us off the street and gave us a chance to compete for scholarships. We also talked about how great it was to have young teachers who were fun and alive. But it had done no good. Every time we talked one of the older men or women would shout us down and say they couldn't afford all these "frills" and the school should get back to basics and stop coddling kids. To them "frills" meant the basic stuff—books, computers, buses. It was unbelievable. One guy was really out of control. He kept talking about the "bottom line," restructuring, downsizing, and accountability. He kept saying the school needed a "businessman" who could keep taxes down. All the kids felt like we were on trial, trying to defend the things in the school that were important to us. But we didn't get anywhere. The senior citizens just stampeded everybody and let the board know that if things didn't go their way, the board would be voted out. And they reminded the board that they had the votes. What power did we have? We couldn't vote or put pressure on people. We were just kids.

There was no one supporting us except some teachers and parents who cared about kids and the coaches. We were in the minority. You know, people like these senior citizens are stupid. They criticize kids for hanging out at the deli and drinking beer in the parks, but there is no place for kids to go at night. Just think how many kids will be on the street if they charge to play sports and do away with the evening and summer recreation. They take away everything that's important to kids and then they criticize them for just hanging out and doing nothing. They always tell you that you should get a job. That's a laugh; the only jobs are at McDonald's or Burger King. There's nothing else. Most of us don't even have enough money for a movie; it costs you twenty bucks by the time you buy a ticket and popcorn. I don't drink but it's cheaper to buy a couple of six-packs and get trashed. That's what the kids do who don't play sports. They just get trashed and drive around knocking mailboxes over and giving people lawn jobs.

Sometimes I wonder if anyone really cares what happens to us kids. It seems the adults are out for themselves. They had their education and sports and now they don't want to pay for us. If the budget goes down, I don't know what I'm going to do. My senior year is coming up and I'm a starter on the football, basketball, and baseball teams, but I could never afford the four hundred dollars they say it will cost for each sport. My parents have three kids in high school and one in junior high and we all play sports. They can't afford two or three thousand bucks! I can't ask them for it. Our whole school is going down the tubes and nobody cares.

A lot of kids are thinking about transferring to private school so they don't have to deal with all the cutbacks. Everyone with any money is getting out. There will be nobody left in the school except the poor kids like me, a bunch of old teachers, and the sports banners of the great teams we had before people like that "businessman" started this downsizing and restructuring stuff and ruined our school. I'd like to give that guy and the senior citizens some downsizing and restructuring! There's a lot of hate out there between the kids and the senior citizens. How did it all happen? It wasn't always like this. What went wrong?

Drinking and Drugging: The Need for Relief from It All

Alcohol, drugs, and cigarettes play a big part in the everyday life of high school kids, their parents, and teachers. Some kids get into alcohol for relief from the pressures of school, the need to get it "right"—the right average, college, girlfriend, weight. The booze works; it eases the stress. It's also cheap, plentiful, and easy to get. Teens can find alcohol whenever they want. A case of beer or wine coolers is cheaper than a night at the movies. It's a cheap night out for kids who can't find a job because the senior citizens and laid-off adults are taking all the part-time jobs. Besides, where is a high school kid going to go on a weekend without cash? The recreation programs in the schools are all closed due to budget cuts and most schools have stopped having dances. The schools say they can't afford to pay chaperons any more. That's part of it. But they also don't want to deal with all the problems that arise when a dance is held. As for the churches, they talk a good game on Sunday but they don't offer any recreation or activities for the kids.

The town leaders all over America have given up on the kids. Remember when every town had a recreation program for kids? Remember when churches had activities like the CYO? It's hard to find programs like that today. Plus you have all these mothers and fathers working two jobs to make ends meet. Often there's no one home to supervise the kids and check on things. Kids are on their own. There's no work, no recreation, and little supervision. The kids have time on their hands, nowhere to go, and the booze is, again, cheap, plentiful, and easy to get—a powder keg situation waiting to blow every week-end all over America. So a lot of kids end up spending their weekends partying at a house where the parents are gone or at some mall parking lot or beach. The booze is plentiful. It takes the edge off the pressures of life. But the booze becomes a problem for some kids. They may not die but they end up in rehab, with a DWI or suspended from school after falling down drunk at a dance. The data are in. There's no mystery. High school kids are increasingly using booze and drugs as a way to deal with pressure and pass the time.

In What's Going to Happen Next? and When Your Worst Fears Come True, the girl and the boy are not so lucky. They do not have a wise parent to help them. The parent is the problem. In What's Going to Happen Next? the girl clearly sees her mother's alcohol abuse while her father and brother look the other way, not seeing or hoping that things will get better. She learns a hard but necessary lesson. She has to leave or somehow she will be drawn further into the sickness. She, too, will learn to look the other way unless she leaves. She has to grow up fast and find other "mothers" and "fathers" she can follow— teachers, coaches. They're out there if you look. Sometimes your own mother and father can't give you what you need. It's best to stop knocking on their door and expecting something they can't or won't give you. Trying to stop your mother from drinking by breaking or hiding the whiskey bottle can become a way of life. Yet it takes great strength, all her power, for the child to flee. In an alcoholic home we never know what's going to happen next. All we have is the terror and uncertainty when the first glass is raised. This is the life we know, in spite of its terror. But in leaving there is another terror, a different sort of fear of what is going to happen next. Kids in alcoholic homes need to make a choice. Hopefully they will have a rabbi, a teacher, someone who will help them find a way. It's hard to do it on your own.

In When Your Worst Fears Come True the child looks to the parent who is not an alcoholic for help. He is asking to be saved from an alcoholic father who frightens him, a parent who is capable of humiliating him publicly—with his own friends—at his own graduation. But the mother's only answer is to say, "Can't you see he's getting better?" She looks the other way, not able to hear her son's pain and fear. She leaves him to work it out alone, with no rabbi, no teacher, no help in sight. June can be a long, long month for a kid who worries that his dad will come drunk to graduation. The best time in your life? Not!

In Drunk at the Dance, the child learns a valuable lesson about life with alcohol. You can get hurt. She didn't see it coming. The red light that says "danger ahead" never came on. Like a lot of high school kids, she was moving in the fast lane with no experience. But there is only one way to get experience. A kid has to get out there and learn. Taking it on the chin, taking your lumps as they say, can serve as a great lesson in life. The girl in Drunk at the Dance is better off than the child whose

Too Good Parent won't let her out of the house to do anything. No one can stop kids from drinking. If you make the rules harder, kids will try harder to break them. If you make the rules harder you may drive kids into the very destructive behavior you are trying to have them avoid. Let us not, in our haste to develop drug and alcohol policies in schools, create conditions that lead high school kids into living lives of lies and hypocrisy. Let's keep it simple. Let's be available with the best resources when the call comes. Let's be near the kids so we can help them when they need us, like those in What's Going to Happen Next? and When Your Worst Fears Come True. When kids like the one who is Drunk at the Dance have skilled caring people in their corner, good programs will follow. It doesn't work the other way around.

What's Going to Happen Next?   My mom has a short temper with me. I can feel her anger. She is always accusing me of going through her things. She says, "I know you're going through my things. I want you to stay out of my room." The whole thing started when I was in junior high. My mom had always been, as my father says, a drinker. She would get drunk a lot during the holidays. My father would yell at her and say she was embarrassing all of us. Then she would start to yell back and tell him, "I'm not drunk and no one is going to tell me what to do." They would yell and scream at each other until she finally went to bed. I remember the Christmas when I was in eighth grade in particular. It was the most hurtful time of my life. I remember walking into the kitchen on Christmas and smelling wine on her breath. She was acting so happy and loving that it scared me. I knew she had been drinking and that things would get worse. I made up my mind then that enough was enough. I went into her room and went through her closet until I found three bottles of wine on the top shelf. I put them in a sweater and brought them out back, where I broke them in little pieces in the woods. I vowed that I wasn't going through another holiday with the drinking and fighting. My father and my brother could put up with her drinking if they wanted to but this was it for me.

But I was scared by the time I got back in the house. I didn't want my mother mad at me, especially at Christmas. I knew she would find out that it was me who took the wine. My father was afraid of her and my brother would put his coat on and leave; that was his way. That's why my mother seemed to like him more; he left her alone with her drinks. But she knew it bothered me. I was always telling her to go to AA but she would just look at me with such hate. I often wondered why I persisted. It never worked; things never changed. When I got back in the house I just waited. Right after we opened our presents, it started. She went into her room saying she wanted to try on a new sweater my brother and I had gotten her.

All of a sudden I could hear her knocking things over. Then she came out and started yelling—"Who took my bottles of wine? I know I had three bottles in my closet!" She looked straight at me and said, "Betsy, I know you took it. You have no right to take anything in my room. Now, where is it? What I do is up to me. Besides, it's Christmas. Can't I even have a drink? I'm sick of you telling me to stop drinking, to go to AA, and looking through my things." She looked at my father and my brother. "Your father and brother don't care; they understand. Now where is the wine? You'd better have it because the liquor stores are closed." I looked at my father but his head was down; I knew I couldn't count on him. And my brother had this smile on his face, as if to say, "Now you're going to get yours. Get wise, little girl, and forget about it." He was watching the scene like an outsider, which he was. It was between me and my mother. I was scared but things had to be said.

I said, "I took the wine and broke the bottles. You hear me? I broke them in little pieces and there's no more wine. Maybe, finally, we can have a real Christmas without you drinking and ruining every holiday. Dad won't stop you and Larry runs away. They let you get away with it and nothing changes. You ruin every holiday. I don't care what you think or do to me. I'll find the bottles every time you bring them home and I'll break them."

My mother just stood there, stunned. My father was crying and saying, "You shouldn't talk to your mother that way. Don't you have any respect?" I looked at him and said, "Respect? She ruins our lives and you let it happen. Instead of doing something about it you just ignore it like Larry. Respect? When is she going to respect us and stop ruining our lives? She doesn't respect us or herself or she wouldn't be doing this." My father just looked at me and put his head down; he knew I was speaking the truth. Larry had gone over to my mother, telling her that it was all right. I looked at him and said, "It's not all right. Why do you deny she has a problem? It doesn't help her. And what about your feelings? Doesn't it bother you to see her like this, to have all this screaming? Don't you want to have a normal family?" Larry just glared at me and said, "Leave her alone. You've hurt her enough."

We all just stood there, Larry holding my mother, my mother glaring at me, and my dad—the poor beaten man—had his head down, waiting for it all to end. Finally my mom said she was going to her room and there would be no dinner. As she went, she looked at me and said, "Don't ever, ever come into my room again, young woman." I'll never forget her look until the day I die. That afternoon my dad got us pizza and we watched a movie. Nothing was said and my mom never came out of the room.

I never went into her room again after that day. That didn't stop her, whenever she was hung over, from accusing me of going through her things. By the time I was a senior in high school, she looked like hell. I knew she was drinking more. Each day she would come home from work and hide the bag filled with wine in the bushes in front of our house. I was sure that all the neighbors saw her. After dinner she would go out to empty the garbage and bring the wine back into the house in the trashcan. We all knew what she was doing—me, my dad, Larry— but no one said anything. I knew it was only a matter of time before something happened to my mom. In some way though, I wanted whatever was going to happen to hold off until I went to college. I'd had enough. The whole thing had left me very tight. It showed in my talk; it was very hard for me to make conversation, especially with a guy. It even showed in my walk. I felt like I had a learning disability but I knew it was all the worries I had about my mom. I just wanted to leave; I didn't want to be home when "something" happened to her. I knew she was getting sick. Funny how you can tell something bad is going to happen to someone, especially your parents, even before it happens. Funny thing, Larry must have felt the same way, although we never talked about it. He decided to stay home and go to a community college, even though he was on the honor roll every year and none of his teachers could understand why he didn't go to some big-name school. I could understand; he wanted to be near my mother when "it" happened. And my dad, he got worse, too. He developed an ulcer and a heart problem. It had all been too much for him. I felt bad for him, for

Larry, and even for my mom. But I had to go. I was different; I wasn't part of the family.

Since the day I broke the bottles, things had changed in ways that I couldn't understand. The day I left for college, my mom and dad were supposed to drive me. Just before we left my mom said she was "sick" and couldn't go. I knew she would be drinking before my dad and I left our street. But I had to go.

When Your Worst Fears Come True   I couldn't wait to get away to college. How many kids had been through what I'd been through? My father had been a drunk as long as I could remember and my mother was never home. She was always out shopping or with her friends from work. I had tried to tell her that it made me afraid to be home when my father came home drunk but she always ignored me, saying, "Your father's a lot better now." She didn't seem to care. She had her own life. It was the same routine every weekend. On Friday night my dad would come home drunk from the teachers' parties (my dad was a teacher) and just sit and stare at me. And then he would start in with the same old question, "Why don't you ever talk to me?" It would go on and on. I felt like I was cornered. My mother would come in around seven o'clock with a pizza (we never had a normal dinner) and she would start in, too, saying, "Why don't you talk to him? He's doing better." I could never get up the guts to ask her what she meant by "he's doing better." She sees that he's drunk every weekend, that he's been in rehab twice and never went to meetings after that, that my older sister and brother never come around because he always caused trouble on holidays and at family gatherings, that they never got invited out or went on vacation, that he was going to lose his teaching job if things didn't change. The school had supported him so far but they had warned him that if he kept missing days, they would have to press charges against him. Didn't she see that we had no family life (they slept in separate bedrooms) and the house was falling apart? That's what scared me most, that sometime, somewhere, my mother had stopped caring about my father and me. Maybe it had all been too much for her. Maybe she just couldn't do it any more.

I know when I was in middle school and my dad would come home drunk and embarrass me with my friends, she would yell at him and try to make things OK. I used to hear her pleading with him at night not to "drag the kids into this." I could hear her through the wall, crying as my father slept in his drunken stupor. In high school I stopped inviting people over. My friends knew the story and understood. I guess I stopped trying, too.

So it's graduation time, June 23, and the other kids have their plans together. For me it's one day at a time. If my dad gets fired, there go my college plans, so I'm walking on eggshells. My mom says not to worry, that things will be fine, but I can see the fear in her eyes. I wonder what will happen to them when I'm gone. Will she get a divorce? She doesn't say, but I can tell something is coming. I can't think too much about that, though, because I've got graduation to get through. For the past year I've had this recurring nightmare that my father comes to graduation drunk and starts yelling "Why don't you talk to me?" over and over. In the dream I yell at my mom, "Stop him, stop him, he's ruining my graduation." And she says, quietly, "He's getting better. Can't you see?" I hope my worst fears don't come true.

Drunk at the Dance   I hadn't planned on getting drunk; it just happened. Karen had asked me to come over to her house before the dance for a couple of beers, just enough to get ourselves "feeling good" after another boring week at school. I told my mother that we were going to the mall to shop before the dance and I would be home at my curfew, twelve o'clock. She believed me. She didn't like Karen—she said there was something about her that made her uneasy. But she said I could go as long as I promised her that I wouldn't drink or take drugs. She said that she had heard that a lot of kids got high before they went to the dance and she didn't want me getting mixed up in that scene. I didn't want to lie to my mother but what was wrong with drinking a few beers on a Friday night? After all, my parents had their wine. I liked the "buzz" it gave me. The beer made me laugh easier and forget all the stuff that was going on in school. I was in the honors program at school and they never let up on the work. It was pressure, pressure, pressure all week and more work on the weekend. I needed some relief somewhere. Besides, I had been drinking since the sixth grade and I knew how to handle it. Some kids went crazy but I always stopped before I got out of control. If my mother knew I had been drinking since the sixth grade, she would have dropped dead. She was always saying, "This is not going to happen to my little girl. You're not hanging out with those kids who go to the beach and have keg parties. You're a bright girl with a future ahead of you." If she only knew.

When I got to Karen's house, the party was already going strong. Her older brother, who was a senior, had bought us a case of beer and a couple of quarts of vodka. He was there with some of his friends to "laugh at the ninth graders trying to party." Karen's mother worked until ten o'clock, so we had plenty of time to hang out before the dance started at eight. Karen's brother started making vodka and orange juice but I told him I just wanted a few beers. The vodka stuff scared me. I had seen what it did to other kids. But he kept pushing the stuff and saying that "the ninth graders can't drink with big boys." Finally I gave in and had a few. All I remember was that it was such a great feeling. It gave me more of a rush than the beer. We started dancing and turning the music up. I kept thinking I should have tried this stuff before. And I liked hanging out with these older guys. None of the kids in my grade did this stuff on Friday afternoon. It was so much fun, dancing and dancing. I remember Karen's brother saying that I was a real party girl.

But that's all I remember. I don't remember going to the dance or dancing when I was there. They say I blacked out. All I remember is falling down in the bathroom and barfing all over myself. I couldn't even get up. Karen tried to help me but I couldn't move. Then I saw the school principal come in. He and another teacher helped carry me to his office. I was so sick and embarrassed; there was barf all over my clothes. I stunk to high heaven. And I was frightened. I couldn't remember anything about the dance. What had I done? Had I made a fool out of myself? And what had I done at Karen's house? The principal said he had to call my parents and have them pick me up. He also said I would be suspended for three days and have to be evaluated by the psychologist before I was allowed back in school. It was a school rule, he said. I couldn't believe this was happening to me. Everyone in school would know what I did. I was so embarrassed.

Then my mother and father showed up. They had dazed looks on their faces. My mother said, "What happened? How could you do this to yourself and to us? We'll be the talk of the town. Everyone will think we're lousy parents." My dad just said, "Do you have a coat? Let's go." The principal told my parents about the suspension and the evaluation. My dad asked what the evaluation was for. The principal said the school had to determine if I had an alcohol problem and needed counseling. This was all happening because I went to Karen's house. If only I had gone home. I didn't have an alcohol problem, did I?

On the way home no one said anything. When I got home my mother told me to take a shower and go to bed. She said we would talk in the morning. From my bed I could hear my mother crying and my father yelling at her that she was too easy on me and from now on he was going to take charge. "She's going to be grounded for a long time. No daughter of mine is going to act like a tramp in front of the whole school. And she's never going near that Karen again. I knew she was trouble from the beginning; I told you that, remember? Her mother is never home to supervise those kids. We're both dumb for not seeing this coming. Where were our heads?" My mother had trusted me and I had let her down big time. I felt so dirty. But it wasn't Karen's fault. I had done it to myself. Somehow I was going to have to get through the next week. I knew I wasn't an alcoholic but why had I done this to myself, let myself get carried away? Was there something wrong with me? I didn't want the morning to come. I knew my parents would want to "talk" with me. All I could tell them was that I wouldn't do this again. I had learned my lesson. But would they believe me? I had never been caught doing anything "bad" in school before or suspended. How had I let myself down so much? It wasn't going to happen again.

Death: You Know You're Growing Up When People Start to Die

Death is a stranger to many high school kids until it comes, often unexpectedly, often as a surprise. When you talk to adolescents about death, you find that many of them have never gone to a wake, a funeral, or seen a dead person. As children they are often shielded from death, from the smell of the funeral home, the closing of the casket, the lowering of the casket at the cemetery.

In today's culture there are few adults who speak to high school kids about the mystery of death. It's easier to talk about college, proms, sports. Kids live in a world of "what's going to happen next," a world of tomorrows that doesn't speak of death. Is there a life hereafter? Is there a heaven? A hell? What about cremation? Many questions go unanswered for kids. Many fears about death go unspoken. So when death intrudes—a parent, a teacher, a classmate dies—most kids are unprepared for an event that will visit them again and again throughout their lives. They think life isn't supposed to be this way, that somehow the death of their parent, teacher, friend, is an anomaly. But death is not an anomaly; it's all around. The wise mother, father, older brother, rabbi, or teacher prepares the child for death and loss they know will come. This work, this teaching, is most important in the readiness of the child for living, as important as reading, writing, or class rank.

In How Can I Wish My Father Dead? the child sees and hears the agony of his father as he slowly dies. He wants his father to be better, to live, but it doesn't happen. He wants his mother spared the everyday trauma of caring for a dying husband. Every night he hears the sounds of his father's struggle to breathe, listening to hear if there will be a "next breath." He doesn't want his father dead and yet he does. He wants the man, the wife, himself, free of the terrible illness. But, he wonders, "How can I wish my father dead?" It's an awful thing to think, and an awful thing to say. Death lingers around too long sometimes. Will it be tomorrow or the next day? For a high school kid, the wait can be an eternity.

In How Can God Allow These Things to Happen? the religious child can't square a "loving God" with a God who allows a favorite teacher to die. He looks for answers from his minister and teachers but there are none. Yet other kids look to him for answers. They know he is religious, that he prays. They think he knows about death. They want him to help them, to take away their pain, to give them clarity. But he is too full of grief to help others. He is one of them. He wishes they would leave him alone just to be, just to cry.

Trying to Commit Suicide Where I'm Safe is a story about near-death. The boy attempts suicide but does it in a place where he is sure to get help, to be rescued. Is it a suicide attempt or a cry for help? The diagnosis, the reasons, the "whys" don't count here. The "whys"— why he did it, why no one saw it coming, why he didn't get help—can cloud the air and miss the real message that the boy has a part of him that wants to live. Death has not won out here. High school kids need to learn that a time might come when they are like this suicidal boy. Living is difficult. There are times when we all want our lives to end. Kids need to know where they can go to save themselves, safe places where their pain will be seen, places where they will be looked after until they are ready to face life again. Near-deaths are all around high school kids and often go unnoticed—a car accident, an alcoholic binge, a drug overdose, a starvation diet. The suicidal boy's act is clear but done in a safe place. How many other near-deaths among high school kids are not so clear and are not carried out in a safe place? How many "accidental" deaths among high school kids are not accidental? Better to fall where you can get help.

In The Bus Stop, the child can never follow in the footsteps of the older brother who died a sudden death in high school. He remembers the day of the death—the police, his parents' reactions; he remembers the emptiness after the incident. The death leaves him paralyzed, not physically but emotionally. He is dead, too, in the sense that he cannot act. An overpowering force lays him out but he doesn't understand it. A death in the family leaves us all off course, sometimes for many years. Sometimes kids need help to figure out what the death of a brother or sister means. They often wonder if a brother or sister dies, can they be next? Death is no simple visitor. It always leaves its mark somewhere on the living. Sometimes, as with the boy in The Bus Stop, we can't fight back after a death. It takes time and support. Understanding that "when God takes you away to heaven you can never come back" is not so easy.

How Can I Wish My Father Dead?   I could hear my dad struggling to breathe. Each breath came so hard, with so much pain. My mom had made the living room into a bedroom for him so he didn't have to walk up and down the stairs. My room was upstairs on the other side of the house, but I could still hear his tormented breathing. There was no getting away from it, especially at night when the house was quiet. I wanted it to stop. I wanted him to either die or get better. It had gone on too long. We all knew he was dying; the doctors had said last year that it was only a matter of time. My dad had emphysema for years. He had chain-smoked himself to death. We had all tried to warn him but he wouldn't listen. He had been smoking since he was a kid. He couldn't, wouldn't, change. My mom and I tried to get him to go to a smoking program or to go cold turkey but he fought us all the way. It was as if we all knew, even my dad, that he had chosen this way to die and that was that. I even went through a time when I would hide his cigarettes or flush them down the toilet, like a kid trying to hide the booze from his alcoholic father. But that didn't work. It only made him mad. He would yell at me and tell me to stay out of his business. I would get frightened every time he lit up; my heart would start pounding and my hands would shake. When I was in elementary school I would get mad at my mom for not stopping him. Now that I'm in high school, I realize she couldn't do anything about it. It was just the way it was. The only thing that was sure in my life was the realization that one day I would get a call at school telling me, "Your father has died," or that I would come home and find the police car and priest there. Over and over in my mind I pictured the priest saying, "He's gone. It's for the best." I would cry and cry as I thought about this picture. Cry and cry as I knew I would when that day finally came.

Sometimes I would try to think how it would be with my dad gone. I wanted my mom to take some of the insurance money and buy herself some new clothes, get a hairdo, and maybe even go on a vacation to Florida or the Bahamas. Maybe we could sell the house and get a nice condo. My dad had been sick so long that our house was falling apart. I tried to do what I could but it was too much. It would be nice to have a new place and not see and hear him so sick. But then I would feel guilty. How could I want my own father to die, the guy who had played with me, taken me to ball games, and been there for me all my life; how could I even think these thoughts? I was so confused. I didn't want him to suffer any more but how could I wish him dead? But with each day, I wanted all of us, my dad, my mom, and me, to suffer less. I wanted to lead a normal life like all the other kids. I wanted to go to school without worrying what would happen when I came home. I wanted to have friends over to the house and laugh again. Since my dad had gotten sick, I hadn't had anyone over. My mom said it was too hard. When my dad first got real sick, all the kids would ask how he was. But now they didn't say anything. They just waited, like me, until that day came.

Sometimes I found myself worrying that my mom would meet someone new and get married again. She was still young. But I didn't want another man taking my dad's place. I wanted her to be happy but the thought of her sleeping with another man scared me.

When death finally comes, it's not like you think it's going to be.

My dad's tormented breathing had become a part of the sounds of the night. It was like living near a railroad track. The sound of his breathing, like the sound of trains, was always there. It was June 14 and I was in my room doing a prep test for the SAT exam when the house suddenly became quiet. I looked at the clock. It was 10:20 P.M. I'll never forget the date and time. I ran downstairs and my mom was sitting on the bed holding my father in her arms. She was crying so hard that her face and nightgown were all wet. She looked at me and said, "It's over, Matt. He died at peace and he told me to tell you he loves you. Come and sit with him before we call the police. He's at peace now. Maybe we can be at peace now, too. Come and sit down and say good-bye before we do what has to be done." I sat down with my mom and we both held my father. I thought I would be terrified of this moment, but I was calm. My dad had such a peaceful look. My mom and I sat there crying. It had been such a long battle but it was over at last. After awhile my mom asked me to call the police, the priest, and the funeral home, so she could spend these last minutes with "her guy."

And so it ended. My mom had wanted my dad to have, as she said, "a good send-off," so he was waked for two days. All the kids and teachers came from the school and a lot of friends from my dad's job. It was hard for me and my mom because the person in the casket didn't look like my dad. His hair had a reddish tint and his face was pasty. It made me angry that the funeral people had made him look so different. But my mom said, "Your dad is in heaven now. That's not him; he's at peace. We have the tough time now. We have to get through this." And we got through it. The funeral Mass was beautiful, with the priest recalling how much my dad had given to other people. It was as if he had really known him. The funny thing is that my dad never went to church, although he made sure that everyone else did. The trip to the cemetery was the toughest part. My mom really fell apart as they lowered the casket into the ground. She grabbed my hand and cried, "You're the man now."

It's been over a year since my dad's death. It's hard for me to believe that so much has changed in a year. We sold the house and now have a neat condo. My friends are over all the time. My mom has a boyfriend, Al, whom she met at Parents Without Partners. The guy seems OK but I hate him hanging around all the time. But she seems happy with the guy and he treats her well. They go out to dinner and the movies a lot and they're planning a cruise for the fall. So I'll have to live with it. At least she'll have someone to keep her company when I leave. I don't like the idea of him coming to graduation, but that's the way it is. At least my mom won't be there alone. I miss my dad, but I know he is at peace. Finally.

How Can God Allow These Things to Happen?   I believe in God and I'm not ashamed of it. Religion has always been a big part of my life. We pray each night as a family and try to follow the Bible in our everyday life. Going to church on Sunday is a big event. We usually spend most of Sunday morning there. My pastor is so understanding; he's always helping someone out. When he speaks about all this emphasis on material things, sexuality, or trying to find peace through alcohol and drugs, I feel like he's talking to me. I try to talk to some of the other kids at our high school about the peace I feel, but they laugh at me. They call me "Pastor Bob" and every time some religious issue comes up in class, they say, "Let's hear what Pastor Bob has to say about this." But it doesn't bother me. I think a lot of these kids are envious of my beliefs and how my church helps me. They know I don't go to parties or hang out. Sometimes in class kids will say, "I'd like to be like you, you know, not go to parties. I'm sick of the whole scene. How do you do it? Every week I plan on staying home and being sober but when the phone calls come on Friday night, I can't say no. How do you just stay home all weekend? How can you be so good? Doesn't anything get to you or bother you?" You see, they have the whole thing wrong, like I'm a saint or some total do-gooder. A lot of things about God and life do bother me. Believing what I believe is sometimes very hard. There's so much evil and terrible things happening that I can't understand how God can allow these things to go on.

Like when Mr. Casey, one of my favorite teachers, died this year. Here was a man who was literally loved by every student he had. He was a legend. When kids came back from college over the holidays, he was "the" teacher they went to see. Each year he would write over a hundred college recommendations and each letter was special. He treated each kid with respect and dignity. There was no fooling around or putting people down in his class. Everyone, even the dirt bags, got into the discussions and no one was ever late. And he was always chaperoning the dances or coaching a team when no other teacher would do it. And then one day he wasn't in school. He came back the next day and said he had some "medical problems" and he would be out for a while. A month later he was back but he looked terrible; his stomach was all bloated and he looked like an old man. I couldn't believe it was the same man. I used to pray for him every night but he just got worse. Just after Christmas vacation, he told us that he was taking a leave but he would be back next year. He died in March.

It was so sad. The church was filled with crying kids and teachers. They even had all the counselors and a psychologist there to help the kids. It made me so sad and angry. How could God take such a good person away from the kids who needed him? I'll never, never understand. It was such a waste. After Mr. Casey died, I tried talking to my pastor about how I felt. I asked him how God, who is supposed to be so loving, could take away people who were really needed. How was I expected to pray and believe in a God who would do that? I felt that all my beliefs were crumbling inside me. He said that most of life is dealing with sadness—death, divorce, illness, all kinds of losses. He said that the happy days are few and that our reward would be in heaven. That's the way life is and to expect anything different would be to invite despair.

I still felt such a loss! And to make matters worse, a lot of the kids in school came up to me the week after Mr. Casey's funeral and asked if I would talk with them about how they could handle losing such a good friend and teacher. Even the counselors asked me to run some support groups to help the kids get through this. But who was going to help me? Again, they had it wrong. I wasn't a saint! I was in as much pain as everyone else. Did they really think that my religious beliefs took away all the pain? Why were they making me into some kind of a savior? How could I help them when I was having so much trouble myself? I wish I had never talked about my religion in school. If I hadn't, then people would be leaving me alone now. And that's what I wanted right then, to be left alone to cry, left alone to be a kid who lost a close, close friend and teacher. I didn't want to be a savior, just a sad, confused kid.

Trying to Commit Suicide Where I'm Safe.   We never eat together as a family. I don't remember ever sitting down for a "family" meal.

You just go to the fridge and get something when you want it or go up to the deli or McDonald's; that's the way it's always been. That's why I'm out of the house all the time. My friends are my family. The psychiatrist said that's why I tried to commit suicide at school. She said that I felt someone would get me help if I tried suicide there. If I tried it at home there wouldn't have been anyone to save me, I would have just died. It's funny, I didn't think of it that way, you know—rationally. I was just so sick of everything. I had been through the whole drinking and drugging thing and it had worn me out. I guess I started drinking when I was in the fifth or sixth grade. Even then I had given up on school. I was smart in elementary school; they said I was gifted and talented. But by the time I got to middle school, I decided I didn't want to work any more. My mom always made excuses for me; when I wouldn't go to school she would call up and tell them I was sick. I hated the pressure on me to do well even then. It was like when I started playing the piano. I was really good at it but as soon as I got good, my mother was always asking me to play for relatives and neighbors. Then she let the people know at school and they had me playing in the school band. I just couldn't do it. In the sixth and seventh grades I started hanging out with people who drank and smoked dope. That lasted right up to my junior year in high school. We would sit around every weekend at somebody's house and get stoned. My dad used to get upset when I didn't come home. I always told my mom I was sleeping over at a friend's house. She bought my reason every time. But I think my dad knew what was going on. On Sunday night he always said to me, "You look like hell. You sure you're not drinking? I never see you doing any homework." My mom would always say to him, "Honey, we have to trust him. We brought him up to make good decisions; I'm sure he's doing the right thing." And that was it. That's the way our family worked. No one looked too deep into anything. As long as I wasn't coming home stoned or failing completely in school, things went along. I guess everyone was trying to keep the lid on all the crap; as long as there were no arguments, life could go on.

But by the time I got to high school, I had gotten more depressed. The booze and smoking, plus not eating anything but pizza, was taking its toll on me. The only way I could sleep was to knock myself out with booze. I would black out every weekend. By Monday morning I couldn't remember half of what I did. Kids would come up to me in school on Monday and tell me all this crap about vandalizing and fighting. I'd answer them with a laugh, but I didn't remember any of it. For the first time in my life, it scared me. When I got to be a tenth grader things really got out of hand. I woke up one Monday morning and found deep cuts all over my arms. I thought I must have been in a fight but I couldn't remember anything. When I got to school I asked some of my friends what had happened. They looked at me kind of weird and said, "You did that to yourself. We couldn't stop you. You just took out your knife and started cutting yourself. We finally got the knife away from you and you went to sleep. There was blood all over Kevin's mother's new sofa; when she came home she was really pissed. Don't you remember? You've got to get yourself some help. We can't be responsible for you when you're like that." But I didn't know what to do. If I told my parents they would be bonkers. I didn't need them in my life. It was too late for them to start playing daddy and mommy. And I couldn't tell the school. They would say I needed counseling and I didn't want any shrink.

So I kept drinking and doping and cutting myself. I would cut myself at home—my arms, my legs, places where no one could see it. My mom had arranged a medical excuse for gym for me so I didn't have to worry about anyone finding out. It was horrible but I couldn't stop. By my junior year I was worn out. I went to school every day but I was doing nothing. The school didn't know what to do with me. I had failed so many courses that I was running out of possibilities. The counselor called me in and suggested that I might like to take a vocational course at the tech center. But I didn't want to leave my friends. They were all I had. But even my friends were beginning to dump me. I was no fun. All I was doing every weekend was getting stoned in the corner; no one talked to me and I didn't talk to anyone. They just left me alone.

Then one day, I don't know what happened, I had just had enough. I went into my mother's bathroom before school and swallowed a whole bottle of tranquilizers. Was I trying to kill myself? I don't know. I just wanted it all to stop, to get off the crazy train ride I was on. I went to school and after homeroom went to the nurse's office and just sat in the corner. I remember looking at the clock: it was first period, 7:45. That's all I remember. When I woke up I was in some hospital.

Actually it was a psychiatric ward. My mother and father were there looking at me. They both were crying and holding my hands. My dad said, "It's all right, we understand. The psychiatrist says you're going to be OK. They want you to go into a rehab program for thirty days. You'll be able to go to school there. You were lucky you sat in the nurse's office; as soon as you passed out, they called the ambulance. The psychiatrist said you weren't trying to kill yourself but just wanted help. Thank God. Now go back to sleep; we'll be here." I could see him hug my mother. I was tired.

The Bus Stop.   The graduation ceremony was almost over. The valedictorian was going on and on. She would have to stop soon. I was so happy. Here I was graduating in the top percentage of my class and going on to the Air Force Academy to become a pilot. I could see my parents beaming with happiness as they sat in the audience. They were so proud of me. Who would have thought that I would be so successful after all the trouble I had in elementary school? While the speech went on and on, I thought about those awful days, particularly in the fourth grade, and how far I'd come. It was the most awful time of my life.

"It," that scary feeling, started when I was going into the fourth grade. I was ten years old. Up to that time I never liked school but I went. I hardly said anything. I was smaller than the other kids and afraid to say very much. I just sat there most of the time and did what I had to do to get through. Because I was so small and scared, I was an easy target. I must have had "that look" that some kids have that says you can do anything to them and they won't fight back. They'll just take all the crap that you give them. That was me. I was always getting beat up on the playground or on the bus. I hated walking to the bus stop in the morning. The other kids were always calling me names, like "runt," and taking my lunch. On the bus I sat up front by the driver but he just let the kids carry on. I was always getting hit in the back of the head by a flying book or a rock. I had no one to help me or stick up for me. Other kids had older brothers who would defend them but my brother got killed in a car accident when I was in third grade.

So each morning I went to the bus stop as late as I could. My mom would always ask, "What's wrong with you? Don't you like school?" I didn't know how to tell her what was happening. What could I say, that I was a chicken and a coward? I really felt that way. I didn't know how to fight back. My dad had always said, "Fighting will get you nowhere. Only bullies fight." When I got to school it was worse than the bus ride. Someone was always making fun of me or pushing me down. Even the littlest wimp would take me on. Each day was World War II. I prayed for the weekends or a snow day. When I got home I stayed in my room and watched TV. I didn't have any friends; no one ever called me. My mom tried to get me to go out or invite someone over, but I had no one to call. I stayed in my room and fantasized about getting stronger and beating up all those kids who were giving me such a hard time. I hated them with such a passion. I vowed that I would learn how to fight and get even some day. I knew my dad wouldn't agree but he didn't understand the beating I was taking. I wanted to be on the other side for a change, making those kids squirm and shake. I wanted to see the girls laughing at them and calling them chickens and runts.

But something happened in fourth grade that changed everything. When September came and school was starting, I couldn't get out of bed to get to school. I knew by the time I got to the bus stop that I would be so scared that I would run home. I didn't know what it was, this awful feeling that came over me. It had never happened before, even though I had all that trouble at the bus stop. I felt like I was going to faint; my legs were like jelly and the sweat poured out of me. My mother didn't know what to do with me. She tried everything! At first she tried walking with me to the bus stop. The other kids never said anything, but I could see them laughing to themselves and whispering "Momma's boy" and, "Mom's got to take little baby to the bus stop." But when I saw the bus coming I would panic and start screaming that I wasn't going. All the other kids looked at me like I was a lunatic. They would laugh and make faces at me when the bus pulled away. It was like a show every morning. Up to that time, the kids thought I was just a chicken but now they thought I was really crazy, disturbed. They didn't understand how frightened I was.

Then my dad took the tough route. If I didn't get on the bus, I wouldn't be allowed to go out and I couldn't have any friends over to the house. He didn't understand how frightened I was either. I still refused to go. I just couldn't do it; I was paralyzed. Finally my mother took me to a pediatrician but she couldn't find anything wrong with me; I was physically a healthy kid. She suggested to my mom that I should see a child psychologist. By now it was mid-October and I hadn't even been in school. My mom would call the school each day and tell them she couldn't get me there. They even sent a social worker to talk with her. She told my mom that I had "school phobia" and I should "see someone."

So I went to see this psychologist. I'll never forget it. This guy had a big beard and his office was really dark; he had one light in the corner. I didn't like him at first. I just sat there while he asked me all these questions about school and home. He asked me a lot about my brother's death. How did it happen? Where was I when I found out? How did my parents react? What was the funeral like? At first I hated all the questions and just sat there. But he was a funny guy and would always joke about how much he hated school. He said he knew how hard it must have been for me to put up with all the school stuff and then, on top of all that, have my brother die. After a while I started to talk. I believed the guy really understood how scared I felt. He asked me to talk about the day my brother died. I told him I heard a police siren and an ambulance around three o'clock. It sounded close by. About an hour later a police car pulled up in front of my house and two cops got out and knocked on our door. I could see some of the neighbors out on the street. The cops asked if my parents were home but I said they were working. Just then my mom pulled up in her car and came running into the house shouting, "What is it?" The cops told her to sit down, that my brother had just been hit by a car while walking home from school and he was dead. It was awful, my mom crying; I just stood there. My brother had been in high school and great at sports and academics. I always wanted to be like him but I was just the opposite, lousy at sports and lousy at school. My dad always said he never gave them a problem. I always felt bad when he said that because I had given them lots of problems. So I told the psychologist the whole thing, about the funeral, my parents being so depressed. I told him I didn't know what to feel. I hadn't been that close to my brother. He used to call me the same names the other kids did: "You're a little wimp to let those kids push you around like that. Don't you have any balls? I don't blame them for letting you have it, you act so spineless." I could never tell my brother how frightened I was or ask for his help. He wouldn't have understood, being the jock he was. He wasn't the brother I needed. I wanted to cry for my brother but I couldn't.

After I had been meeting with the psychologist for a month, he told me he wanted to have a meeting with me and my parents. At that meeting he told them he felt I was a normal kid but had a traumatic experience with school and my brother. My brother's death had been the final straw and it had left me helpless. He said I was worried that something was going to happen to me; that's why I had such trouble taking the school bus. He felt that I was afraid I would never come home. When my brother died on the way home from school, it only confirmed my feelings that something bad—even dying—could happen to me, too. He suggested that I keep coming to counseling but that I also start karate and self-defense so that I could learn how to defend myself and not be everyone's victim. Plus it would be a good way for me to meet other kids. I was isolating myself and that was no good. Finally, he said that I had to take the bus. I had to deal with things. He understood how hard it would be for me to go back to school now; it was November already but I had to do it. It was time. He would meet with me each week and he would be there to help me. "I'll teach you how to fight back and to fit in. I'll teach you the words. All I want you to do now is to get on the bus and get to school. That's a lot to do." So I started back. The first day the kids didn't say anything. They just looked surprised to see me. On the bus no one bothered me. I didn't feel scared or like I was going to faint any more. I didn't know what would happen in school but right now I was OK. I could hardly wait to tell "my" psychologist about it when I saw him. I finally had someone to talk to.

The valedictorian had finished at last and the principal was starting to call out the diplomas. I felt lucky. Somehow I had been saved. I wondered what would have happened to me if I hadn't gone to the psychologist. He had taught me "the words," how to defend myself, make friends, get my schoolwork in order, and grieve for my brother. I saw him for four years. His last words were, "This door is always open but remember, you've handled a lot of things for a young kid. There will always be problems. Remember, you have the resources to deal with things." Sometimes I go by my old bus stop and see some kid standing all alone or getting picked on by a gang. I want to stop and help him, tell him to keep going and not give up, fight that fear, don't run home.

But I don't. He'll have to learn it on his own. I just feel so bad that young kids have to go through so much pain to grow up. Some make it, others don't. I was one of the lucky ones.

Divorce and Other Endings Àre Never Simple for Kids

We live with loss. For high school kids there are the everyday losses—failed grades, lost friendships, broken romances, the big game not won. These losses hurt, sting, but they can live with them. But divorce, that's a different matter. It takes so long to get over a divorce, sometimes years. Even if things between parents have been chaotic for years, the final splitting apart comes with a great price for kids. Moving out of the home they have known for years, having less money, new romances in the parents' lives, changing schools, and lawyers making charges and counter-charges all take their toll. Hidden secrets come out—affairs, abuse, addiction—things often not known to the child suddenly become public. The child of divorce begins to see his or her parents in new, often hostile ways. The child wonders why they have done this. With all the changes of addresses, with all the new schools, with all the unpaid bills, the child wonders if there is any end in sight. Is this the life they will live? Keeping going, keeping balanced, is difficult. Things are different, simple things, like changing their address at school, being asked who is the "custodial parent," making sure that both parents see their report cards, being asked to participate in groups for "children of divorce." Life is different; people know about their situation. Teachers, psychologists, social workers want to help, even if the child doesn't want their help. It's their job to help.

In The Knock on the Door Could Be for You, the child doesn't want help. She doesn't want everyone—the school, the neighbors, the kids—to know about her father's leaving. She is having a tough enough time sorting it all out herself. She wants, even needs, anonymity, at least for a while. But the school wants to help. The psychologist knocks on the classroom door and summons the girl of divorce to come for help. There is no escape for the child. Her story is public. She is forevermore known in the school as a "child of divorce." When teachers speak her name it will always include the data that her parents are divorced. She has a label, a sign, that is known to all, like an ex-prisoner who is always associated with past crimes. So she goes along with the help just as she has gone along with the divorce—she has no choice. If she did, she would sit at home and cry, be sad that such a terrible thing has happened to her, and let nature take its time to heal her. Things, especially divorces, don't get solved overnight. She would seek help when she was ready. But she feels she has no choice, no say in the matter. The knock on the door is for her. She must go. She is a child. But she learns not to tell the school too much. She learns that private stories, her story, can spread even when people say, "What you say here is private and no one outside this room will know." Be careful, child, when the knock on the door is for you.

The Wedding is a hopeful story, a story that begins with violence and abuse for a father and his children and ends with the hope of a new marriage and peace at last. Sometimes in divorce, violence and abuse know no limits. Everyone is fair game for attack, even the children. The genie is out of the bottle. The rules of fair play are off. It's each man, each woman, each child for himself or herself. It's a whirling blade that can chop them up. The police, the priest, can't help. The children and the father run for shelter from the abusive wife and mother. It's hard for the new family—moving, nurturing, working, supervising, sharing. Every act, every move, is about survival. Daily routines—laundry, meals, homework—are patched together. Phone calls become only one more source of trouble: bill collectors, lawyers, social services, threats from the former spouse. School becomes something to get through, not important when your whole life is under attack. They wonder if it will ever end. But the man, the father, meets a woman who is "right"—she wants to be his wife, mother his children. After all the years of running, of violence, the kids and the father can rest. Was this good news, this marriage, merely luck, being in the right place at the right time? Or was it, as the priest said at the wedding, divine intervention, God's will? Must we go through these tough times to find the "white flowers"?

In My Father Left Home When I Was Born, the child is abandoned by his father at birth. The child longs to see his father, just once, so he can deliver the long-awaited beating he feels his father deserves. Life is a nightmare for the child in elementary school. He seems to be at the top of everyone's hit list. Even at home he is bullied by an abusive uncle. He has that look of being fair game for anyone's attack. Every school has its designated "victim." He had no father to show him the ways of the world, how to defend himself, how to find his place. But events change his life. He gets a fresh start. Hang on, abandoned child, one day the losses may stop.

The Knock on the Door Could Be for You.   I remember the day too well. I've tried to forget but I hear the voices as if it were today. I can still hear my mother and father fighting outside the house and then my father driving up the street. My mother.came in the house crying and told me that they were separating but things would be all right. She went to her room and cried all night. I remember it so well because it was my birthday. I was thirteen and in the seventh grade. The family never did celebrate that birthday. When my mother came out of her room she promised that she would make it up to me, but how can you make up for such hurt? You can't. The next day I went to school hoping that no one would know. After all, my parents never did fight real loud. Maybe no one knew. But word travels fast. After recess, my teacher asked if everything was all right and said that she was there for me if I needed to talk. She had that look; you know what I mean, that she knew about the separation. Then some strange lady came into the classroom and asked my teacher if she could talk with "Eve." She motioned to me (how did she know who I was?) and took me outside. There she told me she was Mrs. Jenkins, the school psychologist, and she wanted me to come to a group for "children of divorce." I was in tears. How had the school found out and why was this woman after me to join some group? Now all the kids would know that I was some weirdo and everyone would know my business. I had nowhere to hide. I followed Mrs. Jenkins through the school, trying to avoid the eyes of all the kids and teachers who now knew that I was different. You see, I had no choice. I realized at that moment, even at that young age, that I had become one of their "cases," where my story would be written up in files and passed along from grade to grade. I was screwed by my parents and now, within twenty-four hours, I was being screwed by the school. No adult can ever realize the terror a kid goes through when there's a knock on your classroom door and the knock is for you. The terror only gets worse when you are taken to some office and some adult says, "Whatever you say stays here." You know you're in trouble when they say that to you. One thing is certain: your story will get passed around the school. Privacy in schools is hard to keep and being "helped" can sometimes bring great harm to a kid.

But I went along, even though I had a passing thought to run out the closest exit. What good would that do? My mother would only bring me back and reprimand me for being disobedient. Then I would be in trouble with her and they probably would have to have a meeting with the principal and with my dad. Then everyone would know for sure and my file would be placed right at the front of the files of "kids at most risk." My parents had not even been separated for forty-eight hours and I was sure the school thought I needed counseling. God, I hated my parents for doing this to me!

In the counseling room, Mrs. Jenkins introduced me to the other kids (there were about seven other kids all looking like they would like to be out of there) and said, "Eve's parents have just separated and her mother called me to see if I could help Eve through this traumatic time. I suggested that Eve join our group and share her pain with ours." So that was it! My mother had called the school without even telling me and let our story be spread all over the school and community. Before tomorrow, everyone would know. Things weren't bad enough with my father leaving, but now I was a "child of divorce," a "kid at risk." I felt like someone on the four o'clock TV show. Then Mrs. Jenkins looked at me and asked, "Would you like to join the group, Eve?" I remember wondering what the hell I was supposed to say. I felt like saying, "My name is not Eve, my name is Rachel. You've made a mistake; can I go now?" But then they would really think I was nuts and put my folder in a file by itself. Then I thought I could pretend that I was sick and somehow go on home tutoring for the year and not face this woman and the kids. I knew that there was no escape. Mrs. Jenkins' job depended on people like me so she wasn't going to let me off easy. If I said that I didn't want to join the group, they would label me as, how do they say it, a resistant child. They had me. So I joined the group and just never said much. I just prayed for June and to be sick on group day. When Mrs. Jenkins pressed me for information on how I felt, I would tell her that things were getting better at home. It seemed to work. Most of the kids said they didn't want to be in the group but went because they couldn't figure out how to get out of it. What rights do kids have?

So I made it to June. My father and mother got back together for a while, but I knew it wouldn't last. Sometimes kids know more about their parents' marriage than the parents do. At least it got me out of group for a while. They had the final split-up when I was a junior in high school. The big "D," the divorce, had finally happened. When it happened my mother played the "my daughter needs support" card again. Good intentions can hurt a kid. The day of the big "D" decision, I was in chemistry class. I knew my parents' marriage was over. I just wanted to graduate and get to college. Then there was a knock on the door. I could see Dr. Melnick, the assistant principal. I knew the knock was for me. He motioned to me and asked if he could talk to me for a minute. He brought me to his office and after some small talk about my grades, he said, "Your mother called and she said she and your father have decided to get a divorce. She wanted me to offer you some support." It was so strange. I felt like I was back in the seventh grade and Mrs. Jenkins was knocking on the door. God, I thought, maybe this whole thing is finally over and I won't be called into these offices any more. When you're a kid and called into an office, you can bet that there's a problem! I told Dr. Melnick that I was fine and the divorce was no surprise. Besides, I had to get back to chemistry class. Bye!

It had finally happened. I was just glad it hadn't happened in my senior year, with college and all that. It's amazing how many kids' parents split up after they graduate. You know the theme: "Let's stay together until the kids are out of school." Well, that really happens a lot. Maybe it was good that it had happened earlier. At least I knew where things were at and that life isn't perfect. I also learned that I didn't have to "get help" unless I wanted it and that I, myself, could choose what help I wanted. During my senior year counseling interview, the counselor laughed when she read my folder. I asked her what was so funny. She gave me the folder to read and told me to pay special attention to the note from Mrs. Jenkins in grade seven: "Eve comes to group and shares at a minimal level. She is not depressed and seems to be handling things all right. Clearly she does not wish to come to group and sees my intervention as intrusive. She tolerates me but I doubt if I will see her next year in group. She is looking for a quick exit. She is unhappy, not disturbed." Mrs. Jenkins wasn't so dumb after all. My only advice to kids whose parents are divorced is to make believe things are OK. If the school finds out your real story, there will come a knock on the door and then everyone will know and people will look at you as a "case" and your folder will be filed under "kids at risk" whether you like it or not. And one more thing: keep your parents from calling the school and spilling the beans. Why does your life have to be revealed for the whole school just because they screwed up? Divorce American style—everybody gets into the act!

The Wedding.   It's going to be a fun wedding. We're all in the wedding party, me, my brothers, and my sister, plus my father's girlfriend's kids. The reception is going to be at this fancy hotel with plenty of stuff like shrimp and champagne. We're going to have a ball and we deserve it. Then my father and his new wife, my new mom, are going to Bermuda on a big ocean liner. All the kids are staying home and watching over the house and the wedding presents. You bet the party is going to keep rolling. I'm so happy for my dad; he stuck with us kids after my mom threw him out five years ago. I'll never forget that day. I was in seventh grade. I came home after soccer practice and saw all my father's clothes and tools thrown all around the front yard, with a sign saying, "Yard Sale." He was running around trying to pick up his stuff while my mother was yelling at him from inside the house, "Get your crap out of here and never come back again! I told the neighbors to come over and pick up all your stuff; they don't even have to pay me." My dad was crying his head off. When he saw me he turned pale. "I don't know what's going on. I found all my stuff out here. She's even changed the locks so I can't get in. She's lost her mind." I could see all the neighbors looking out their windows at what was going on. Some kids walking home from school crossed the street when they came near our house. I guess they didn't want to embarrass me by standing around. There were even cars stopping to watch what was going on. I was so embarrassed, for myself, for my dad, for my whole family. Then my mom yelled at me to "get in the house and stop talking to that bum." So I went in and went to my room and cried while I watched my dad pick up his stuff. Finally it got dark and he drove off, leaving a lot of things there. After my mom went to bed, I went out and picked up what I could—his old Army hat, fishing poles and tackle, high school yearbook, his "good" suit—and hid them under my bed.

After my dad left, my mom got really crazy. She wouldn't let us talk to him or go visit (he had a small apartment in town). I didn't know what had happened for her to throw him out, but I knew she wasn't right mentally. She'd sleep all day, never make any meals, and always be yelling that we weren't helping out. I knew she needed help but even though I was the oldest, I didn't know what to do. My dad would wait for us after school and ask how things were going. We would tell him how bad things were and ask him to please find a way to come home or take us with him. I still remember the tears in his eyes whenever he left us. He would always say the same thing: "Take this money and buy yourself some food. Make sure you eat lunch and take care of each other. Remember, don't tell your mother you saw me; she'll just take it out on you. We'll get through this somehow." I was always so afraid that when I got home, my mom would find out that we had talked to him. I was the oldest; she would hold me responsible. One day I stayed after school for soccer without telling her. When I came home she said, "I know you've been with your father. Well, I've had enough. The school called me and told me that he's been talking to you all in the parking lot. Well, if you love him so much, you can all get out." She was yelling at the top of her lungs. "You get packed and tell your brothers and sister to do the same. I'm calling your father right now to pick you up. Let's see what he does with four kids in that little apartment of his. What's he going to do with his girlfriends now?" So my father came out and got us and I hardly ever saw my mother again except at Thanksgiving or Christmas. I don't know why she is like she is. Maybe when I'm older I'll find out what happened to her, why she changed so much.

So we all moved in with my dad. I have to give him credit. He did the laundry; made us breakfast, lunch, and dinner each day (the other kids in school always marveled that my dad made such good lunches); and kept the house clean. We were always having to move because of problems with the landlords or the plumbing. We must have moved four times before my dad met his wife. I was always going to the school office to change our address. But my dad kept everything on a schedule; we had to do our homework, go to church, do our chores, no matter where we lived. He always went to school for open house and conferences. And he did all this while working and paying my mother alimony and mortgage money. I never could figure that one out; here he gets thrown out of his house and has to take in his kids and he ends up paying my mom? I don't know how he did it all. Some nights he would come home and I could see he was tired; he'd fall asleep watching TV right after dinner. I'd always cover him up with a blanket before I went to bed. I used to worry so much that he would get sick and die. Then I, being the oldest, would have to bury him and take care of the other kids. I was always telling him to slow down and go for a physical; it was like we were being fathers to each other.

But everything changed when he met my new mom. She is so kind and loving to my dad. Her husband had died, leaving her three kids and lots of money. She told me that she knew right away that my dad would be a great father to her kids; "He has such love and patience." So they bought this big house with her money; "That's what money is for," she said, "to spend." And we all, all seven of us, have our own rooms. I'm happy for my dad, for me, and for my brothers and sister. The worst is over, at least for a while.

My Father Left Home When I Was Born.   The early beginnings were a sign of things to come. I have never known my father and I hope I never see him. I'm afraid of what I might do to him for all he did to me. He left, so my mother says, when I was born. It was the first of many blows to come my way in life. I hate my father without having ever set eyes on the man. How can that be? After I was born we moved in with my mother's father and her brother. My grandfather was a wonderful man, like a father to me. My Uncle Frank was a bully who bossed and physically pushed everyone around. I guess you would call him an abuser today. If we were watching TV and he didn't like the show, he would change the channel without asking anyone. If anyone—my grandfather, mother, or I—said anything, he would say, "Shut the hell up or I'll give you something to complain about." Even then I vowed that I would get even with him for bullying us; he would get what was coming to him.

When I went to school it was really strange. I found myself hating the other kids who had real parents, nice clothes, lunch boxes. I felt different, especially when we had to fill out those forms asking for your parents' address, birthday, place of work, and so on. When it came to my father, I forced myself to write "unknown." Sometimes I wanted to lie, to put down father as a doctor or lawyer, but I couldn't do it. I knew the teacher knew because the mail sent home from the school was always addressed to "Mrs." and not "Mr. and Mrs." That's why I hated the other kids. They could fill out those forms and show they were from a normal family. I was sure there wasn't another kid whose father had left! I tried to get rid of this hate, it bothered me so, but I couldn't. And the worst part was that it showed. I couldn't hide it. All through elementary school and middle school, teachers would tell me to "lighten up" and "hang out" but it wasn't something I knew how to do. I knew the teachers were right, but I felt like I was in a box and couldn't get out. Even my poor mother and grandfather noticed it and tried to get me involved with Boy Scouts, church, and Little League. But I hated it all. I was a lousy athlete and I hated always going to the games by myself while the other kids had their dads and family. My mother and grandfather were always working and I certainly didn't want Frank there. I tried to make friends but the other kids stayed away from me. They thought I was weird and maybe I was. I couldn't fit in. But when they started calling me "gay" and "homo" in the middle school, it was more than I could take. Why did they say those things, those awful things? Hadn't I had enough? I didn't think I was gay, but what did it matter when everyone else said I was? In the eighth grade I missed a lot of school. I just couldn't, wouldn't, go and take that name-calling day after day. I was bullied at home and now at school, too.

Then my grandfather died. It was just before my graduation from eighth grade. It was the worst time in my life, again. He was the only person besides my mother who loved me. At the funeral some of the kids from school and their parents came. It was the first time anyone had ever been nice to me or showed they cared. It helped but I was too busy worrying what was going to happen with the house. It didn't take long to find out. My grandfather hadn't been dead for a week when Frank told my mother that he was selling the house and we would have to move. My mother was a wreck. Where would we live? What if we had to move to another school district? She relaxed more when I told her I wanted out. I needed to move and make a fresh start. So we got a cheap apartment and you know, it's really good. We don't have Frank to deal with and nobody in the new school knows anything about me and they don't seem to care. It's high school and no one cares whether your father is dead or alive. No one calls me "gay" or "homo" any more. All you have to do is show up, keep your mouth shut, and do your work. I can do that. Besides, I have a part-time job now and a car and I can go anywhere. In some ways my grandfather saved me again. When he died, my mom and I could move on. He gave us the gift of a fresh start. I don't feel so boxed in any more.

Setting a New Course after the Pain

For high school kids, there are special moments when decisions must be made, moments when they decide either to stay—stay at home, stay stuck in a destructive relationship, stay addicted—or move on. It's not easy for a kid to move on, to choose the unknown. Who really wants to go to rehab, get your own apartment, or give up a relationship? It takes a fight, a fight within yourself and a fight with your world, to leave even the worst situations. We may not like, we may even hate, what we have, but at least we know it. The landscape is familiar even if it is hostile. We know what time Dad starts to drink; we know the holidays will bring trouble; we know the divorce is coming. We go down wrong roads, avoiding, moving on. When kids decide to move on, there are no real bearings, only fog, turmoil, uncertainty.

The perfect child who never challenges his or her parents or situations stays the perfect child, always at home whether in a foreign port or around the corner. We all know these people; maybe we are one of them. These are the kids who follow the "errant signs, delusive flashes, phantoms" of the right college, the right relationship, the right job, the right family, the right SAT, the right weight, the right win and loss record. Pursuit of the "right" world creates a shaky security for these kids and their parents, a world of "if only I do this, I will be all right." Choosing this way can lead kids and their parents way off course, to danger, quicksand.

The stories in this section are about kids asking, telling, parents that "I'm not bringing home prizes any more and you're going to stop waiting for me to bring them home. I'm just what I am, that's all." In The Pitcher the boy achieves stardom early in his high school career. He is pursued by college coaches and big league scouts. His father pushes him. Baseball becomes a full-time job, summer, winter, and spring. Finally he tires; he can't go on. Luckily he doesn't have to wait until he is thirty-four. He and his father have a chance again to do child things before he moves on.

Sometimes an injury, a fall, seems so horrible to the child star but it is a gift for a new life, a course that was the right course after all. In fairy tales about childhood every miracle requires an initial disaster. In I'm Homeless and My Parents Think I'm OK, the girl knows that the course that her parents have set out for her is dangerous. It will lead her away from her real talent and spirit to a world "voided of all substance and light." But she feels she must follow her parents' way. She is only a child. She knows early that she is not bringing home any prizes. If she just gets through it will be a miracle. Her parents choose a way that fits them, not the girl, a shaky security that they need. The girl tries, her best shot, but she is out of her league, in a world of clouds and fog. She drifts, staying away from home, the home of requirements and demands she can't fulfill. She becomes homeless in a sense. Don't we all stay away from pain as long as we can? Disaster comes in the form of failure. But in the fall she finds allies, hope—teachers, mentors who can challenge the parents' unwise and cruel course. School can be a friend when the real voice of the child is heard and supported. Schools can be places for kids where miracles take place, places where the child is supported for being "just who I am, that's all."

Anorexia in the Air speaks about the false security of the young girls who search for the right weight. Girls, children really, who early on get seduced into looking "right," being thin, wearing black dresses, and working out. Danger is all around and no one sees it. No one cries "fire." There is no red light. What seems right is all wrong. "Errant signs, delusive flashes, phantoms" are followed. But one girl sees danger. A disaster, again, leads to help, a new life. Things have to get bad before they improve. In the perfect life, the perfect child's pain goes unnoticed. Clear flights with no fog can lull you into thinking that's the way it will be all the time, forever. Easy living on easy street. Going to rehab, getting your stomach pumped out, being hospitalized for anorexia, failing courses, getting arrested, can all be necessary wake-up calls, wake-up calls that tell kids and their parents that they are off course.

In They Don't Send Kids to Jail for Shoplifting, Do They? the girl does not have a course. She does not know the way. She is playing with danger in an adult world that can come down hard. It doesn't take a lot to throw you in jail. Just spend some time at a local courthouse and watch what happens to high school kids without mentors and rabbis. This girl doesn't see the danger that is suddenly there. Disaster, trouble, but no miracles here, not yet. A faint wake-up call. Sometimes setting a new course takes time, years. We go down wrong roads. Some kids try to move on by getting things right. Others, like the girl in this final story, try to move on by getting things wrong. She, too, is saying, "I'm just what I am, that's all." Seeing our children as they really are isn't so pretty sometimes, particularly when they choose ways to move on that cause them harm. Wake-up calls are necessary but never easy.

The Pitcher.   Winning all those games and going to the State Championships in tenth grade was my downfall. All the papers said I was headed for the majors and that schools like Louisiana State were after me. My dad started saving all the newspaper clippings and sending my stats to all the big baseball schools: Stanford, Miami, Texas, Florida State. He even had videos made of me that he sent along with this cover letter that he wrote. The letter was supposedly from me; I signed it, but he wrote it. That summer he arranged for me to play with this team in New Jersey that traveled all over the country. We played a night game at the home field (the field was an hour and a half from our home on Long Island) on Wednesday and a doubleheader Saturday and Sunday in different cities. The team was made up of major league potentials who were still in high school, kids like me who had made the papers. The team, the Trenton Tigers, had these great uniforms and traveling bags donated by major league teams. And we traveled first class, either by chartered bus or airline, and stayed in these nice hotels. It was like being in the majors. In each city there were college and pro scouts with the notebooks and speed guns to check the velocity of the pitchers. The Tigers even had a brochure with each player's picture and stats that they sent to all the local papers and to college coaches. Most of the cost for the team was paid for by sponsors, but my dad still had to pay five hundred dollars. He said it was worth it for all the "exposure" I was getting. He drove me to every home game and went along on every weekend doubleheader. He kept a notebook on every game I pitched—how many balls, strikes, hits, runs, innings pitched. After each game he would go over every detail with me and point out the things I did right and things I needed to improve on. It was a full-time job for him, more important than his own work. The other kids and the coaches loved him because he was always cheering and yelling at the umpires if they made a bad call. Sometimes the Tigers coaches had to tell him to tone it down because he would get so carried away with the umpires, particularly when I pitched. He was always saying, "Did you see how that S.O.B. changed his strike zone all the time? No wonder you couldn't buy a strike." My mother never went to the games because she said she couldn't put up with his constant yelling and attacking the umpires and the other team's coaches. She said it was no fun for her and she wondered how I put up with it. It bothered me but he'd always been like that, ever since Little League. I was used to it, I thought.

I could always predict how he would react, depending on how I did in the game. If I had a good game, he was happy. We would stop at McDonald's and go over all the right moves I had made. But if I was having a bad game, I could see "the look" come over his face. His eyes would get heavy and he would start yelling, "Stay within yourself! Stay under control! These guys can't hit you." But sometimes they did and I lost. After these games he would say the same things: "Did you warm up enough? I told you to throw a hundred pitches. Did you? You're not following through with your motion; you've got to bend your back. I told you to take deep breaths between pitches. You're hurrying too much. You've got to slow down." Or he would attack the other kids for making errors or the coaches for playing certain kids. I hated that because he didn't keep it to himself. If a kid made a bad play or an error while I was pitching, he was always yelling, "Get him out of there before he loses the game for us." I hated it when I lost or we played a bad game. I knew he would have a lot to say. He had every game on a video, since I started playing in Little League. He was always the first parent there, setting up his equipment. He even made copies for the other kids' parents. All the videos were on bookshelves in our basement. There must be two hundred of them. After McDonald's we would go home and look at the tapes. Even in the off season he had a weight lifting and running program for me. I spent more time on baseball than on school. That was the way it was. I thought I was having fun.

But in my junior year things fell apart. A lot of the good players from our championship team had graduated and the defense was pretty poor. Plus my arm began to feel tired. It was hard to explain; it just felt different. At first I thought it was because I had pitched so much that summer for the Tigers and then had signed on to play fall baseball with the snowbird league. I had been pitching from the previous March right through November without a rest. When we started practice in March all the papers were picking me for the State All-Star team. My dad said this had to be my "big year" because the college teams went by the junior year. They wanted their recruits to commit by the fall of their senior year. He had a pile of letters from Division I coaches who were interested in me. Some of the major league scouts were also interested in me and said if I signed with them, they would pay my college tuition. There was a lot of pressure on me when the season started. But I couldn't get anyone out. My control was lousy and I had lost the hop on my fastball. I didn't know what had happened. My arm felt like it was detached from my body when I pitched. And the pressure was on from the other teams. I could hear the players on the bench saying things like, "You're going nowhere, pal. You can't even get the ball over the plate. What happened to the child star?" It was brutal. Even the other parents got on my case for blowing games; they were acting like my dad did with their kids. I couldn't do anything right. Here I had a chance for a Division I scholarship and I was blowing it. I wished I was an outfielder; then I could just catch fly balls and hit. I wouldn't have to worry about every pitch—what location, was my curve breaking, did I have my fastball? My coach tried to help but he couldn't do much except say things like, "We'll get them next time. Keep working on your mechanics."

After a while, the other kids lost faith in me. I couldn't believe this was happening. I had always been the "go to" guy, the guy they wanted to have the ball when the pressure was on. I could hear them making comments under their breath that I was burnt out. But my dad was the worst. After every game—I had lost my first five games—he would go over every pitch and talk to me about "concentration," "focusing," and "staying within myself." He kept it up. Even at breakfast he was giving me advice. After a while I didn't even know what he was talking about. What the hell did "stay within yourself" mean? And then my mom got involved. After I lost my fifth game she came downstairs while we were watching the video. She looked at me and said, "All this stuff has to stop. It's making me crazy to see all the pressure that this stupid game is putting on you. Look at you—you're pale and tired out and hardly eating. If this keeps up you'll be in the hospital. It's not worth it for a game that should be fun. It's only a game, remember." Then she looked at my father and said, "You've got to stop this right now. Something happened to his arm; it's probably all this summer and fall pitching. He hasn't had a minute to do anything else. He's just a kid still and all his life he's had to deal with the pressures of this silly game. All this business about Division I and scouts is your doing. You've driven him since he was a kid and now, when he can't do it, you're putting more pressure on him. Can't you just have fun with him without baseball? What if he broke his arm tomorrow? What would you do? All you know about your own son is baseball. I blame myself for not stepping in sooner. I knew he couldn't go on forever; he's only human." Then she said to me, "Maybe this is a blessing in disguise. There are other things in life—music, books, girls, friends. I think you should quit. I can't believe I'm saying this! Then we can do family things and have some fun without all the pressure of getting to some game and making sure you have your ice pack and drinks. We haven't eaten a regular meal together in years. Next year you're graduating and you'll be gone. It's not worth it. Think about what I'm saying. Get out while you have your dignity. There are plenty of other things you can do with your life. We all have to get to know each other in some way besides baseball!"

Well, I finished out the season. My arm never really came back. I won three games and lost nine. I didn't even make All County, forget about All State. After my mother yelled at him, my dad didn't say much. It was strange; he even stopped coming to my games. He said he was doing it to take the pressure off me. I told him I didn't want him to do that but he never came by. The other kids' parents always asked me where he was. I had no answer. He put the video camera in his closet and never used it again. It was like something died in him. Sometimes I felt I had let him down. He had put all his energy, his life, into helping me get to the show, the majors. But I couldn't do it. After the season the coach arranged for me to see this bigshot doctor who was the team physician for the Yankees. He had me take an MRI and X-rays. Afterward he met with my parents and me and said I had a serious rotator cuff injury and that I would never be the pitcher I was before. He recommended that I give up baseball. On the way home it was quiet in the car. I didn't know what to think; I was crushed. I couldn't get it through my head that it was over, all the scouts, the Tigers, the plane trips, the newspaper articles. I was done. I wanted my father to say something but he was quiet, just driving and looking ahead. Finally I said, "What do you think, Dad? What should I do? Should I try another position? I can still hit. Maybe I can play first base; you don't have to throw much there." I wanted something from my father, I didn't know what. I wanted him to say something, anything. After a few minutes he said, "Well, why don't we let that go for a while. I think what your mom said was right. Maybe this is an omen or something. Maybe we can plan a family vacation; I was just thinking we've never gone any-where as a family except to ball games. Other people go to the beach in the summer. You gave it a hell of a shot. I'm so proud of you, partic-ularly the way you handled yourself this season. You've got more guts than I do; I couldn't even deal with it. I'm sorry for not coming to the games. I thought I would help you by not being there; I didn't mean to leave you all alone. Besides, I always wanted to learn how to play golf and tennis. How about you?" Suddenly I felt relieved. I didn't know what I was going to do with my time now but I knew my father wasn't mad at or disappointed in me. Maybe he was right—I had given it a helluva shot.

I'm Homeless and My Parents Think I'm OK.   I got off to a bad start in high school. My parents made me take French even though I barely passed it in junior high. Plus they made me take sequential math and biology, things I hated. And I had the stupid orchestra that took one period each day. I had no lunch and no time to see my friends. I couldn't fit the art courses I really wanted to take into my schedule. My parents said I could take those courses once I got through with the col-lege requirements. They were both teachers and they said that they knew what was best. When we had my program appointment with the eighth grade counselor, I kept telling them that I wouldn't be able to handle all that stuff. They just sat there and said, "You're an under-achiever but once you get to high school and the real world, you'll be able to do it. We know you will." They didn't like the junior high; they said that the school was "all fun and games" and that "learning wasn't taken seriously there." I had no chance to take what I wanted or what I could excel in. The summer before high school I did my best to put it all out of my mind. Maybe my parents were right. Maybe I would do fine.

In September things went along OK. But by October I hadn't a clue what was going on in math, science, and French. My first report card was horrendous—three Fs, two Ds, and a C in orchestra. I told my parents that I couldn't do it. I cried and did everything I could to get them to understand but all they could say was, "You have to do it. Take notes, go for extra help. We'll even get you a tutor. But you have to stick it out." So they got me a tutor for math, science, and French. Now I had no time. I had to give up soccer for the stupid tutors. And on top of all that, they grounded me on weekends "so you can make sure you do all you can do to get through these courses."

I found myself not going home after school. What was the point? All that was waiting for me was a tutor and more talk about how school was going. So I lied. I told my parents I was staying for extra help or going to the library to study. In reality, I just walked the school corri-dors by myself or sat out on the football bleachers. I used to think that this must be what it's like to be homeless, just wandering around. Once in a while a teacher would stop me on their way home and ask if every-thing was all right. I always told them I was getting the late bus home. Even the six o'clock bus driver said, "You must be a great student, staying after school and studying every day. Your parents must be proud of you." I laughed to myself; if only he knew the real story. When too many people took notice of me, I would walk all the way home, even in the rain or snow. It was better than being home. I had created my own little world between three and six o'clock. It was my time! My parents couldn't find me and I could do what I wanted, more or less. Each day I would figure out something to do. I had my places. Some days I would go to the exercise trail in back of the high school and just walk. Other days I would sit by the bus stop and watch the kids that took the late bus home. The kids would look at me kind of funny but I didn't care. Sometimes I would walk up to the deli and get a Coke and chips. That would take thirty minutes each way. I was always after some destination that would take time. Meanwhile my parents seemed happy; they were proud that their "little girl was finally taking her academics seriously." I had to laugh; I was homeless and they were happy. If only they knew the real story. They had their own little world and I had mine.

By December I was hopelessly behind. All my teachers were suggesting that I drop to a lower track. But I didn't care. Report cards weren't due until January. I laughed to myself that I still had a whole month to be "homeless." But then it all ended. I got a call to report to the assistant principal's office. He said that he had gotten a lot of reports that I had been seen around the building long after the other kids had gone home. He said that he had checked the sports programs and the library and found I did not belong to a sports team or a study group. He sat back in his chair and asked, "Why are you hanging around the school every day? Don't you have a home to go to? What do your parents think about this? I checked your records and you're failing every course. Please tell me what's going on; I'll try to help you." I burst into tears and told him how my parents wouldn't let me take the art courses and how I couldn't pass the math, science, and French no matter what I did. I told him that I hated going home and all I did each day was wander around until the six o'clock late bus. He laughed when I said I felt like I was homeless, but he stopped when he saw how serious I was. Finally he said, "I know you don't want me to do this but I have to call your parents and get them in here tomorrow. I promise that I won't tell them about what you have been doing after school unless they ask me a direct question. This can't go on. You'll get sick or break down. I promise I'll do what I can to change their minds about the courses."

When I got home my mom said that the assistant principal had called and wanted to see both her and my dad first thing the next day. She said, "What's this all about? What do you mean, you don't know? This never ends with you, does it? It's been one thing after another since you got to high school. Now we have to take a day off to deal with this. Your father will love this when he comes home. And just when we thought you were beginning to take some responsibility." At the meeting the next day, the assistant principal started off by telling my parents that he felt that the program I was enrolled in was too difficult for me. He told them that all this pressure for college courses wasn't worth the anguish that they were putting me through. "Besides," he said, "this must be making you miserable as well. Your daughter has no self-esteem or satisfaction in her work. You can't feel good about that. Is all this worth seeing your daughter so unhappy?" As soon as he said that I could see the look on my parents' faces. They had heard enough. They didn't like school administrators or counselors; my mom always said, "All they do is sit around their offices and mess into peoples' lives." And they didn't like anyone suggesting that their daughter take the "easy way out." This wasn't going to work.

Then I started to cry. It just happened. I looked at my parents and said, "Dad, Mom, look at things. I'm dumb. Well, maybe not dumb, but I can't pass these courses. I've tried to tell you in every way I could think of but you can't hear me. I've had a tutor, gone for extra help, given up my social and sports life. What do you want from me? Do you want to kill me? I'm over my head; even the teachers are telling me to quit. Why can't you listen?" I was crying so hard that the secretaries and kids in the office could hear me, but I didn't care. This wasn't fair. I looked at my parents and said, "I'm not doing this any more. I'm dropping math, science, and French, and orchestra, too; I hate playing that stupid flute and I'm no good at it. I'm going to take some art courses next semester. If I don't graduate in four years, so what? I'm going to major in art and go to art school after graduation. That's what I'm good at, not French, math, and science. That's not me and you can't force me back into those courses. Call the police, the courts, tell the principal. I don't care; I'm not doing it any more. I'm over my head and I'm sinking. I'm not doing it!" My parents just sat there. They couldn't believe I was saying these things and neither could I. Finally my mom said, "Well, this is not the time or place for this. We'll talk about this tonight as a family. You've done quite enough to embarrass us." I looked at my mom and said, "We are not talking about this later. We are talking about it now! You understand me? Now! You think I'm embarrassing you now? You haven't heard anything yet. You think I've been staying after school every day to study? Well, that's a lie, a lie.

I've stayed after because I don't want to go home. I'm homeless, you hear me? Homeless! All I do is wander around the school or the sports fields until the last bus. I'm like a freak; all the other kids look at me like I'm a bag lady or something, but it's better than going home to tutors or your whining about my grades. That's the real reason you're here today, because the assistant principal has gotten reports about me hanging around. It's so sad that it's funny. You both don't even know or care what's going on in my life. It's all your idea of grades and college. Don't you want me to be happy? Don't you want me to come home every afternoon and be happy, not have to hide out like I've been doing? Well, I don't care any more what you think. I am dropping the math, science, French, and orchestra—that's it!"

I had them. There was nothing they could do. I had won. I couldn't believe it. I felt like a swimmer who had escaped the undertow, lying on the beach exhausted. My father said, "Well, it's your life. Maybe it is better that you change. All this conflict isn't worth it for some stupid college acceptance. I can't take much more either." He looked at the assistant principal and asked, "Where do we sign to allow these changes to happen?" And so I changed and took my art courses. I loved the courses and did well. A lot of the conflict in our family ended with that meeting. My parents never again tried to pick my courses. Sometimes I wonder what would have happened to me if I hadn't fought back. Why did I have to become so crazy for them to understand? If I had been a good little girl and gone along, I would have drowned. Maybe I really would have become homeless. It's not good, ever, to go along with anyone or anything just because "they" think it's good for you, even your parents. Sometimes things have to get crazy before they get better.

Anorexia in the Air.   When I was a kid growing up, I never thought about how much I weighed or about being "too fat." Sometimes my mother would say things like, "You're eating too much," or, "You shouldn't wear that; it makes you look too fat." But I just let it go. I figured that was her problem. But in the eighth grade that all changed. All of my friends suddenly became very, very weight conscious. All the talk was about how "fat" we were. It seemed like my whole group stopped eating at once. We would drink a diet shake in the morning and nibble at our dinner. And we all started wearing black clothes to make us look thinner. The whole thing didn't seem to bother me too much, but some of my friends began to lose a lot of weight. It scared me a lot because I could see them getting more and more into this "being thin" thing. I felt like Joan, one of my closest friends, was really getting sick, physically sick, with this nonsense. She had stopped eating altogether except for hiding food under her bed. She would eat some of the food during the night and then throw it up. Each day she would complain to us, "I'm getting so fat I can't get into any of my clothes." The truth was that her clothes were falling off of her and she was all skin and bones. I was scared and wanted to get out of the group but these were my friends since first grade. Besides, if I deserted the group now, what would happen to Joan? At least I could try to help her if I stayed around. Around school we became known as the "black dress girls" but none of the other kids or teachers seemed to notice what was really happening. Joan was sick and some of the other kids were on their way. I was glad when eighth grade graduation came. We all wore black at the ceremony and our parents, laughingly, took group pictures of the "slim gals." I remember looking at Joan's parents and wondering if they saw how terrible their daughter looked. How could they miss what was happening? I thought about talking to them but I knew Joan would be off the wall if I did. So I kept things to myself. To make matters worse, our eighth grade yearbook carried a full-page picture of our group dressed in black with the caption, "Junior High Girls Strive for Healthy Minds and Bodies." I looked at the picture and thought, "That's healthy?" I was glad to see the summer come. I was going on a trip with my parents and to camp. I could eat again without all that pressure. Maybe high school would be different.

But high school wasn't different. In fact, the pressure to lose weight and be thin got worse. It seemed the whole school, except for the dirt bags, were into working out in the weight room. The place was packed from six in the morning until ten at night. My group would work out before school, play sports after school, and then go back to work out after we did our homework. It was crazy. We were into some kind of sickness we couldn't get out of. I envied the dirt bag group because they didn't care about weight or health. They just hung out and smoked and drank Bud. As the year went along, Joan got worse. Her weight dropped to eighty pounds and she couldn't keep up in basketball. In the spring she tried out for softball but decided to quit. She had no energy. It was then that I made up my mind that I had to do something. I was convinced that this girl was going to die if things kept going the way they were. First, I tried talking to her but it went nowhere. She said, "I'm fine and you have no business telling me that I'm getting sick and I need help." I could see that she couldn't help herself. The next night I went to Joan's house to talk to her parents instead of working out. I knew Joan would be at the weight room. When I started to tell Joan's parents my concerns, they both started crying. They said they had been trying to get Joan to go for help but she refused to go. They were at their wits end and were even thinking of calling the Child Protective Services to force Joan to get help. The parents said they had been to their church pastor who in turn had set them up with a support group for parents of anorexic adolescents. Their first meeting was next week.

I felt so relieved talking to them. At least they saw the problem and were doing something about it. Suddenly I felt like I wasn't a kid any more. Things weren't so safe and secure. I was seeing that kids could really get screwed up even when they had everything going for them. Joan was a bright, beautiful girl, a good athlete, with good parents, a nice home. And look what was happening to her. I realized that this could have been me instead of her. Then the phone rang. Joan's dad answered the phone. I could sense that whatever the message was, it wasn't good news. He said, "I'll be right there." He hung up the phone and said, "Joan has fainted at the weight room and they're taking her to the hospital. We'd better get going." At the hospital they admitted Joan to the Adolescent Psychiatric Unit. I didn't get a chance to see her. On the way home her parents seemed relieved. At least she might get help now. When I got home my mother asked me how the workout went. I started to cry and told her the whole story. My mother said she was very proud of what I had done and I was truly a good friend. Joan is still in the hospital, but she is getting better. The whole thing has had a big impact on my friends and me. We don't work out so much any more, or wear black. I'm even a little more like the dirt bags. Maybe those kids know a little bit more about life than I gave them credit for. Maybe hanging out makes more sense sometimes than working out. I was glad that all of this had happened before I went to college. I knew

I had learned something, I wasn't sure exactly what, that would help me out in life. I was lucky.

They Don't Send Kids to Jail for Shoplifting, Do They?   I've been stealing things for years and never got caught. My friends say I'm a "klepto," you know, like in kleptomaniac. My friends always dare me to take this and that. I'm good at it. I've got one of those faces that can make you believe anything. Besides, I'm a great b——s——person; if anyone comes up to me in the stores, I drown them with b——s——. When I'm checking out of the store, I always start up a conversation with the cashier; usually it's some older lady. I always tell her how good she looks and what a nice dress she has on. Then I go into the grandchildren bit—how many grandchildren does she have and what are their names. You wouldn't believe how many times they just stop what they're doing and take out pictures of these kids. It's a riot, like they really believe I care. Like I said, I'm good at b——s——ing people. I should be majoring in that in school. I sure as hell would be doing better than I'm doing now. If the Grandma bit doesn't work, I usually pretend I'm sick, like telling the cashier I just got my period and I'm about to faint; women always fall for that one. It always works in school, too; tell that to an assistant principal or a teacher and you're home free. My friends can't get over that I never panic. It's like a game with me. Besides, I really don't need half the stuff I rip off. It's just something to do, to fill up the time. My mom is always wondering where I get the stuff I bring home but I b——s—— her, too. I tell her that my friends buy things and then decide not to wear them. She's easy to fool. I've even taken her credit cards and run up big bills and she never makes a big stink about it. She just says, "Please ask me first. It's not like I want to deprive you of anything, but you have to ask first." I always say, "Yeah, yeah, Mom. I will next time." And I mean it. But I never do. My stepfather gets all uptight when he finds out about it. He's very, very straight and thinks my mother is a fool for letting me get away with this stuff. He tells my mother, "She's going to land in jail unless you stop her stealing from you. She's not going to stop with your credit cards, believe me. If I were her real father there wouldn't be a next time. I'd bring charges against her." But my mother couldn't do it; I know it, she knows it, and my stepfather knows it.

My mom always felt bad for me because of the divorce. I was only ten when my real father left. He always tormented my mother about how dirty the house was and what a lousy cook she was. He was a gambler and never let my mother have any money; she had to beg him for food money. He never paid any bills so there was always some bill collector calling the house. After he left we lost the house and our car and had to move into this welfare apartment. It was a poor neighborhood and all the kids' parents were divorced and on welfare. Every month we had to take this long bus ride to Social Services to fill out these forms for heat and food. I remember the white line in front of the receptionist's desk there. There were big letters above the line: "Do not cross this line until your case number is called." The people there were so unfriendly. My mom was always having to show a million papers to prove who she was. Sometimes there would be one paper missing and we would have to go all the way home and come back with the paper before we got our food stamps and heat allowance. It made me so mad! You'd think it was their money they were giving away there. I used to wonder why people who had the job of helping other people acted so miserably. My mom and I would always joke before we went to Social Services that we were going to "Scowl Heaven." When things were really bad my grandmother would help out but my mother hated that because she always knew my grandma would have the last word. She would always say, "I told you not to marry him. I knew he was no good. You could have gone to college and met a doctor or lawyer. Now look at you, on welfare and with a child." My mom didn't need to hear that and neither did I.

After a few years my mom got a good job in an insurance company and we got off welfare. No more trips to Social Services. Thank God! And then she met this guy who was a widower, an older man, and before long they got married. I didn't mind it because we moved into his nice house and he treated my mother like a princess. He had no kids so it made things easy for me. You see, you get the point, my mother always felt sorry for me for those terrible days with my dad (I never saw him again after he left) and when we were on welfare. When she married my stepfather, I got whatever I wanted. That's when I started stealing. It was crazy. Here was the first time in my life I could have whatever I wanted and I start ripping things off. It happened so fast that I couldn't believe it.

When they got married I started twelfth grade in a new high school. Most of the kids there were preps who had known each other since first grade. I was an outsider and things never changed. I didn't know how to relate to all this rah-rah-preppie stuff. I had spent the last four years in a welfare apartment and in a school loaded with rejects. My mom kept telling me to join some clubs, get involved, but it was too late. I stayed home every weekend; the phone never rang for me. After a while I started hanging out with some of my friends from my old school at the mall. They would play this game of who could rip off the most stuff each day. I didn't need anything but I got into it; I liked the excitement, the danger, the risk. Maybe, I thought, I had my dad's gambling genes. Within a short time I became the major player in the gang. They called me Miss Right because I looked so honest. I was always among the top three when it came to totaling up what we ripped off each week. And I never got caught. Some of the other kids would end up being caught and brought down to the precinct. But they usually got off with a reprimand or placed in their parents' custody. Not me.

That all changed just before Christmas. We were in Macy's trying to steal some neat sweaters. We put them on in the dressing room and put our own sweaters on over them. We had done it a million times. Besides, Macy's is a "safe" store; they have hardly any help, even at Christmas. Someone said they were in bankruptcy. But just as we were walking out, two guys came up and told us we had to go with them. I was shaking all over. What were we going to do? They took us to an office and called the police. In about ten minutes two cops came and took us to the precinct. They said they knew we had stolen the sweaters; some employee had seen us go in with sweaters and come out with nothing. This one cop said we were being charged as adults because we were over eighteen. He said, "You can go now. You'll be notified of the court date. You'd better get a lawyer."

Get a lawyer? Jesus, what would my mother say? I didn't even know that you could be charged as an adult when you're eighteen. Some thief! I haven't told my mother yet. How can I tell her this? I'm still trying to figure out how to get a lawyer. One of my friends said to call Legal Aid but every time I do, the line is busy. Someone else said they cut their budget. I even thought about going to Social Services for help. They must have some social worker who would know what to do. But all I could think of was the white line—"Do not cross this line until your case number is called." I didn't want a case number. I even tried calling my dad; I figured he would know about these things. But he wasn't listed in the phone book. I guess I'll just wait until the court date and go in without a lawyer. My friends say then they'll have to appoint a lawyer for my case. Besides, what's the worst that can happen? Everyone gets probation or community service or something. They don't send kids—I mean adults—to jail for this nickel and dime stuff. Do they???

NOTES

1. Beverly Lowry, "Crossed Over," *New York Times,* 23 August 1992, 1, 21 (7).

2. William L. Fibkins, *What Schools Should Do to Help Kids Stop Smoking* (Larchmont, NY: Eye on Education, 2000), 132–39.

CHAPTER 5

Preparing Secondary-School Teachers to Be Effective Advisors and Adult Role Models

The focus of this final chapter is on how we can prepare teachers in our secondary schools—high school, junior high school, and middle school—to become effective advisors and to develop schools in which every teacher is an advisor who can provide and open doors through which students can walk and get the help, support, and advice they need to make sound decisions about their present and future lives. This chapter is divided into the following sections:

1. An overview of the need for teachers to become effective advisors.
2. Helping teachers assess their level of commitment to the advising process and reviewing the barriers and opportunities involved in the advisor role.
3. Helping teachers assess their advising skills. What areas are working well and what areas need improvement?

An Overview of the Need for Teachers to Become Effective Advisors. Encouraging and expecting all teachers to perceive themselves as advisors and adult role models and giving them the necessary skills to accomplish this important task begins with asking educators to abandon the flawed notions that a few guidance counselors can carry out this mission; that this teacher-led intervention can be accomplished only with a formal advisory system; or this kind of close student–teacher contact cannot occur in large schools. We need to honestly assess where our students have the greatest opportunity to connect with credible adults. As Anthony W. Jackson and Gayle A. Davis advocate, every student should be well-known by at least one adult.[1] Students should be able to rely on that adult to help them learn from their experiences, comprehend physical changes and changing relations with family and peers, act on their behalf to marshal every school and community resource needed for the student to succeed, and help fashion a promising vision of the future. We need to provide teacher-centered alternatives to our current process of directing students to doors that are earmarked for help and advice but that are often closed.

Education reformer Ernest L. Boyer reminds us that when students turn to counselors for advice concerning future opportunities, this often leads only to frustration.[2] In his study of high schools, Boyer found that at every high school he visited, the counselors were shockingly overloaded. Boyer gives two examples of the professional box counselors find themselves in. At Sands High School in the Southeast, John Pierovich, one of four counselors, starts his day on the run. "I begin seeing students at 7:15. I'll meet twenty to twenty-five every day plus two or three parents each day." Pierovich is responsible for 450 students in all. At 8:00 one morning at DeSoto High, a parent sat with her child in the guidance office, waiting to see a counselor. None was present, explained the secretary, because they were giving tests that morning. Soon one of the counselors happened to appear. After being introduced to the parent he confirmed the situation. "We're tied up with tests this morning. I couldn't see you until eleven." The parent said she couldn't wait and left with her daughter.

The bottom line is that teachers do have very specific classroom opportunities to become engaged with individual students. Let's recall counselor educator Harold L. Munson's observations about the potential helping and advising role of teachers that I reported on in chapter 2:

Teachers are human. They can be accepting, understanding and trusting. Some teachers, if we can accept the reports of youth, are better at providing these conditions than some school counselors. If a teacher can relate with a student in this manner, he should be encouraged to do so. To restrict such relationships is to infringe on the freedom of the teacher and to destroy the humanness of the teaching-learning relationship. Perhaps his communication skills and techniques are not professionally developed yet he has the potentiality for a human relationship with every student. Communication about the student's progress, ability and interest in the subject may spill over to personal matters outside the realm of teacher concern and responsibility. This should be anticipated, and when the teacher feels capable, and confident to deal with these issues, he should be encouraged to do so.[3]

Again, Munson is right on target concerning the teacher model we need in our schools right now. In my experience the school's teachers who care about a student or students who care about a teacher are apt to communicate about very meaningful and sometimes confidential topics. And I know many teachers can be accepting, understanding, and trusting if those behaviors are expected and rewarded.

James Garbarino, Nancy Dubrow, Kathleen Kostelny, and Carole Pardo suggest that not only are schools one of the most continuous institutions in children's lives, they, after the family, represent the most important developmental unit in modern social systems.[4] Furthermore, as a public institution, schools are more accessible than the family as an appropriate unit of intervention. Despite the overwhelming pressures in the environment, 75 to 80 percent of children can use school activities as a support for health adjustment and achievement when schools are sensitive to them and their burdens.

Here is an example of the kinds of positive experiences that can happen to students when schools are sensitive to them and their burdens. Author Patsy Walker recalls how her school experience gave her a ticket out of a troubled family life. Here is her story:

My secret was so much liking everything we did in school . . . but I did like some of it, and a few teachers. Not a lot of them, but you don't need a lot of them. Fact is you only need a few . . . 'cause what they were both telling me was, okay, you want to make a secret out of it, that's cool. But we could either forget you and let you fall away like everyone else, or we can, like I say, plant a little seed in you. That's what both of them did, too, plant little seeds. Took a long time for those seeds to grow into something, but they did. What they were telling me, see, was you play the game, but we want to tell you we'll support you playing a whole 'nother game if there ever comes a time you feel like you might be ready. Maybe they were daring me . . . but like, what they did was plant those time capsules of the kind like they were saying, Hey, you might like to see what's inside you one of these days. Might like to find out there's more than one way to go in this world, game or no game. Fact, they never did say, think about it. Neither one did. They just took a chance. Probably took it with lots of kids. Damn strange somebody seeing inside you to where you keep your secrets, where they know you keep your secrets. I had a secret, too, going to my school. Used to say to myself: "School, get me a ticket out of this life. And baby, make it one way!"[5]

Wise words from Patsy Walker that every teacher needs to hear. What she needed in her life was a few teachers she liked who quietly planted seeds of hope, suggested that there's more than one way to go in this world, dared her to be different, and took a chance on her and probably with lots of other kids. They never said, "Think about it," but just kept planting those time capsules of theirs, waiting patiently for Patsy to develop some self-awareness that yes, school is a ticket out of this life. No, we are not all as wise and able as Patsy's teachers. We are often rushed and want quick changes of behaviors from our students. Planting seeds and being available and accessible, daring them now and then to be different, may well be the best approach with our students who have lost interest in school and hope for change. Real change and developing resilience and hope take time. As Patsy Walker reminds us, "A child grows up in what you could call two homes. Home where he's born and home where he goes to school. One fails him, but he's got the other. It can work either way. But if they both fail, he can call the music to an end. I was up to calling my own music to an end several times there myself. Family life didn't do too much good, and I wouldn't have thought the schools were going to be any different. But they did their job. I didn't think so at the time, but they were grinding away."[6]

Yes, sometimes it takes a teacher grinding away, offering concern and care in the face of rejection, to help students find their tickets out and take their place in the world. Clearly Patsy's teachers played a major role in helping her maintain resiliency in the face of a difficult home life. As James Garbarino points out, a favorite teacher appears to function for resilient children in one or more capacities: an instructor of academic skills, a confidant, and a positive role model for identification. We should keep in mind, however, John I. Goodlad's wise reminder that a teacher's pedagogical knowledge must be tempered with humility; to try again and differently with a pupil is to admit humbly that one's earlier teaching efforts did not suffice.[7]

I would suggest that "favorite teachers" do not magically appear. Becoming involved with students often takes persistence. Initial overtures to have a closer and more caring relationship are often rebuffed. Becoming a role model and confidant doesn't happen overnight, nor should it. Most students are not fools. They want to be sure of what they are buying into. Can this teacher be trusted? How much should I reveal of myself and my life? Teachers have to accept these rebuffs humbly, be tough, and not turn their backs at the first sign of rejection. They must try to understand that their feelings of disappointment are part of the process. This is not to say that accepting rebuffs and being disappointed about not being able to help and advise some students comes easy for successful professionals. Researcher and author Robert Coles describes the professional angst associated with these disappointments.[8] Coles was involved in a research project to gather data about the lives, hopes, and worries of pregnant teenage girls in a Boston ghetto. As part of his investigation he met with a group of physicians, nurses, youth and social workers, ministers, and teachers who, day in and day out, try to connect with, and be of help to, these pregnant girls. The group talked about the psychological, social, and moral struggles of the young people with whom they worked. They also talked, rather grimly, about the disappointments they had experienced in the course of their efforts, the women and men with whom they failed to connect, whom they failed to understand in important ways, no matter what the effort. One of the doctors said, "I think I know how to help some of these kids. I try to teach them how to take care of themselves and the babies they're carrying. But they are kids, and lots of times I feel I missed something; they're not telling me what's on their minds. Maybe they don't really know, I mean, what's giving them trouble. A lot of them are in trouble, and so am I, because I'm trying to figure out what to do, how to be of help, and the kids won't let me because they can't seem to level with themselves."

As Gary Fenstermacher suggests in chapter 3, teachers, like physicians, may at times wish for social distance from the complex, tangled, and sometimes destructive lives of their students, but they cannot both teach well and ignore the many dimensions of the lives of their students. Teaching well requires a broad and deep understanding of the learner as possible, a concern for how what is taught relates to the life experience of the learner, and a willingness to engage the learner in the context of the learner's own intentions, interests, and desires. Social distance of the variety favored by many physicians inhibits the capacity of teachers to do their job well.

When we go about understanding the dimensions of our students' lives, we may indeed find out more information than we wanted. Deep emotions may overtake us. The events, the stories, in our students' lives will naturally come forth in a trusting teacher–student relationship. It comes with the territory. Many students have been silent too long about their personal issues and are ready to talk, if they are encouraged to do so. We can't as teachers say we are caring and concerned and then suggest to our students that some subjects are not to be discussed. Simply put, teachers can't open the door and then say "stop" just because they are uncomfortable, anxious, and unsure with their students' stories. Being uncomfortable, anxious, unsure, even afraid in fact makes up a large part of any successful teacher's day. As Parker Palmer wisely observes, "I will always have fears, but I need not be my fears, for there are other places in my inner landscape from which I can speak and act."[9] I believe as teachers we must continually grapple, sometimes stumbling, for ways to connect with our students, even when our fear and discomfort level begin to soar. These feelings tell us we are onto something important and worthwhile. We must strive to stay rather than to run and hide, to be connected, so neither our students nor we are cut off.

Education reformer James Comer suggests that we can help our students accomplish socializing gains and make academic gains at the same time.[10] They need not interfere with each other. Sometimes socializing gains can take more of our personal and professional investment than academic gains. Yes, there is a paradox here for teachers. Many go into the profession with one vision—to be academic teachers. Now, in our changing world, they are asked to address their students' nonacademic, personal, and well-being issues, to be confidants, models, and so on. There has to be tension for them in this new role. But as Palmer suggests, we need to find new ways to understand the tension we feel when we are torn between the poles. New habits are required.

We stumble and grapple with ways to bring the poles into some symmetry. We search for integration keeping in mind Goodlad's imperative that creating havens of resting, sharing, and caring is one of the most critical and challenging problems of our time. Children and young adolescents should never be far from the attention of caring adults.

We need to keep in mind that there is a professional and a personal price that teachers pay when they increase their social distance from students. For the creation of social distance in the teacher–student relationship, as in all other relationships, allows discontent and mistrust to fester. As Palmer observes, the lenses through which many teachers view the young these days tend to distort who, and how, our students really are.[11] As Palmer reports, "When I ask teachers to name the biggest obstacle to good teaching, the answer I most hear is 'my students.' When I ask why this is so I hear a litany of complaints: students are silent, sullen, withdrawn; they have little capacity for conversation; they have short attention spans; they do not engage well with ideas; they cling to narrow notions of 'relevance' and 'usefulness' and dismiss world ideas." And as Palmer relates, "whatever tidbits of truth these student stereotypes contain, they grossly distort reality and they widen the disconnection between students and their teachers. Criticizing the client is the conventional defense in any embattled profession, and these stereotypes" conveniently relieve us of any responsibility for our students' problems or their resolution.[12]

It is important to remind teachers that being an effective advisor requires more than kindness and being a nice person. The role, not unlike that of the successful subject-mastery role, requires teachers to connect with students with overtures that require a response from students who may be hiding behind a domain of silence. Being nice, being kind, may help break the ice but it is not a useful skill when students need tough talk, confrontation, and tough love. In the long run, advisors who rely only on kindness in addressing the needs of their students are ill-equipped to help teenagers. The following is an example of how medical doctors hide their lack of skills to help patients behind their kindness mask. It is important for advisors to avoid the same pitfalls.

Dr. Abigail Zuger reports, "I once worked with the nicest doctor in the world. She was a true marvel of kindness and dedication. Day or night, her patients could reach her for anything, and they adored her.

She was their friend, their advocate, their savior, grieving at every mishap from divorce to pneumonia, and rushing to heal the pain. There was just one little problem. She was a spectacularly bad doctor. Watching her work was an education in one of the most counterintuitive truths in all of medicine: the most sympathetic people do not always make the best doctors."[13]

As Dr. Zuger suggests, patients are instinctively on their guard against hostile or uninterested doctors. But kindly doctors with smooth bedside manners can manage to provide vast quantities of substandard medical care. I believe the same can be said of the teacher–student relationship. Students are on their guard against hostile or uninterested teachers. But kindly teachers may fail to persist in the needed efforts to find out what is really going on in their students' lives, fail to ask the tough questions and instead accept hollow, unrevealing responses that are intended to end the conversation as soon as possible. For example, "Sherry, how is your parents' divorce going?" "Oh, it's coming along." "Well, you know I am here for you. You can call me any time." This is a conversation in which the advisor is acting kind but failing to elicit important information or feeling: "Oh, it's awful. My dad is threatening my mom, saying once the divorce is approved she'll have to sell the house. What will happen to me and my brothers? I don't want to leave this school. All my friends are here. I hate my dad. He's become so cruel since he became involved with his new girlfriend. All he does is spend money on her. Last month they were in Bermuda for two weeks. Meanwhile my mom is working two jobs and all I do is baby-sit and cook. He's off having fun and all of us are suffering. No wonder my grades are down. I was on the honor roll every year before this happened. My mom was always involved in school activities and now she's hardly around. It's not her fault. Everything is just screwed up, including me."

It is clear that the teacher in the classroom is best positioned to attend to students' social, emotional, and physical well-being and help his or her students become knowledgeable, responsible, and caring students and future citizens. As Maurice J. Elias and colleagues suggest, all Americans recognize that schools play an essential role in preparing our children to become knowledgeable, responsible, and caring.[14] However, behind each word lies an educational challenge. For children to become knowledgeable, they must be ready and motivated to learn and capable of integrating new information into their lives. For children to become responsible, they must be able to understand risks and opportunities and be motivated to choose actions and behaviors that not only serve their own interests but also those of others. For children to become caring, they must be able to see beyond themselves and appreciate the concerns of others; they must believe that to care is to be part of a community that is welcoming, nurturing, and concerned about them. Few realize, however, that each element of this challenge can be enhanced by thoughtful, sustained, and systematic attention to children's social and emotional learning. Indeed, experience and research show that promoting social and emotional competence is the "missing piece" in efforts to reach the array of goals associated with improving schooling in the United States.

As Elias and colleagues state, today's educators have a renewed perspective on what common sense always suggested: When schools attend systematically to students' social, emotional, and physical well-being, the academic achievement of children increases, the incidence of problem behaviors decreases, and the quality of the relationship surrounding each child improves. Social and emotional issues are at the heart of problem behaviors that plague many schools, communities, and families, sapping learning time, educators' energy, and children's hope and opportunities. Effectively promoting social and emotional competence is the key to helping young people become more resistant to the lure of drugs, teen pregnancy, violent gangs, truancy, and dropping out of school. Schools have become the one place where the concept of surrounding children with meaningful adults and clear behavioral standards can move from faint hope to a distinct possibility, and perhaps even a necessity.

However, as Munson suggests, teachers need to feel capable and confident to deal with personal matters that have been for too long considered outside the realm of teacher concern and responsibility.[15] They also need to feel capable and confident that they can act as significant adults who can provide support and direction during difficult times. They need to feel capable and confident that they can enhance their students' social, emotional, and physical well-being. We need to remind ourselves that encouraging and exhorting subject-mastery teachers to be advisors and adult role models is not enough. Well-intended speeches, slogans, and too-generalized professional articles about the need for teachers to be caring and concerned don't make the grade. There is often no "how-to," no nuts and bolts, in these approaches. There are calls for action without training. Recall Arthur G. Powell, Eleanor Farrar, and David Cohen's advice in chapter 2 that education reformers rarely helped teachers take the next step.[16] Few explained how to do it. We need to remember, as Theodore Sizer advises, that the Horaces of the world hate to admit that some sort of change is necessary, major change. He hates his compromise but he is comfortable with the familiar routines, however inadequate. The fear that another practice might be even more inadequate makes him chary.[17] I suggest that moving teachers in the direction of being competent advisors will occur only when they begin to believe that they are capable of carrying out this new role successfully and are given the tools to forge these kinds of close relationships with their students. They must see that it's not just another add-on to their job as a result of the latest education fad that has no relation or payoff to their subject mastery role.

Helping Teachers to Assess Their Level of Commitment to the Advising Process by Reviewing the Concerns Teachers Often Voice about Becoming Advisors and the Opportunities in this New Role. Here is a list of concerns and opportunities:

Teachers concerns about becoming an advisor:

1. If they get involved as an advisor they will be entering new and uncharted territory with students.
2. If they get involved as an advisor their new role will detract from their academic teaching.
3. They won't know how to behave as both an academic teacher and an advisor.
4. If they get involved as an advisor they will be acting in different and more proactive ways with students than other teachers who may choose to look the other way or refer a failing or troubled student; they will be out of step with other teachers and the academic culture of the school; they will be seen as a savior, messiah, or surrogate parent.

5. If they get involved as an advisor they won't be able to deliver the level of support and guidance needed by students.
6. They were hired as academic teachers and are not being paid as advisors.

The opportunities in the advisor role for teachers:

1. When teachers become advisors they will have an opportunity to help students enhance their academic success and their personal, social, and emotional/physical well-being; they may help students avoid isolation, risky behaviors, school failure, and dropping out.
2. When teachers become advisors they can help students resolve problems early so they don't fester and become worse in later life.
3. When teachers become advisors they can help students regain hope and follow their stars, to become useful school and community citizens rather than heading toward the margins.
4. When teachers become advisors they become learners again. When teachers enter the profession they develop an academic curriculum and presentation style that usually remains the same throughout their teaching careers; they may over time stop learning and changing. In becoming advisors they begin learning a whole new set of helping skills that become a part of their presentation style. They, like most new learners, become energized, curious, and a little confused and uncertain. This newfound energy and uncertainty will help them recapture the thrills and risks associated with teaching.
5. When teachers become advisors they become more effective teachers for all their students. Becoming an advisor provides a way for teachers to become involved with all their students. Changing from a strictly academic teacher to a teacher who can also help students will dramatically change the way students are addressed. Teachers who become advisors begin to view the whole student—personality, culture, background, successes and failures, wellness, motivation, achievement, relationships, family life, hopes, and dreams. In an advising role teachers will be

there when troubling changes begin to take place in the lives of their students—poor attendance, weight loss, death of a loved one, loss of family income, suicide of a friend; all these events will be noticed and attended to.

6. When teachers become advisors they become more coupled with other teachers. Academic teachers often appear self-sufficient; they usually work alone and tend to be isolated from fellow teachers. They don't appear to need the advice and support of colleagues. When teachers become advisors, that changes. Even teachers who are skilled advisors will encounter student problems that will leave them uncertain and confused about how to respond. They will have a group of colleagues to serve as their support network, offering feedback on how best to intervene. Concomitant with their helping role is the need for a support system. The relationship between individual teachers and among groups of teachers will become more interactive, therapeutic, and student centered.

7. When teachers become advisors they learn new skills that enhance their overall performance. Academic teachers usually work with a large group and tend to view their class as a whole. When teachers become advisors, they will learn to work more with students as individuals. They will acquire the skills needed to set up helping groups and also to meet with students on a one-to-one basis. They will learn how to engage students, listen, be empathetic, give constructive feedback, and offer support. They will become skilled at questioning, observing classroom interaction, giving feedback, encouraging participation, and allowing students to give feedback on their teaching style and performance. They will stop relying solely on the lecture model.

8. When teachers become advisors, administrators and counselors learn they can rely on teacher advisors to intervene when the first signs of trouble appear in the lives of students. A big load will be taken off their backs. Teachers will be able to intervene and quickly offer help when students exhibit problems. Administrators and counselors will no longer have to endure the frustration that often accompanies the long process of teachers referring students to counselors. The logjam of backed-up refer-

rals will be broken; complaints that nothing is being done to help students will diminish. Counselors will no longer feel overwhelmed and will be able to make a more positive contribution by helping train teacher advisors and counsel the most at-risk students. Administrators will begin to assess the helping skills of teachers. The school will become a more caring place and a new sense of community and purpose will evolve.

9. When teachers become advisors, the quality of interactions with parents improves. Teachers who become advisors will often speak of their students as "my kids." They will take on, to some extent, a parent's role of concern and care. They will know what a parent and student are going through when trouble comes into their lives. They will begin to share a new relationship and bond with parents based on helping the troubled student—and the troubled parent. This new bond will replace the old teacher–parent relationship that was based solely on academic concerns. In this new role the teacher will try to help both the students and the parents to work through the thorny issues of teenage life. The advisor will become a helper for parents as well as students, hearing the parents' anguish and concerns. He or she will direct them to sources of help and support by having a list of referral sources at his or her disposal and will follow up referrals with support. Parents will learn that they can rely on the teacher advisors for guidance and direction.

10. When teachers become advisors they become more involved in helping their students resolve community problems. They will become more aware of the hostility and conflict among teen subgroups in the community. They will learn first-hand from students that the fights and confrontations that occur in school often have their roots in the community. They will begin to understand that the divisions among the adults in the community—racial, economic, religious, political—impact on students and often carry over into the school. Advisors will be in a position to help students better understand, value and accept each other. A direct benefit of the teacher advisor project is the opportunity to help students learn how to reach across bound-

aries that separate groups and create new ways to communicate, without hostility and violence.

11. When teachers become advisors they become more aware of their own personal issues. The advising process will heighten their sensitivity to others and to themselves. In the process of helping others we often begin to learn a great deal about ourselves. When teachers begin to serve as advisors they will quickly find out that they themselves experience many of the same issues faced by their students. Teachers learn that their new insights into the helping process will often serve as motivation to find ways to solve their own personal problems, an unintended and unexpected benefit for teachers.

Helping Teachers Assess Their Advising Skills.   What skills are working well and which ones need improvement? Here is a list of questions and issues that administrators and teacher leaders can ask teachers to reflect on in the effort to get every teacher on board the advising process:

1. What educators helped guide you during your adolescent years?
2. What skills did these educators have? Were they good listeners? Nonjudgmental? Encouraging? Capable of delivering criticism in a positive way that made sense? Were they intimate, knowable, and accessible? When you were involved with these educators, did you feel comfortable and at home?
3. What words of encouragement and support did these advisors use when talking with you? What words worked best to help you?
4. Have you modeled your own professional life after these educators? Many teachers, coaches, and administrators go into teaching because they have encountered positive advisors in their own school experience and want to pass on the care and guidance advisors have given them.
5. Do you employ some of the same skills you learned from your advisors in your teaching? Are you a good listener, nonjudgmental, encouraging, able to deliver criticism in a positive way that makes sense, intimate, knowable, accessible?

It is also useful for teachers to recall those advisors who had a negative impact on them. Many educators set out with good intentions to help students but in fact lack the skills, caring, compassion, and ability to work one on one in an intimate relationship. Consider the following points:

1. What educators set out to guide you and were unable to deliver in this role? We all get exposed to educators who are unable to connect with us in any positive way. .

2. What advising skills did they lack? Were they poor listeners, judgmental, discouraging, critical, not intimate or knowable, inaccessible? When you were involved with these negative advisors, was something amiss or even threatening?

3. What words did these advisors use that convinced you that you were in an unhelpful relationship?

4. In developing your own teaching persona, have you deliberately tried to avoid becoming like these negative advisors? Or have some of their negative behaviors and attitudes crept in silently and taken hold of your persona? As teachers we enter the school setting priding ourselves on our ability to work effectively with every student. The reality of school life soon strikes with a creeping awareness that we are not as open and inclusive as we thought. We sometimes have communication and relationship problems with certain students. It is relatively easy to overlook this dilemma, wish it would go away, or even say it doesn't exist. But in resisting the use of this data to change our teaching strategies we, over time, often become negative advisors for these students. Has this excluding, denying, process become part of your teaching persona? Have you become a negative advisor for some of your students? Are you a victim of settling, not willing to change to be inclusive?

5. What skills have you developed as a teacher to avoid the characteristics of the negative advisors in your teenage life? Being an effective advisor for students takes ongoing self-awareness, work to form new habits of interaction, practice, and patience as we integrate this new role. It is all too easy to slip back into a negative mentoring stance. Schools are hectic places in which rela-

tionships and communication are easily strained. The negative press of some schools calls for teachers to be critical of students who are different and of teachers who are committed to close connections with students. There is a fine line between being helpful and being critical. Being helpful and supportive of students is not always in vogue. That is the school climate we need to challenge so real help can flow to our students.

It is also useful for teachers to become aware of the kinds of characteristics of students they want to help and those they wish to avoid. Recall Horace's experience for a moment. He "chooses" to become more involved with students who interest him or who press themselves on him. He views his other students as "acquaintances" or as a "genial blur." Every teacher is drawn to certain students because of their own backgrounds and values. Yes, some students are just more interesting and engaging. They satisfy many of our own personal needs for a positive connection in our often-stressed teaching role. The danger here is that we, like Horace, end up satisfying our own needs and distancing ourselves from students who are different from us. We end up serving and interacting with only a small portion of our students while the rest remain on the outskirts, anonymous. In order to counteract this process, I believe it is helpful for teachers to focus on the following questions. I believe these questions will help teachers become more aware of which students they choose to include and which students they tend to keep at a distance.

1. What are the characteristics of the students you like? For example, do you feel more comfortable with female than male students? The brightest and most articulate students? Students who are well-behaved? Students who praise you?
2. What part do issues of gender, color, personality, culture, appearance, motivation, and ability play in determining whom you like to help and guide?
3. What needs of yours are met through interaction with these favorite students? Are your needs for praise, affirmation and support met by interacting with these students? We all come to our work setting with personal needs to be met. But is your overall

efficiency as a teacher being diminished by focusing too much on students who are most like you and interest you?

4. What kinds of student problems do you like to help with or gravitate toward? For example:
   - School problems such as failure, underachieving behavior
   - School problems such as advisee conflict with a teacher
   - Parent–advisee conflicts
   - Family crisis, such as divorce
   - Peer problems
   - Problems related to death and loss
   - Problems related to suicide issues
   - Problems related to physical/emotional/sexual abuse and/or neglect
   - Problems related to eating disorders
   - Problems related to alcohol, drug, or tobacco abuse
   - Multiple problems such as underachieving in school, conflict with parents, alcohol abuse, and peer relationships

5. Looking at the above list, identify the kinds of student problems you "could" handle but prefer to avoid. These are the so-called sticky problems that you, maybe we all, would find uncomfortable. Do kids sense this and maybe back off? Remember, these are problems you could handle—if you chose to.

6. What are the kinds of student problems you know need immediate referral to a reliable resource in the school or community? These are problems we know we can't handle. Our work then is to move the helping process along—fast—and remain close by for support. Effective advisors know when to refer and how to go about the process. They are aware of their strengths and weaknesses as helpers, what they can and cannot do to help students. There are times when students need professional help. The task of the advisor is to know when that occurs and how to direct the student and his family to more care. The advisor needs to be straightforward and clear when a referral is in order. They must avoid being tentative and putting the onus of the referral on the student. When a referral is necessary action must be taken. It is the responsibility of the advisor to carry out this action in a successful manner. The life and well-being of the student may be at

stake. What the student needs most in a time of crisis is to know that the teacher advisor is not abandoning him or her and will be present throughout the helping process to offer support. The advisor needs to communicate to the student that "we are in this together."

It is also useful to advisors to increase their awareness about what students they tend to keep at a distance and give short shrift to. The following questions can help in this process:

1. What are the characteristics of students you tend to avoid and find difficult to guide? For example, students who seem passive and uninterested? Students who act out and cause mischief? Students who confront you and test you? It is important to reflect on those students you avoid. We all arrive at the classroom door with our own set of biases, judgments, and prejudices. The work is to try to figure out our avoidance process and work at building our tolerance and inclusion level, developing new habits that allow us to interact with all students.

2. What part do issues related to gender, color, culture, personality, appearance, motivation, and ability play in determining which students you avoid helping and guiding?

3. What kinds of inner conflicts arise when you become involved in helping and guiding students who are out of step with your image of a successful student? Resistance within you and the students you have trouble relating to is a troubling condition, one that leads to neither party welcoming a personal interaction, that can lead to anonymity or open conflict for both teacher and student, a condition that is not life giving. As a teacher you have much to gain from coming to terms with the real you and overcoming your resistance to helping certain students. That requires acknowledging that you have a dark side that senses caution, threat, and the unknown when you encounter certain students. You may feel that they are not on your side or they are not worth the effort. In fact, they are worth the effort if you are to become a complete academic teacher and advisor. Advising and teaching only those you are comfortable with is only half the game. As we

proceed through our teaching careers it is important to stay aware of our own biases, acknowledge whom we push away and daily try to right this situation.

Finally, administrators and teacher leaders can use the following questions to help teachers honestly assess their present advising skills and use this data to build ongoing school-based in-service opportunities.

1. What are your strengths as an advisor? These are the skills you can build on. For example:
   - Are you a good listener and non-judgmental?
   - Can you establish a trusting, caring, and supportive environment?
   - Are you loyal and able to keep a confidence (unless a serious health or suicide issue emerges)?
   - Do you know how to hold successful one-on-one conferences with students and parents?
   - Do you know when, where, and how to make a good referral when trouble emerges?
   - Can you advocate for your students with colleagues, administrators, and parents?
   - Do you know how to maintain close and intimate contact with your students without crossing over professional boundaries?
   - Do you know how to deal with endings? That is, do you know how to help your students to move on to the next level, not hold on and prevent them from moving forward to new relationships?
2. What are your personal goals in wanting to help your students, parents, and colleagues? What personal and professional growth opportunities are in it for you?
3. What are your nonstrengths as an advisor? These are skills that need improvement.
4. How do you view yourself as an advisor? As a success? Average? Mediocre? Failure? Self assessments, if not too harsh, can show us the path to improvement.
5. How do colleagues, administrators, and family/friends perceive

your role as an advisor? As a success? Average? Mediocre? Failure? Are you perceived as a valued advisor? Do your family members and friends understand this important aspect of your work?

It is important for administrators and teachers to keep in mind that there are teachers and counselors on staff who have highly developed advisory skills. They need to be identified and called on to become trainers for their colleagues. It has been my experience that if teachers begin to believe that advising is a positive addition to their subject mastery role, they will get on board. In my experience of providing advising training as director of the Bay Shore Junior High School–Stony Brook University Teacher Center (Long Island, New York), I found that teachers would opt to use their lunch, free periods, and before school time for training, training that was led by teachers and counselors who in the process of providing training added a new dimension to their subject-mastery role. Bay Shore Junior High had a student population of over 2,200, many of whom were minorities and new immigrants to America. The effort to provide easily accessible and ongoing training led by school staff members helped to reduce anonymity in this large school for students, parents, and not surprisingly, for teachers. Many of them learned for the first time how to communicate on a personal level with their students and be willing, able, and most importantly, expected to help students solve non-academic issues.

No, it wasn't perfect. While many teachers were able to use their newly developed advising skills in both their personal and academic relations with students, some teachers did have trouble buying into the advising role and learning advising skills. As a result they did not become star advisors. But they understood that they were being held accountable and their best effort, albeit imperfect, was expected.

Any effort to move teachers in the direction of becoming effective advisors needs to be championed by administrators, teacher leaders, and hopefully by counselors now boxed in by the many demands of their role. While I believe the time has come for the emergence of a mutually satisfying subject mastery and pedagogy role, it will not see the light of day without this expectation being clearly spelled out by school leaders. The focus needs to be on creating new expectations for teachers, not just for students. And the process can't be left to a few dedicated teachers who see the value in close relationships with their students and be ignored by the majority of faculty members. A clear and visible benchmark needs to be established that says, "This is the way we interact with all our students." There has to be an expectation in the school, no matter how large and complex, that advising students is an important part of teachers' work. And teachers have to be rewarded and recognized for this important contribution to their students in the same way they are rewarded and recognized for the academic achievement of their students. As I have argued, carrying out close and intimate contact with students and understanding the personal side of their lives in an effort to improve their academic performance and aspirations can be career enhancing for teachers, opening up new ways of viewing their work and requiring new skill acquisition, seeing their role as more than lecturing and feeding facts to their students and creating the expectation that their presence in the school is valued and of value to their students. They must recognize that they indeed do have a reservoir of life experience from which their students can learn, which will be of use in changing their own life paths. As Brown and Woodruff report, James P. Comer, the founder of the School Development Program, indicates that nothing is more important to successful schools than the quality of relationships among students, staff, and parents. Comer notes that "where there is a good climate of relationships there is academic achievement and you can accomplish the business of socializing kids and making academic gains at the same time. One need not interfere with the other."[18]

Clearly, as Goodlad suggests, it is reasonable to expect teachers to be responsible stewards of the schools in which they teach. Teachers are to the school as gardeners are to the garden, tenders not only of the plants but of the soil in which they grow. And, as Walker recalled her school experiences, "there are some teachers who plant little seeds of hope and opportunity. They took a chance. Probably did it with a lot of kids. School, get me a ticket out of this life." They were saying to Patsy, in essence, "You are valued and you can take your rightful place in the world." I believe this is the vision we must be seeking, a culture in which teachers plant seeds of hope and opportunity and tend to these aspirations, sometimes gently and sometimes with confrontation, making sure they don't atrophy and die. Our work needs to be about challenging our present practice that allows and encourages many teachers to remain distant and uninformed about their students, a school culture in which the particular data about each student is either ignored, shifted off to the already overburdened guidance staff, or simply paid lip service, with no real intention to act. It is a culture, as David D. Marsh and Judy B. Codding suggest, in describing George Washington High School in America's heartland, in which there is little sense of accountability for student results and no one seems able, even if anyone was willing, to improve the learning environment for students.[19] Tradition is comfortable and satisfactory in a school where instruction is teacher directed and textbook driven. The school and the district are awash in information about students, but administrators do little to analyze the information to form important decisions about students. In these schools, caring and the information that is elicited from students in the caring process about their personal lives, problems, hopes and dreams, and fears of failure take a back seat. There is no priority to understand and use this data about each child in both the teaching and administering process.

This is also true for schools in which there is an overemphasis on academic achievement and churning out numbers that demonstrate that the school is succeeding. Yet in these schools' communications with parents and community members, some schools tout their teachers as being caring and concerned, not letting one child fall through the cracks. But the reality is that teachers are quietly given the message that caring is not their main function, not their domain. In these schools caring atrophies. The kind of school culture that spawns this kind of behavior needs to be challenged. It is not healthy for students, teachers, counselors, administrators, and parents.

NOTES

1. Anthony W. Jackson and Gayle A. Davis, *Turning Points 2000: Educating Adolescents in the 21st Century* (New York: Teachers College Press 2000), 8.

2. Ernest L. Boyer, *High School* (New York: Harper and Row, 1983), 131–32.

3. Harold L. Munson, "Guidance and Instruction: A Rapprochement," in

Guidance for Education in Revolution, ed. David R. Cook (Boston: Allyn & Bacon, 1971), 337, 341–43.

4. James Garbarino, Nancy Dubrow, Kathleen Kostelny, and Carole Pardo, *Children in Danger* (San Francisco: Jossey-Bass, 1992), 121, 131–33, 154.

5. Thomas J. Cottle, *Children's Secrets* (Garden City, NY: Anchor Press, 1980), 262–65.

6. Cottle, *Children's Secrets*, 265.

7. John I. Goodlad, *Teachers for Our Nation's Schools* (San Francisco: Jossey-Bass, 1990), 44.

8. Robert Coles, *The Youngest Parent* (New York: Center for Documentary Studies, 1997), 5.

9. Parker Palmer, *The Courage to Teach* (San Francisco: Jossey-Bass, 1998), 40, 57, 83.

10. Fay E. Brown and Darren W. Woodruff, "Getting the Most from Students," in *Child by Child,* eds. James P. Comer, Michael Ben-Avie, Norris M. Haynes, and Edward T. Joyner (New York: Teachers College Press, 1999), 227.

11. Palmer, *The Courage to Teach.*

12. Palmer, *The Courage to Teach.*

13. Abigail Zuger, "From Doctor, an Overdose of Kindness," *New York Times*, 1 October 2002, 5 (F).

14. Maurice J. Elias, Joseph E. Zins, Roger P. Weissberg, Karin S. Frey, Mark T. Greenberg, Norris M. Haynes, Rachael Kessler, Mary E. Schwab-Stone, and Timothy P. Shriver, "Promoting Social and Emotional Learning," *Association for Supervision and Curriculum Development (ASCD) Online*, 1997, http://www.ascd.org/readingroom/books/elias97book.html (accessed 7 May 2002).

15. Munson, "Guidance and Instruction."

16. Arthur G. Powell, Eleanor Farrar, and David Cohen, *The Shopping Mall High School* (Boston: Houghton Mifflin, 1985).

17. Theodore E. Sizer, *Horace's School: Redesigning the American High School* (Boston, Houghton Mifflin, 1992).

18. Brown and Woodruff, "Getting the Most from Students," 227.

19. David D. Marsh and Judy B. Codding, with associates Robert Rothman, Philip Daro, Sally Hampton, Jacqueline Kraemer, John Porter, Marc S. Tucker, and Michael Strembitsky, *The New American High School* (Thousand Oaks, Calif.: Corwin Press, 1999), 10, 139.

Bibliography

Allen, Rick. "Big Schools: The Way We Are." *Education Leadership* 59, no. 5 (February 2002): 36–41.

Angus, David L. and Jeffrey E. Mirel. *The Failed Promise of the American High School, 1890–1995*. New York: Teachers College Press, 1999.

———. "At 17, A Star and Suicide Victim." *New York Times*, 1 October 1995, 1 (6).

Associated Press. "Study Links TV to Teen Aggression." *Newsday*, 29 March 2002, 4 (A).

Barth, Roland S. "The Culture Builder." *Education Leadership* 59, no. 8 (May 2002): 8.

Bear, Thelma, Sherry Schenk, and Lisa Buckner. "Supporting Victims of Child Abuse." *Education Leadership* 50, no. 4 (December 1992–January 1993), ASCD Online, *www.ascd/readingroom/edlead/9212.htmil* (accessed 7 July 2002).

Betts, Kate. "The Tyranny of Skinny, Fashion's Insider Secret." *New York Times*, 31 March 2002, 1, 8 (9).

Bireda, Martha R. "Education for All." *NASSP Principal Leadership Online* 1, no. 4 (December 2000), *www.nassp.org/news/pl_ed4all_1200.htm* (accessed 6 June 2002).

Bowers, Judy L. and Patricia A. Hatch. "The ASCA National Model: A Framework for School Counseling Programs." (Alexandria, Va.: American School Counselor Association, 2002): 7–9.

Bowman, Darcia Harris. "School 'Connectedness' Makes for Healthier Students, Study Suggests." *Education Week* (24 April 2002), *www/edweek .org/ew/newstory.cfm?slug=32health.h21* (accessed 7 July 2002).

Boyer, Ernest L. *High School*. New York: Harper and Row, 1983.

Bracey, Gerald. "11th Bracey Report on the Condition in Public Education." *Kappan Online, pdkintl.org.kappan/k011obra.htm* (accessed 28 May 2002).

Brown, Fay E. and Darren W. Woodruff. "Getting the Most from Students." In *Child by Child*, edited by James P. Comer, Michael Ben-Avie, Norris M.

Haynes, and Edward T. Joyner, 227. New York: Teachers College Press, 1999.

Bunn, Austin. "Terribly Smart." *New York Times Magazine*, 3 March 2002, 17 (6).

Center for Disease Control & Chronic Disease Prevention. "Teen Pregnancy." Center for Disease Control (CDC) (1999), *www.cdc.gov/needphp.teenhtm* (accessed 3 July 2002).

Children's Defense Fund. *The State of Children in America's Union: A 2002 Action Guide to Leave No Child Behind.* Washington, D.C.: Children's Defense Fund, 2002.

Clemetson, Lynette. "For Teenager, Troubling Bond in Chaotic Life." *New York Times*, 27 October 2002, 1, 36 (A).

Coleman, James S. *Adolescents and the Schools.* New York: Basic Books, 1965.

Coles, Robert. *The Moral Intelligence of Children.* New York: Random House, 1997a.

———. *The Youngest Parent.* New York: Center for Documentary Studies, 1997b.

Conant, James B. *The American High School Today.* New York: McGraw-Hill, 1959.

———. *The Comprehensive High School: A Second Report to Interested Citizens.* New York: McGraw-Hill, 1967.

Cook, David R. "The Future of Guidance as a Profession." In *Guidance for Education in Revolution*, edited by David R. Cook, 517, 523–24, 529–31, 548. Boston: Allyn & Bacon, 1971.

———. "Guidance and Institutional Change." In *Guidance for Education in Revolution.* edited by David R. Cook. Boston: Allyn & Bacon, 1971.

———. "Guidance and Student Unrest." In *Guidance for Education in Revolution.* Ed. David R. Cook. Boston: Allyn & Bacon, 1971.

Cornell, Craig Sones and Anna-Maria Petricelli. CinemaSense.com Movie Review 2000, *www.cinemasense.com/Reviews/billy_elliot.htm* (accessed 28 September 2002).

Cottle, Thomas J. *Children's Secrets.* Garden City, N.Y.: Anchor Press, 1980.

Cuban, Larry. *How Teachers Taught: Constancy and Change in American Classrooms, 1890–1990.* New York: Longman, 1984.

Damon, William. *Greater Expectations.* New York: Free Press, 1995.

Dewey, John. *Democracy and Education.* New York: Macmillan, 1916.

Edmundson, Mark. "Soul Training." *New York Times Magazine*, 18 August 2002, 8, 10 (6).

Elias, Maurice J. "Easing Transitions with Social-Emotional Learning." *NASSP Principal Leadership Online* 1, no. 7 (March 2001), *www.nassp.org/ news/pl_soc_emo_lrng_301.htm* (accessed 7 June 2002).

Elias, Maurice J., Joseph E. Zins, Roger P. Weissberg, Karin S. Frey, Mark T. Greenberg, Norris M. Haynes, Rachael Kessler, Mary E. Schwab-Stone, and Timothy P. Shriver. "Promoting Social and Emotional Learning." *Association for Supervision and Curriculum Development (ASCD) Online* (1997), *ascd.org/readingroom/book/elias97book.html* (accessed 7 May 2002).

Elkind, David. *The Hurried Child*. Reading, Mass.: Addison-Wesley, 1981.

Falkowski, Carol. "What's New in Youth Substance Abuse?" *Hazelden Voice* (Winter 2002): 11.

Farkas, Steve and Jean Johnson. "Kids These Days: What Americans Really Think about the Next Generation." *Public Agenda* (1997): 8–9, 11, 13, 16–19, 25–26.

Fenstermacher, Gary D. "Some Moral Considerations on Teaching as a Profession." In *The Moral Dimensions of Teaching*, edited by John I. Goodlad, Roger Soder, and Kenneth A. Sirotnik, 137. San Francisco: Jossey-Bass, 1990.

Fibkins, William L. *What Schools Should Do to Help Kids Stop Smoking*. Larchmont, N.Y.: Eye on Education, 2000.

———. *An Administrator's Guide to Better Teacher Mentoring*. Lanham, Md.: Scarecrow Press, 2002.

Foderaro, Lisa W. "Suburb's Residents Not Pacified by Charges in Students' Death." *New York Times*, 24 August 2002, 4 (B).

Garbarino, James, Nancy Dubrow, Kathleen Kostelny, and Carole Pardo. *Children in Danger*. San Francisco: Jossey-Bass, 1992.

Gay, Geneva. *Culturally Responsive Teaching*. New York: Teachers College Press, 2000.

Goleman, Daniel. "Eating Disorder Rates Surprise the Experts." *New York Times*, 4 October 1995, 11.

———. *Emotional Intelligence*. New York: Bantam Books, 1997.

Goode, Erica. "Boy Genius? Mother Says She Faked Tests." *New York Times*, 18 June 2002, 1, 12 (A).

———. "Progress Can Be Fragile for the Young Witnesses of Sept. 11." *New York Times*, 14 May 2002, 1, 4 (B).

Goodlad, John I. *A Place Called School*. New York: McGraw-Hill, 1984.

———. *Teachers for Our Nation's Schools*. San Francisco: Jossey-Bass, 1990.

————. *Education Renewal*. San Francisco: Jossey-Bass, 1994.

————. *In Praise of Education*. New York: Teachers College Press, 1997.

Goodman, Ellen. "Sex—Is There Joy in Not Knowing?" *Newsday*, 27 October 2002, 30 (A).

Grant, Gerald. *The World We Created at Hamilton High*. Cambridge: Harvard University Press, 1988.

Gratz, Donald B. "High Standards for Whom?" *Kappan Online* (May 2000), *www.pdkintl.org/kappan/kgra0005.htm* (accessed 14 March 2002).

Gross, Jane. "Teenagers' Binges Lead Scarsdale to Painful Self-Reflection." *New York Times*, 8 October 2002, 1, 7 (D).

Hampel, Robert. *The Last Citadel*. Boston: Houghton Mifflin, 1986.

Hartocollis, Anemona. "For City School Children, the Healing Starts Here." *New York Times*, 9 May 2002, 2 (B).

Healy, Jane M. *How Computers Affect Our Children's Minds: For Better or Worse*. New York: Simon & Schuster, 1998.

Hirsch, E. D., Jr. *The Schools We Need*. New York: Doubleday, 1996.

Jackson, Anthony W. and Gayle A. Davis. *Turning Points 2000: Educating Adolescents in the 21st Century*. New York: Teachers College Press, 2000.

Jeffrey, Nancy Ann. "The Organization Kid." *Wall Street Journal*, 6 September 2002, 1, 4 (W).

Katz, Lilian. "Some Generic Principles of Teaching." In *Essays On Teachers' Centers,* edited by Kathleen Devaney. San Francisco: Teachers' Center Exchange, 1977.

Kleinfield, N. R. "In Nightmares and Anger, Children Pay Hidden Cost of 9/11." *New York Times*, 14 May 2002, 1, 4 (B).

Kohn, Alfie. *The Schools Our Children Deserve*. New York: Houghton Mifflin, 1990.

Kwawer, Jay S. and Miriam Arond. Letters to the Editor. "Is the Boy a Genius or a Victim?" *New York Times*, 8 March 2002, 20 (A).

Lararee, David F. *How to Succeed in School Without Really Learning*. New Haven: Yale University Press, 1997.

Lenhardt, Anne Marie and H. Jeanette Willert. "Involving Stakeholders in Resolving School Violence." *NASSP Bulletin* (June 2002), *www.nassp.org/news/bltn_invstake0602.html* (accessed 5 May 2002).

Levine, Arthur. "Rookies in the Schools." *New York Times*, 29 June 2002, 15 (A).

Lowry, Beverly. "Crossed Over." *New York Times*, 23 August 1992, 1, 21 (7).

Maeroff, Gene I. *Don't Blame the Kids*. New York: McGraw-Hill, 1982.

Marsh, David D. and Judy B. Codding, with associates Robert Rothman,

Philip Daro, Sally Hampton, Jacqueline Kraemer, John Porter, Marc S. Tucker, and Michael Strembitsky. *The New American High School*. Thousand Oaks, Calif.: Corwin Press, 1999.

Meier, Deborah. *In Schools We Trust*. Boston: Beacon Press, 2002.

Morris, Lois B. and Robert Lipsyte. "What Itzhak Pearlman Learned at Camp." *New York Times*, 8 August 2002, 1, 5 (E).

Munro, Neil. "Brain Politics." *National Journal*, (3 February 2001), *www.pbs.org/wgbh/pages/frontline/sjows/medicating.reading/brainpolitics/html* (accessed 4 February 2002).

Munson, Harold L. "Guidance and Instruction: À Rapprochement." In *Guidance for Education in Revolution*, edited by David R. Cook, 337, 341–43. Boston: Allyn & Bacon, 1971.

———. "Guidance in Secondary Education: Reconnaissance and Renewal." In *Guidance for Education in Revolution*, edited by David R. Cook, 179. Boston: Allyn & Bacon, 1971.

National Center for Chronic Disease Prevention and Health Promotion. "Adolescents and Young Adults." Center for Disease Control (CDC) (2002), *cdc.gov/nccdphp.sgr/adoles.htm* (accessed 3 July 2002).

National Center for Education Statistics. "The Principal/School Disciplinarian Survey on School Violence, 1996–97." *NCES* (1998), *nces.ed.gov/pubs98/violence/9803001.html* (accessed 3 August 2002).

National Center for Health Statistics. "More American Children and Teens are Overweight." Center for Disease Control (CDC) (2001), *www.cde.gov/nchs/releases.01news/overwght99.htm* (accessed 3 July 2002).

National Center for Injury Prevention and Control. "Youth Violence in the United States." Center for Disease Control (CDC) (2002), *ede.gov/ncipc/factsheets/vvfact.htm* (accessed 3 July 2002).

———. "Dating Violence." Center for Disease Control (CDC) (2002), *www.ede.gov/ncipe/factsheet/datviol.htm* (accessed 3 July 2002).

———. "Suicide in the United States." Center for Disease Control (CDC) (2002), *www.cdc.gov/ncipe/factsheets.suitfacts.htm* (accessed 7 July 2002).

New York Times Staff. "A Star and Suicide Victim: An Athlete Dies Young, But by His Own Hand." *New York Times*, 1 October 1995, 1 (6).

———. "Scarsdale School Suspends 28 Students for Drunkenness." *New York Times*, 27 September 2002, 6 (B).

Ochs, Ridgely. "They're Not Getting Physical: Girls too Inactive, Study Finds." *Newsday*, 5 September 2002, 20 (A).

Palmer, Parker. *The Courage to Teach*. San Francisco: Jossey-Bass, 1998.

Pang, Valerie Ooka and Velma A. Sablan. "Teacher Efficacy." In *Being*

Responsive to Cultural Differences, edited by Mary E. Dilworth. Thousand Oaks, Calif.: Corwin Press, 1997.

Powell, Arthur G., Eleanor Farrar, and David Cohen. *The Shopping Mall High School*. Boston: Houghton Mifflin, 1985.

Purdy, Matthew. "A Teenage Party, a Punch, and a Choice That Can't Be Reversed." *New York Times*, 1 September 2002, 29 (B).

Purnick, Joyce. "In Schools, A Hidden Toll of Sept. 11." *New York Times*, 13 May 2002, 1 (B).

Putnam, Robert D. *Bowling Alone*. New York: Simon & Schuster, 2002.

Rasmussen, Karen. "Schools and Social Service." *Association for Supervision and Curriculum Development (ASCD) Curriculum Update* (Fall 1999): 6.

Ravitch, Diane. *Left Back: A Century of Failed School Reform*. New York: Simon and Schuster, 2000.

Ravitch, Diane and Joseph P. Viteritti, eds. *New Schools for a New Century*. New Haven: Yale University Press, 1997.

Rothstein, Richard. "Schoolchildren of Welfare Parents." *New York Times*, 5 June 2002, 8 (B).

———. "Dropout Rate Is Climbing and Likely to Go Higher." *New York Times*, 9 October 2002, 8 (B).

Salomone, Rosemary C. *Visions of Schooling, Conscience, Community, and Common Education*. New Haven: Yale University Press, 2000.

Sanacore, Joseph. "Home at School." *Newsday*, 2 August 2002, 20 (A).

Sanders, Thomas H. and Robert D. Putnam. "Rebuilding the Stock of Social Capital." *School Administrator* (1999), *www.assa.org/publications/sa/1999_09/sander.htm* (accessed 14 March 2002).

Schemo, Diana Jean. "Mothers of Sex-Active Youths Often Think They're Virgins." *New York Times*, 5 September 2002, 20 (A).

———. "For Schools, No Shutdown But Spread of Lockdown." *New York Times*, 23 October 2002, 18 (A).

Shoben, Edward Jr. "Guidance: Remedial Function or Social Reconstruction." *Harvard Educational Review* 32, no. 4 (Fall 1962): 430.

Sinclair, Robert L. and Ward J. Ghory. "Last Things First: Realizing Equality by Improving Conditions for Marginal Students." In *Access to Knowledge: An Agenda for Our Nations Schools*, edited by John I. Goodlad and Pamela Keating. New York: College Entrance Examination Board, 1990.

Sizer, Theodore R. *Horace's School: Redesigning the American High School*. Boston: Houghton Mifflin, 1992.

Sizer, Theodore R. and Nancy Faust Sizer. *The Students Are Watching*. Boston: Beacon Press, 1999.

Sontag, Deborah. "Who Was Responsible for Elizabeth Shin?" *New York Times*, 20 April 2002, 58 (6).

Spindler, George and Louise Spindler, eds. *Pathways to Cultural Awareness.* Thousand Oaks, Calif.: Corwin Press, 1994.

Substance Abuse and Mental Health Services Administration. "3 Million Youth are Suicide Risks." *Newsday*, 15 July 2002, 14 (A).

Tanner, Lindsey. "Hispanic Kids Face Health Crisis." *Associated Press* (2003), *detnews.com/2002/health/0207.03–529270.htm* (accessed 7 July 2002).

Tobacco Information and Prevention Sources (TIPS). "Tobacco Use among Middle and High School Students—National Youth Tobacco Survey 1999." Center for Disease Control (CDC) (2000), www.cdc/gov/tobacco/research_data/survey/mmwr4903fs.htm (accessed 3 July 2992).

Traub, James. "The Test Mess." *New York Times Magazine*, 7 April 2002, 48 (6).

Tyack, David and Elisabeth Hansot. *Managers of Virtue.* New York: Basic Books, 1982.

Udovitch, Mim. "A Secret Society for Starving." *New York Times*, 9 September 2002, 18, 20 (6).

Waldholz, Michael. "To Tame Kids' Junk Food Urges: Fewer Speeches, More Fruit Bowls." *Wall Street Journal*, 25 July 2002, 4 (D).

Woodall, Martha. "There's No More Teachers' Dirty Looks." *Newsday*, 12 March 2002, 25 (A).

Zuger, Abigail. "From Doctor, An Overdose of Kindness." *New York Times*, 1 October 2002, 5 (F).

Index

Aber, Larry, 115–16
advanced placement, 187–90
advising skills, 258–64
Alberty, Harold, 27
Allen, James E., 33
American School Counselor Association (ASCA), 33, 39, 141
anorexia, 229–30, 238–41

Bay Shore Junior High–Stony Brook University Teacher Center, 264
Benoit, Marilyn, 108–9
Blum, Robert, 92–93, 105–6
Breggins, Peter, 106
Brown, Sarah, 119

Capra, Fritjof, 112–13
Caswell, Hollis, 29
Chapman, Elizabeth, 107
Chapman, Justin, 107
child abuse, 97
Child Protective Services, 162
children of divorce, 221
Children's Defense Fund, 97
Covello, Leonard, 23

Davis, Ellen, 101
Dewey School, 24
Diller, Lawrence, 106
Dingman, Thomas A., 109
Doherty, William, 109

eating disorders, 100–101
Ebbes, Valerie, 96
emotional intelligence, 93–96
Eth, Spencer, 114

family patterns, 85, 87–90
Franklin High School, 51, 54, 57
Freud, Anna, 143

Gardner, Howard, 93
gay teens, 179–80
Generation Stress, 109
Greene, Geraldine, 104
Greenfield, Pamela, 112

Harrison High School, 104
Haycox, Marry, 118
health and learning, 95–96
Hellard, Joy, 91–92
Hoecherl, Donald, 91–92

immigration, 85
impact of 9/11, 114–17
information technology. 112–14

Johnson, Jeffrey, 113
Johnson, Kirk A., 92
Johnson, Spencer, 109

Kilpatrick, William Heard, 29
Koplan, Jeffrey, 99

large schools, 90–91
Longitudinal Study of Adolescent Health, 92
Louis Armstrong Intermediate School, 134, 136

Maguire, Sue, 96
Malvo, John Lee, 117–18
Manpower Research Demonstration Project, 97
marginal students, 127
McCully, Harold, C., 39
medicating students, 106
Muhammad, John Allen, 117–18

National Association of Secondary School Principals (NASSP), 46
National Campaign to Prevent Teen Pregnancy, 119
National Center for Chronic Disease Prevention and Health Promotion (CDC), 99, 101, 103, 105
National Center for Injury Prevention and Control, 98
National Commission on Excellence in Education, 48
National Defense Education Act, 36, 141
National Household Survey on Drugs Report, 101
National Model for School Counseling Programs, 141
National Organization for Victims' Assistance, 106
National Research Counsel, 110
National Science Foundation, 46
A Nation at Risk, 47, 48, 49
New England Assessment Project, 39
New England Journal of Medicine, 99

New York State School Counselor Association (NYSSCA), 138–39

obesity, 99–100

Paige, Rod, 21
Parents Without Partners, 161, 210
Pearlman, Itzhak, 10–13
physical activity, 99
Pierovich, John, 245
Pogue, Linda, 112
Poussaint, Alvin, 118
pregnancy, 105–6
Principal/School Disciplinarian Survey on School Violence, 98
Progressive Education Association, 25
Progressive Education movement, 24
Project Spectrum, 93
Public Agenda, 76, 81, 120

Renfrew Center, 101
Rice, Joseph Mayer, 23
Rodriguez, Alberto, 91
Rukaj, Patrick, 105, 120, 131

Salovey, Peter, 93
Scarsdale High School, 104
School Development Program, 265
sexual abuse, 106
Shin, Elizabeth, 109, 125
Shoreham-Wading River Middle School, 134, 136
Snelbecker, Glenn, 114
Sputnik, 29, 133
Steinberg, Laurence, 50
stress, 106–12
substance abuse, 103

suicide, 101–3, 159–60, 212–15
Switzer, Anna, 114

Tepp, Alan, 104
Thum, Carl, 108–9

University of Chicago Laboratory
    School, 24

violence, 98–99
Viscome, Rob, 104–5, 120, 131

Walker, Patsy, 143, 247–48, 265
Wechsler, Norman, 91–92, 135
welfare, 97–98
Western Pennsylvania Cyber School,
    113–14
Williams, Delcy, 118

About the Author

William L. Fibkins is an education consultant, writer, and lecturer specializing in training school administrators, teacher leaders, and school counselors on how to develop school-based teacher training and student support services. His training programs include teacher mentoring; training teachers to be effective advisors; restructuring school guidance and health services to address the growing personal, health, and academic needs of students; leadership and peer counseling training for students; and establishing positive parent/community/school connections. Fibkins holds degrees in education, counselor education, and school administration from Syracuse University and the University of Massachusetts.

Fibkins's publications include *An Administrator's Guide to Better Teacher Mentoring, What Schools Should Do to Help Kids Stop Smoking, The Empowering School: Getting Everyone on Board to Help Teenagers, The Teacher-As-Helper Training Manual, Preventing Teacher Sexual Misconduct*, and *Tobacco Interventions*. He is also the author of numerous professional monographs on restructuring secondary schools, training secondary school teachers to be advisors and mentors, implementing group counseling programs, restructuring secondary school guidance and health services, and developing school-based health centers to address teen health issues.

Fibkins's in-school experience includes serving as founder and director of the Stony Brook University–Bay Shore Public School teacher training center, school-community project director for the Queens College–Louis Armstrong Intermediate School, and founder of the student assistance counseling program for the Shoreham-Wading River, New York, school district. His university experience includes serving as professor in the school administration program at Queens College and the department of counseling and development at Long Island University.